THE
AWAKENED LIFE

Communicating with Spirits

D1604617

RITA BERKOWITZ AND DEBORAH BAKER

Publishing: Mike Sanders
Senior Acquisitions Editor: Janette Lynn
Book Producer: Lee Ann Chearneyi/Amaranth@LuminAreStudio
Art Director: William Thomas
Copy Editor: Rick Kughen
Cover Designer: Jessica Lee
Book Designer/Layout: Ayanna Lacey
Indexer: Brad Herriman
Proofreader: Polly Zetterberg

Published by Penguin Random House LLC
001-322404-OCT2021
Copyright © 2021 by Amaranth

International Standard Book Number: 978-0-7440-2919-2
Library of Congress Catalog Card Number: 2021931000

23 22 21   5 4 3 2 1

Interpretation of the printing code: The rightmost number of the first series of numbers is the year of the book's printing; the rightmost number of the second series of numbers is the number of the book's printing. For example, a printing code of 21-1 shows that the first printing occurred in 2021

Printed in the United States of America

Note: This publication contains the opinions and ideas of its authors. It is intended to provide helpful and informative material on the subject matter covered. It is sold with the understanding that the authors, book producer, and publisher are not engaged in rendering professional services in the book. If the reader requires personal assistance or advice, a competent professional should be consulted.

The authors, book producer, and publisher specifically disclaim any responsibility for any liability, loss, or risk, personal or otherwise, which is incurred as a consequence, directly or indirectly, of the use and application of any of the contents of this book.

All identifying information, names, and details of client cases have been changed to protect the confidentiality of clients with whom Dr. Rippentrop has worked. Client stories provided in the book are often conglomerates of different cases to provide examples of how chakra work can be informative and therapeutic in the counseling setting.

Most Alpha books are available at special quantity discounts for bulk purchases for sales promotions, premiums, fund-raising, or educational use. Special books, or book excerpts, can also be created to fit specific needs.

For details, write: Special Markets, Alpha Books, 1745 Broadway, New York, NY 10019.

Reprinted and updated from *The Complete Idiot's Guide® to Communicating With Spirits*

For the curious
www.dk.com

—*"just up to the white" say to myself again & again(while not quite awake):all the mystery of life being(as I now feel) between the darkness of a pencil & the tone of a paper;"you don't need to seek anywhere else,everything which God intends for you is findable within these from-darkness-to-lightness gradations—are they not,after all,infinite?"*

—E. E. Cummings

Contents

Part 1   The Spirit World   1

Part 2   What's on the Other Side?   53

Part 3   Calling Out to Spirit   109

Part 5   The Essence of Spirit Is Being   225

Part 6   Soul Lessons and Karmic Cycles   289

Introduction

Regardless of whether we are awake to the knowledge, all of us are surrounded by Spirit—all of the time, we touch the Divine. As a medium, Spiritualist minister, and Spirit artist, Rita encounters many people who have a desire to connect to the Spirit world. We have many reasons for wanting to communicate with loved ones who have passed to the Higher side. Perhaps circumstances didn't allow you to be with your loved one at the time of passing to say "good-bye" or "I love you". You may want to know that your loved one is "okay" on the Higher side or to let your loved one who's passed on know that *you* are "okay." Perhaps there were unresolved issues or concerns between you. Or, perhaps the relationship was difficult, even one of estrangement.

Maybe you simply feel a need to maintain a connection to Spirit; you want to know your beloved or your dear family is there for you, nurturing you from the Higher side. Perhaps, as well, you are eager to establish evidence you can trust, proof through Spirit of the continuity of life.

The Awakened Life: Communicating with Spirits provides a foundation for you to explore how to work with a medium and also how to discover and develop your own mediumistic abilities. Connecting to Spirit is a powerful way to bring your being into harmony with the Universe. When you understand the continuity of life, you gain confidence and faith in the Divine love that links all living things—whether on the Earth plane or in Spirit—giving your life strength and purpose. Those you love are with you yet, and all lives on in Spirit.

About the Authors

Rita Straus Berkowitz is an Ordained Minister of the Spiritualist Church and pastor of the First Spiritualist Church of Quincy, located at 40 West Street, Quincy, Massachusetts. A Certified Medium herself, she holds a Master of Science in Psychological Counseling. As a Spirit artist, Rita has impressed large audiences throughout the world by drawing portraits during readings that are likenesses communicated to her by clients' loved ones who have passed on to the Higher side. She holds a Bachelor of Fine Art from the Pratt Institute, Brooklyn, New York, and has attended the School of the Museum of Fine Arts, Boston. Rita has taught both drawing and painting at the college level and has shown her own work in galleries throughout New York and New England; her current fine art paintings explore Spirit in landscape. Rita offers private sittings and classes and has trained many professional mediums; she is featured on BBC television UK and in bestpsychicmediums.com. Her Spirit Portraits are tangible evidence and validation of the continuity of life. Learn more about Rita's remarkable Spirit art at RitaBerkowitzArt.com, or find her on Facebook or Instagram. Rita lives in her quiet home in Scituate, Massachusetts.

Deb Baker has co-authored many books on health and wellness. She lives and writes in the Pacific Northwest.

About the Spirit Art

Rita, as an ordained Spiritualist minister, certified medium, and commissioned healer, shares her gift as a fine artist for drawing portraits from Spirit of loved ones who have passed to the Higher side. Throughout this book, *The Awakened Life: Communicating with Spirits,* we use original art, stories, and examples from Rita's experiences. To protect the privacy of others, we've changed the names—but the stories are real.

What comes through for Rita as a medium, she can draw or paint for her clients during readings. Although the veracity of the information she conveys during a reading is compelling enough by itself, seeing the image of a loved one arise from Rita's pencil and paper is irrefutable evidence of the continuity of life beyond physical boundaries. Often there are many spirits surrounding someone at the start of a reading. Usually, the spirits work it out among themselves to decide who has the most compelling need to connect and to be drawn, and that spirit will step forward for Rita. This does not mean the other spirits fade away. It just means that one spirit will generally come forward as the dominant spirit for the reading.

Often the spirits portrayed in Spirit drawings consult with Rita, giving her specific instructions on how exactly they want to be drawn. This includes receiving details of setting ("Make it a blue sky overhead."), age and dress ("Show me as a young man in my uniform—as I appear to you now."), accessories ("I'm wearing the pearl bracelet he gave me."), accompaniment ("Picture me holding our beloved white cat with a gray smudge right where I'm showing you."), and even hairstyle ("Make sure my hair has that *wash and go* feel to the style."). Working together with the spirits, Rita is able to create striking and uncanny portraits that capture both the likeness and the character of loved ones' essential natures. You see who they are at their core of being.

Rita's spirit drawings appear throughout the book, along with photographs of the person from physical life, where possible. (In some readings, a spirit will ask to be drawn because there is no existing photograph or artwork to document their appearance for loved ones.) The stories of these people—and the spirits attending them—are real, and we thank them for being willing to share their amazing experiences of communicating with Spirit with us—and with you.

About This Book

There are six parts to this book:

Part 1, The Spirit World, looks at different perspectives on life, physical death, and the continuation of the spirit's existence. The four chapters in this **part** explore burial customs, the connection with the Divine, the Spiritualist religion, and the answers we look to spirit communication to provide.

Part 2, What's on the Higher Side? explores the differences between the Earth plane and the Spirit world. The four chapters in this **part** examine the various ways contact with Spirit happens and many reasons we welcome and seek it, look at why spirits choose to come through in communication, and why some spirits find it difficult to leave the Earth plane.

Part 3, Calling Out to Spirit, investigates the validation and symbolism of communication with spirits. The five chapters in this **part** provide information about and exercises to develop the psychic and psychical skills that facilitate spirit contact, including learning about what a medium does and how to understand messages you receive from Spirit.

Part 4, Activating Your Spirit Senses, looks at some of the more advanced techniques that help mediums make connections with Spirit. The four chapters in this **part** include exercises to help you develop these skills, including psychometry, dreams, telepathy, and psychical mediumistic skills—clairvoyance, clairaudience, and clairsentience.

Part 5, The Essence of Spirit is Being, explores the healing aspects of Spirit. The four chapters in this **part** look at the different ways Spirit energy connects you to the cycles of this lifetime—your past, your present, and your future—as well as the nature of time, space, and the continuity of life.

Part 6, Soul Lessons and Karmic Cycles, examines the ways you can use Spirit energy right now to nurture spiritual energy in your personal relationships, at work, in your community, rippling out over the globe. These three chapters give you ways to accept the gifts of Spirit, apply the soul lessons you learn to enhance your experience of this life, and use Spirit to heal karmic cycles and help humanity come together, healing the world with Spirit energy.

Appendix A, When Grief and Sadness Overwhelm, will help you learn how to process the waves of grief and sadness that can threaten to throw your world off balance. Spirit is always large enough to hold your strongest emotions and deepest feelings with safety and love.

Acknowledgments

It takes many people to turn a good idea into a good book. Rita and Deb deeply appreciate the efforts of all those who worked to bring this book into existence. We give thanks to (and for) the wonderful team at Alpha Books, including publisher Mike Sanders and editors Brandon Buechley and Janette Lynn, whose remarkable patience and support for *The Awakened Life: Communicating with Spirits* has our sincere gratitude. Special thanks go to Lee Ann Chearneyi of Amaranth, for her extraordinary vision, acceptance, and support.

Rita thanks these people: my husband David and daughters Deborah and Erica for all your love and support and not thinking it too strange that I spend so much time with "dead people." I want to thank Stephen O'Leary, Career Counseling Professor, for saying the right words, "Use your gifts." Thanks to Bob Miller, founder of the Silver Birch Healing Sanctuary, dear friend, and mentor, for always teaching me that all spirit communication is for healing. And thanks especially to Bob Olson, who walked into church one morning and asked for a spirit drawing and changed both of our lives. I can't begin to express the great appreciation I and so many others feel about his work. Thank you, Bob, for all that you do.

Deb Baker thanks Dianne for her observations and insights; Ava for having the courage to speak the truth; Lee Ann for her incredible vision, direction, and patience; and Rita for her insight, good humor, flexibility, and enthusiasm.

And last, we thank the many people who have been willing to share their stories, experiences, and Spirit drawings with us to include in this book. These people and events are real, and they validate the continuity of life as nothing else can.

Trademarks

All terms mentioned in this book that are known to be or are suspected of being trademarks or service marks have been appropriately capitalized. Alpha Books and Penguin Random House cannot attest to the accuracy of this information. Use of a term in this book should not be regarded as affecting the validity of any trademark or service mark.

The Spirit World

Spirits are all around us. They make themselves present to
us throughout our lives in many ways and for many reasons.
We want to make contact with spirits because we seek answers
and validation of the spirit's (and of life's) continuity—and because
we yearn to reconnect with our lost loved ones. Throughout history
and across cultures, humankind has shared a common belief in the
continuation of life after death. Although the physical body dies, Spirit
lives on. This essential belief in the eternal nature of Spirit forms the
basis of numerous religions and faith systems. Spiritualism is a practice
founded on the concept that the individual soul experiences a continuing
existence after death. As an ordained Spiritualist minister and certified
medium, Rita receives spirit communications through the veil between
our Earthly world and the world of Spirit.

CHAPTER
1

The Healing Bond Between Life and Death

The beauty of a face well-loved—the knowing of every line and soft curve. The sound of a dear one's voice filled with the cadences of mood; every tone inviting your soul to join in a harmony of call and response, asked and answered. The scents of their days, drawing near enough to catch out the bits of the world that cling as experiences lived through time—scents of garden or books or of spices, sweat, or spirits that linger to reveal and fade. Enjoying the tastes of a shared family meal, whether caught on the run and digested whole or savored in the rich mouth-feel of courses lovingly prepared. The joy of a touch remembered; it could be as simple and fleeting as the glancing brush of a hand, as warm as the complete abandon of a child's hug, or as significant as a beloved gesture felt all the way to the heart.

In this life, we experience love through our physical senses. Sight, sound, scent, taste, and touch become imprinted on our minds as sense memories that embody the bonds we share with those we love. This sense of empathy with those we love, a shared feeling of being truly felt by a loved one is nurtured by a part of the human brain called the mirror neuron system. This system allows our brains to hardwire the connection experienced through the physical sensesbetween our minds and the minds of others. With this mindsight, human beings are able to mirror the intentions and the emotions of others. This powerful mental bond allows us to anticipate another person's actions and emotions.

These empathetic bonds that connect us to others in our physical lives also extend beyond physical boundaries. We often sense the presence of loved ones when they are not physically with us. How often do you receive a text at the precise moment you're thinking of its sender? We welcome, and even expect, these connections as evidence of the depth of our relationships. Many people expect to stay in contact with loved ones *even after they pass on*. And we expect this contact to take place along the bonds formed in our physical lives. Spouses, parents, children, and dear friends—people connected through love in the physical world and separated by death—want to establish and maintain contact with them that transcends life and death.

Many people who want to communicate with spirits desire to make contact with loved ones who have passed on. This can be especially true for those who cannot be with loved ones near the time of their passing. And many spirits that initiate contact with the physical world have the same desire for connection. This contact can be for comfort, to protect or shelter, to explain or forgive, or simply to continue a loving relationship.

The Continuity of Life

You might think of spirits as ghostly images drifting around just beyond the boundaries of physical experience. And in a sense, this perception isn't wrong … it's just incomplete. Spirits are all around us. We can see, hear, and touch some—those who, like us, inhabit physical bodies. We may not recognize others that are present as *discarnate* spirits; spirits who have no physical body. Discarnate spirits might be spirits who once lived or are yet to live in the *physical or Earth plane* or they might be spirits who exist solely in the *Spirit plane*. The Earth plane is the level of existence at which spirits take physical form (our physical, biological world). The Spirit plane is the level of existence at which there are no boundaries of tangibility, time, or space.

The cycle of life and death has fascinated humankind for all of its existence. Through our spiritual and religious pursuits, we ask what defines the start and end of this cycle. This line of questioning is itself limited by the boundaries of physical existence. But what if we reverse this thinking? Instead of looking at human beings as physical bodies that have spirits (or souls), what if we look at human existence as spirits inhabiting physical bodies? Then the cycle of life and death becomes a continuum of being.

The Greatest Journey Begins with Preparation

Many ancient cultures buried their dead as though they were leaving on grand, extended journeys. Excavated burial sites on nearly every continent show bodies carefully prepared and surrounded by valuables, food, and other items the departed might need in the afterlife. Scientists have dated some of these sites to be as old as the Neolithic period 10,000 years ago. Consistencies among sites in certain locations provide evidence that cultures often followed precise rituals in burying their dead. The ancient Egyptians meticulously removed the body's major organs, sealing them in clay jars placed around the body so the spirit would find them ready as it entered its next life.

The Healing Power of Love

While there are many reasons why people want to communicate with spirits, all paths lead to only one purpose: healing. Healing can take numerous forms, from emotional closure to physical health. It can be understanding, insight, knowledge, or acceptance. Rita speaks of this healing as being "guided by the light," which means that it is undertaken with the protection of the Divine (however you define the Divine within the framework of your belief system).

Comfort from the Higher Side

Countless people who are grieving the loss of loved ones find comfort in contact with the other side, which is what Rita calls the Higher side. Sometimes, it is loved ones who have passed who initiate the contact, reaching from beyond to comfort and even protect those on this side. Sometimes, contact comes indirectly from other spirits who want to reassure the living that those who have passed are at peace.

Often, relatives who have passed become regular visitors to the Earth plane. In their spirit communications, they have joyous stories to share. They want to be of comfort and to establish that existence continues beyond what we mortal humans view as the boundary of death. As a result, people who have experienced such contact may live the remainder of their physical lives in regular communication with spouses, parents, grandparents, siblings, other relatives, friends, and associates who have passed. Once having communicated with spirit, such people lose whatever fear of death they might have had, as they become confident that existence continues. There is a healing bond between the living and the dead.

Unfinished Business

Communicating with those who have passed gives us an opportunity to achieve healing resolution. People can leave us with things left unsaid or undone. Often, you are not able to say a last "I love you" to someone who needs to hear it or to share a last touch or embrace. There simply isn't time. For those who know the pain of not being able to say a proper good-bye when a loved one passes, spirit communication may offer a balm of comfort and a chance to heal the experience of loss when we feel torn apart abruptly from someone who has passed.

For those of us with difficult relationships, healing is also possible. Unfortunately, family members are sometimes at odds with each other here on Earth: lovers quarreling, siblings squabbling, friends bickering. It happens; it's a part of life. But we seldom know in advance when we've reached the end of our physical lives. Sometimes a physical life ends before the disagreement does, leaving the survivor in the relationship steeped in grief and guilt.

Contact with the spirit who has passed can give both parties in a difficult relationship the chance to mend rifts. Sometimes the contact is direct, in which the spirit of the departed appears to the living loved one, and there is a one-to-one communication. Sometimes the contact is indirect, as when a third-party spirit appears to say, "Robert is here. He wants you to know he is fine, and he's sorry for that argument right before his heart attack. It wasn't your fault, and his love for you will never die." There is great comfort in being able to apologize, explain, forgive, reconcile, or say "goodbye" or "I love you"—whatever communication needs to take place.

What about spirits who are apparent strangers to us and don't have a message from departed loved ones and who instead just want to communicate with whatever physical entities they can reach and who will respond? Such spirits typically have their own reasons for making contact. In some way, they need help from you so they can continue their evolution on the Higher side. Perhaps you're the contact point because you are in a space, such as a house, that belonged to or was familiar to the spirit in its physical existence. Maybe there is something about your life mission that intersects with the spirit's mission. Such a spirit has unfinished business, and you can help bring completion and resolution for the spirit. We talk more about this in later chapters.

Taking Familiar Form

Spirits often find it necessary to interact with us in ways that we, as physical beings, can experience. We like to see, hear, and touch our environment and all that is within it through our senses. After all, that's the essence of our physical existence. And especially if communication with the spirit world is new to us, we're more comfortable when we can experience such contact in familiar ways. You might see an image of the person, hear their voice, or even experience a scent associated with the person (such as the sweet smell of hay in a stable to an equestrian or of linseed oil to a painter).

Sometimes, the contact might come through someone else, not necessarily a *medium*. (A medium is a person who acts as a link, through their sensitivity, between the spirit and physical worlds.) Sometimes contact might come through a friend who might say something like: "I don't know where this is coming from because your mother has passed away, but I have this image of her in my head, and she wants me to tell you that you should not go to the lake this weekend. Instead, you should stay close to home. And she's saying, 'For heaven's sake, paint the living room sage, not beige.'" If the words and tone sound just like your mother, don't panic. It's just your mother's spirit with a message for you and coming through in a way you recognize and through a source you trust. So, for heaven's sake, stay home and paint the living room sage!

Personal Growth, Insight, and Empowerment

Communication with the Higher side might be common (more common than you may believe right now), but it is also special. Put it to good use! This is your opportunity to learn about yourself and your purpose in this life. Use the insights you gain to further your life's work and to leave a positive imprint on our physical, Earthly world.

Knowledge empowers. It can help you to understand why you feel and act as you do, so you can direct your energy in positive ways. What you learn through your contacts with spirit entities can help you heal emotional wounds and physical ailments, and it can help you get your life on track.

Sometimes the insights that come to you through spirit communication are intense or even disturbing. It can be helpful to have someone to whom you can turn, to discuss your feelings and concerns. There are professionals who combine psychic consultation with conventional therapeutic approaches. Chapters 13 and 24 provide more information about moving from insight to changes in your life.

Do *You* See Dead People?

Rita is a certified medium and ordained minister in the Spiritualist Church. She began drawing faces when she was a child. At the time, she thought these portraits were of imaginary people and didn't recognize the true meaning of what she was drawing; she just drew what she saw. Now, as an adult with many years of education and experience that have broadened and deepened her knowledge, understanding, and skills, Rita knows she receives spirit communication through drawing and other forms, too. (We talk more about Rita's mediumistic abilities in later chapters.)

Do *you* believe you might (or *know* you might) receive spirit communication? Answer these questions to find out if you have natural mediumistic ability!

1. **Have you felt sudden changes of temperature?** If you're a woman in midlife, we're not talking about hot flashes here! Often, spirit presence results in sudden and unexplainable temperature jumps up or down. Cold, in particular, is associated with the presence of a spirit. You might walk down a hallway and feel as though you've walked into a refrigerator. Less commonly, you might be sitting in your favorite chair when it feels like someone's cranked up the heat.

2. **Do you see sudden lights?** Spirits are energy, and light is an expression of energy. Floating or flickering lights often suggest the presence of spirits. Orbs (also called ghost orbs, ghost lights, or earth lights) are a particular form of presence that is well documented and often photographed. Although in this book, we discuss seeing sudden lights in the context of what this might suggest about the presence of spirits, it's important to recognize that this phenomenon can also suggest certain eye disorders. If you notice any interference with your vision, contact your eye care professional.

In October 2001, Rita went to Arthur Findley College in Stansted, England, to spend a week studying mediumship. Earlier in the day, Rita experienced an independent voice while walking through the beautiful gardens on the grounds. She decided to take a photograph of the gardens from the window of her room, and the image of shimmering light appeared.

3. **Have you ever seen an image out of the corner of your eye? Can you identify that image?** Many people who have healthy vision report seeing vaguely human shapes or shadows in their peripheral vision. If they don't give it too much thought or analysis, some can further report that the figure was a young girl in a nightgown or that it sure looked like Uncle Albert, even though he's been gone for 15 years now. Yet turning your head to look directly at the image generally reveals nothing, which might cause you to doubt whether you actually did see anything. How do you distinguish these images from tricks of light? Carefully examine whether there is an explanation for what you've seen. For example, a quick glance at a white box in a corner shadow might appear to be a fleeting vision of your childhood Maltese dog, Max. Where there appears no perceived explanation, you may have actually seen your beloved Max.

4. **Have you had a discarnate spirit visit you in a dream?** It's often a source of comfort to those grieving the loss of loved ones to have their loved ones appear in dreams. Sometimes the dreams are re-enactments of events that took place when the

loved one was still on the physical Earth plane. Other times, the dreams appear to be messages from the dear one, attempting to reassure and convey a message with love. Pay attention to how the spirit will present in the dream … at what age and in what context.

5. **Has your mind suddenly (and out of context) been brought back to a specific time and place with a loved one who has passed?** Somewhat like a waking dream, this phenomenon could be the work of a spirit who wants you to know it is still with you and remains part of your everyday life. Activating the memory of an event that was meaningful to both of you is one way the spirit can validate its identity to you and demonstrate the continuity of life.

6. **Do you sometimes smell a specific scent that reminds you of a particular loved one?** It could be that this scent still lingers in places the two of you frequented, such as your home or car. And sure, it could be that someone else is wearing the fragrance or has a similar smell, but smell is a sense that activates the emotions and memory, again creating validation. Many times, it is a particular incongruous smell (such as brewing coffee where there is none to be had or a heritage rose in a landscape bereft of their signature blooms). This smell is uniquely associated with the person who has passed and provides clues that the person's spirit is present with you in that moment.

7. **Have you ever felt a touch, or maybe the sensation that you're walking into a silken spider web?** Sometimes, a spirit attempts to "reach out and touch"—which, of course, isn't especially practical for an intangible, discarnate entity! You might feel the energy of the spirit's presence making contact with your skin. Remember that the silk of a spider is both delicate and inordinately strong. Poet Stanley Kunitz in *The Wild Braid* compared the Universe to a web: "Touch it at any point and the whole web quivers."

   Also, there is a phenomenon called *transfiguration* in which a spirit's *ectoplasm* flows around you. Transfiguration takes place when a spirit's physical characteristics superimpose over a medium's features, presenting an image of the spirit entity. Ectoplasm is a substance produced by spirits to make themselves visible. The word comes from the Greek words *ecto,* meaning "outside," and *plasma,* meaning "a thing formed."

8. **Do you ever hear voices when you know you are alone, hear incongruous sounds, or hear things, such as music, no one else hears?** You might have the sense of "hearing" a particular word, phrase, sound, or even a song or piece of music. It might be obvious enough that you can connect it with a person who has passed, or it might puzzle you because what you are hearing doesn't seem connected to anything in particular. This phenomenon is called *clairaudience.* With focus and

concentration, you can often gain increasing clarity until you actually decipher the message that has been sounded.

9. **Have you had a sense something has happened to someone you love and later found out that the person was in an accident or experienced some other traumatic event?** Not all spirit communication takes place across the border between the Earth and Spirit planes. Spirits inhabiting physical bodies also can make contact across temporal space. The most common such contact is a phenomenon called *crisis telepathy* in which you get an image of an event or even just a sense that something has happened (or will happen) to a loved one. For example, an old childhood friend once called you out of the blue years ago to tell you it would be safer to travel on a later plane on a different day. Your friend had no way knowing that you'd just clicked to confirm an online booking for a flight that would have put you in the air on 9/11.

10. **Have you been to a place or touched an object and gotten an image or sensory activation (sound, smell, taste) of a person or an event?** Perhaps you walk into the office and immediately *know* that a colleague is pregnant even before she's felt comfortable telling anyone in the office! She can't figure out how you know, but it's really just *psychometry*—the ability to "read" energy information given off by people and objects. You might be able to touch an antique table and instantly visualize the image of a pioneer woman in her white blouse and long skirts placing a letter, quill, and ink on the table. With concentration and focus, perhaps you can read all or part of the letter's address.

Experiences such as these are far more commonplace than most people realize. Other people who are with you at the time might also feel a spirit presence, as often happens in a *circle*, although it is less likely to happen when the spirit making contact is not personal to them. A circle is a group of people, usually having mediumistic abilities, who gather to connect with spirit entities.

While in England studying at Arthur Findley College, Rita toured Bath and stopped for lunch at the Priory, a beautiful hotel and restaurant. Again, the shimmering light appeared. The Abbey in Bath proved quite magnificent, with an overwhelming feeling of spirit presence. Rita's photos depicted a beautiful light radiating at the bottom of the photo, with no explanation for its presence.

Activating Your Mediumistic Abilities

Everyone has the ability to communicate with spirits. Many people simply don't use this ability, just as they might not use other abilities they have, such as singing or writing. But spirits are always all around us. Discovering spirit presence and establishing connections just requires awareness and focus.

Sometimes this is as simple as sitting in a quiet room and allowing yourself to experience all the energies in the room. From this is likely to emerge a sense of the presence of others—spirits. With practice, you can focus on certain spiritual presences to the exclusion of others, gaining a clearer image or impression. And with more practice, you can focus in such a way as to establish contact with a particular spirit (provided the spirit is willing).

Just as it's important to learn the proper techniques for any activity that blends ability and skill, you need to learn what to do and how to do it, so that your experiences remain positive and provide knowledge and healing.

In Your Dreams

A common setting for communication between we mortals and those of the Spirit realm is the dream. In the dream state, the conscious filters of your brain are turned off. As a result, dreams often teem with vivid and otherworldly images that seem as natural and real as the world we inhabit when awake. We don't doubt or question these dream images; at best, we look at them as insights or lessons, and at worst, we simply dismiss them as "just dreams." This makes dreams a natural environment for spirit contacts that we might otherwise reject or ignore.

Spirit contact in the dreamscape can take any number of forms. Sometimes departed loved ones appear as living, tangible beings—often younger and more vibrant than in life as we remember them. (This is often how the spirits of loved ones in other visitations appear, too; more on this in later chapters.) We might engage with dream images much as we are used to in real life. We might dream of the challenges and thrills of travel through a beloved city. Or our dreams may have no correlation to real events and circumstances. This is the beauty and the power of dreams: anything goes.

One of the themes in spirit contact dreams does indeed relate to travel. For example, the dreamer might be driving along a familiar road and stop to pick up a hitchhiker they recognize as a loved one or go to the airport to meet a loved one's incoming flight. These settings make sense; after all, visiting spirits are on a cosmic journey of sorts, traveling through time and space to call on us.

Occasionally, a dream visit from a spirit brings a message or even a warning. This could be about anything. Some of the most common and dramatic messages relate to health issues. A departed mother, aunt, sister, or female friend might appear in a dream complaining of constant abdominal pains and asking whether you can feel the pains too. Ignoring the dream message could cause your dreams to become more persistent and perhaps more graphic or startling. Until finally, you "get it" and see your gynecologist for a health screening to address that persistent tightness you've felt for a while now and to ease your mind by ruling out a cyst or cancer.

Sometimes spirit visitation dreams are more symbolic than practical, and it takes some detective work to figure out their messages. If such dreams puzzle you, don't just dismiss them as nonsense. There are many good books on dream interpretation that can help you understand the meanings of the symbols and images that occur in your dreams. Write the dreams down. Keeping a dream journal can also help identify your personal dream symbols, dream patterns, and their meanings for your life. If possible, keep a handwritten journal; studies show that the act of writing by hand creates distinctive neural connections in the brain and reinforces meaning and memory.

The tone of most spirit visitation dreams is one ultimately of comfort and reassurance. The loved one might feel your sadness and sense of loss and want you to know that the connection remains strong despite the physical separation. The spirit typically appears as whole, happy, and healthy; instantly, we know all is well. And this is the point. The visit is to reassure you, through images and experiences that make sense in the context of your physical world, that everything is okay. The message is clear: "Feel happy for me, because I am at peace." If the spirit presents to you in a visitation with the appearance of illness or injury, it may be a sign that healing needs to occur at that point in memory or that some issue remains unresolved or addressed. Something in the relationship must be healed or transformed to allow the energy to let go and move forward in peace.

Calling All Spirits

Spirits aren't usually waiting around on the Higher side, waiting for opportunities for contact with you. (Well, most aren't, anyway.) Often, you need to ask them to make themselves available for communication. However, when the spirit is called from the body abruptly, without opportunity to make proper goodbyes, as has happened with the tragic pandemic that began in 2020, a collective spiritual yearning builds, which softens the veil between the Physical and Spirit planes. The desire and need for healing connection, on both sides, is great.

In the chapters that follow, we help you identify and clarify your interests and reasons for communicating with the Spirit realm, and we give you methods and approaches to help you make the contact you desire. In Chapter 10, we talk about how to find a qualified, competent, and honest psychic professional who can guide you in your efforts.

Tell Me What You Want, and I'll Give You What You Need

When you're new to the processes of consciously communicating with spirits, you might feel disappointed and even skeptical when the contact or information that you receive isn't what you wanted. Relax. This is fairly common. Because they are more knowledgeable beings than us physical beings, discarnate spirits tell us what we are ready to hear.

As physical beings, we have a tendency to want The Answer. What is the meaning of life? Is there a God? When am I going to find love? Does it hurt to die? We aren't always seeking, or willing to accept, just simple answers or, less definitive still, just fragments of information. We want to know it all—nothing less then the secret of Life. Yet just as it is the small stuff, it's the everyday stuff that matters in physical life. It's the little things that matter in the bigger picture. And sometimes we physical and spirit entities have differences of opinion about *what* matters.

On the verge of separating from her husband of 20 years, Caroline came to Rita for a reading. In the sitting, Rita got an image of the Braintree Split, a local landmark that formed a fork in the road. In this image, Rita saw the skies open up and the vision of Caroline's grandparents, whose identities were clear to Caroline. They said, "Stay with him, work this through." Caroline didn't really want to hear this message but decided to give it a try. She's now been happily married for 33 years!

If you've made contact with the Spirit world, and you're not getting the information you want or don't understand the information you're receiving, take a look at what you're asking. Does your question match up with what you really want to know? Sometimes we ask one question, though we actually want information of a different sort than the answer will produce.

The more specific your question, the more clear your focus and the more likely you are to receive the response you seek. You might ask, "What is it like on the Higher side?" when really what you want to know is, "Do you still love me, even though you've passed on and now exist in a realm I can't share with you?" Your loved one's contact with you is, in itself, evidence that the answer to your real question (even if unasked) is a resounding "Yes!"

With experience, you'll gain understanding and confidence that will help you ask the right questions and make sense of the answers that you receive. Chapter 4 provides more information about this. There's really no great mystery to getting useful information from the Spirit world!

When You Just Know: Trust Your Intuition

Sometimes we speak of intuition as the sixth sense (the other five being those of tangibility we are familiar with: seeing, hearing, smelling, tasting, and touching). Intuition makes use of the other senses and can also enhance them. Typically, when we talk about intuitive messages, we say things like, "I feel" or "I sense." A person who is in tune with this sixth sense might say, "I intuit." Intuition is a different kind of felt knowing than the mindsight of our brain's mirror neuron system. While mindsight is informed by empathy, an in-tune knowing or intuition is informed by immediate cognition.

You just *know,* instantly and unequivocally—and often act accordingly on intuition. This means you might suddenly turn left when your usual commute route turns right. Later, you read in the local news that there was a horrible accident just beyond the intersection at which you would've turned right had you followed your regular route. Chance or coincidence? We don't think so! Allowing your conscious mind to override your intuition can make your intuition appear faulty when it's really right on target. Intuition is immediate; anything longer is intervention from your conscious mind.

When it comes to contact with spirits, intuition becomes your most powerful tool and your most reliable guide. Your intuition can tell you whether you're right on … or whether it's time to move on. However illogical it might seem at times, your intuition will never lead you astray.

How do you know when it truly is your intuition and not just your feelings of grief, sorrow, or longing? This isn't always easy, particularly if your feelings are intense. If you are concerned about whether an apparent contact or communication is authentic, consider consulting a medium. This brings in a "third party" who doesn't have knowledge of your past or the many little details only someone who was close to you would know.

As a medium certified with the Spiritualist Church Rita has extensive training and skill in validating a spirit's identity before sharing the contact with the person who is requesting it. Spirits typically offer authenticating information in the form of knowledge no one else—at least not the medium—would have. This might be a nickname or recollection of an event, or mention of a beloved pet or favorite food—whatever can conclusively establish that the spirit is who they say … or you believe they are. Suppose a medium cannot authenticate a spirit's identity. In that case, you can be fairly certain other factors are at play, such as your strong desire to connect to Spirit in a specific way to reach a specific person. (Or it could be that someone is coming through with a message only your sibling or child would be able to identify and understand.)

Bringing Us Goodness and Light

The most important thing to remember about communicating with spirits is that such communication is a gift through which you can do good for yourself and for others. Spirits allow or initiate contact so they can help us … and many times we can help them.

Is there a dark element to the realm beyond physical being? Inasmuch as there is a dark element in our physical world, probably. There are always those who seem capable of distorting the good to do bad. Horror stories and movies make the most of this potential. But what they're really doing is exploiting our fears, especially the fear of the unknown and unprovable. And judging by the popularity of this genre, there's plenty of fear to exploit!

But communicating with spirits is not about fear, evil, or darkness. Rather, spirit communication is about love, goodness, and light. If you believe that goodness guides existence, as Rita does, then you know that the spirits of loved ones who have passed on, guardian spirits, and other spirit entities want to help us, not hurt us. (And sometimes they want us to help them, too.) The pursuit of goodness frames our existence and purposephysical and spiritual.

That is the focus of *The Awakened Life: Communicating with Spirits*—to help you communicate with your spirit guides, spirit guardians, and loved ones to find comfort, reassurance, and answers.

You might be seeking closure, reconciliation, or guidance on the passage through your physical life. Your reasons for wanting to communicate across the boundary of physical existence are as unique as anything else about you. Rita seeks to provide you with the understanding and tools you need to make the contact you desire.

Let your healing journey begin!

Divine Purpose

There is a Divine purpose in spirit communication, and its history throughout humanity stands as incontrovertible evidence. Nearly every religion or faith system in the world today, and indeed throughout history, incorporates some element of belief in an existence beyond life in the physical world. These beliefs transcend the boundaries of religion to demonstrate a nearly universal acceptance of the soul's ongoing existence.

Such beliefs do not contradict religious frameworks that support reincarnation, the promise of Heaven, a unity of Spirit, or other tenets that define a particular faith or religion. Beliefs in the soul's continuation beyond the death of the physical body are part of many faith systems, supported by and supporting a diverse and vast number of faiths. And they share in common the fundamental principle that knowledge and light lead the way to communication that is for goodness and healing.

Preparing for the Afterlife

Through the ages, there have been many diverse customs and practices related to the passage of a person's spirit from the physical world to the Spirit world—death. However, they are consistent in their reflection that human beings have probably always believed in the continuation of the soul's existence after the physical body dies. Throughout history, most cultures have viewed death as a passage to another level of being. Burial traditions remain as tangible evidence of this view.

Still considered the most staid and venerable of reference resources, *Encyclopedia Britannica, Fifteenth Edition,* says: "Death rites and customs stem from an instinctive inability or refusal on the part of man to accept death as the definitive end of human life; they thus reflect the belief that human beings survive death in some form and represent the practical measures taken to assist the dead to achieve their destiny …."

As the earliest archaeological evidence dating to about 50,000 B.C.E.—the time of *Paleolithic Era,* or Stone Age, demonstrates, human beings have always viewed the end of this life as a preparation for the next. The Paleolithic period began 2.5 million years ago and is considered the dawn of modern humankind. The Stone Age was the time when humans began creating tools and implements out of stone and other natural materials. This was the point of development at which humans became clearly distinct from other animals. So, it seems that from the very beginnings of humanity, human beings possessed the urge to honor the human spirit and the belief in its endurance beyond life with rituals that soothed the grieving and lovingly prepared the soul for what lay beyond Earthly existence.

Throughout history and across cultures, many of the preparations for a life after death involve the physical body, from dressing it in the finest attire to embalming it to prevent its deterioration. Although in modern times, we might think of these procedures as simply part of the funeral preparation, they are persistent evidence of our conviction that there is, so to speak, life after life. Even the tradition of cremation that has emerged in some cultural traditions such as Native American and Hindu reflects a releasing of the spirit from its physical body to be free to exist as a spirit.

Will we need these physical bodies we now inhabit when we move beyond our current lives? Nearly all prevailing belief systems say no. Rather, they hold there is a discarnate (without a physical body) existence beyond the physical existence, in which a body is not necessary. However, earlier cultures were less certain of this and often buried loved ones with a supply of food, water, and sometimes even furnishings, jewelry, and other accouterments that might be necessary or useful for survival in the next world.

Today, the impulse to surround a loved one who has passed with favorite possessions, photographs, and tokens of love and a life well lived act as a balm for the living and a hope of remembrance and comfort for loved ones in the afterlife. Carefully adorning the physical body with clothing and accessories of significance is more than an act of love; it holds the hope that the loved one will carry their identity onward. Delicately dressing a beloved grandmother in a favorite dress, with all the details from hat to pumps to pearls and earrings, as if ready for Sunday service and family brunch, honors our most ancient human traditions. Including one of her perfect vintage purses filled with letters, cards, documents, and photographs from her life holds the intention that she will have with her what she needs to remember herself and all she loved.

Awaiting Rebirth

So, let's go back in time to those ancient humans for evidence. If you're about to enter a new existence, it makes sense that you should be in the proper position. This seems to have been the belief of the Paleolithic peoples who once roamed the plains of what is now Europe. Archaeologists have uncovered numerous skeletons curled into fetal positions, apparently in readiness for birth into their next lives. Uncovered burial sites also contained food and stone implements such as hammers and knives.

We don't have any way of knowing conclusively what these early humans actually believed about life or death. There are no written records or even drawings to document these prehistoric times. But the archaeological findings strongly suggest that Paleolithic humans viewed death as a transition, not an end. They greatly anticipated and eagerly welcomed the birth of each new child; it seems reasonable to conclude that they would also celebrate and honor the passing into the next life.

Just as they communicated among each other in the physical world, perhaps they communicated with those in the Spirit world. From archaeological evidence, such as drawings and etchings on rocks and in caves, we know that later humans did have such beliefs. And we know that the few remaining indigenous cultures today, who have not experienced contact with the modern world, also appear to have such beliefs.

With the inner eye of your imagination, it's easy to see a small group gathered around a fresh mound of earth that marks the place where a tribesman has been returned to the womb of Mother Earth, singing and dancing in celebration of this transition. This tribe might gather similarly in joy and happiness to welcome an infant's birth.

Crossing the River

By the time the ancient Greek and Roman civilizations dominated much of the Western world, the realm sometimes called the "other side" had become a tangible place. This perception grew from the mythology of the time and became a crucial element of the era's philosophy. Mythology gave the ancient Greeks and Romans their gods, which then framed their philosophical beliefs and social customs.

In this ancient mythology, Hades was the god who ruled the souls of those who passed from physical life. Because the living resided on the ground and the gods inhabited the heavens, the kingdom of Hades was underground, or the Underworld. Its location within the Earth established it as a place the living could not go and provided for a physical separation between the world of the living and the world of the dead.

There was no judgment of good or evil involved, and Hades was not the counterpart to the devil we know of later belief systems. Hades was not a place, even though the word became a handy substitute in seventeenth-century England for what had become a vulgar term, "Hell," which was a most unpleasant location indeed!

Because the Underworld was a place from which no one returned, mythology evolved a barrier to separate the world of the living from the final home of the eternal soul, the river Styx. Upon the body's death, the soul had to make what could be a treacherous crossing to get to the other side, where happiness and loved ones who had already passed awaited. The boatman who ferried souls across the river Styx was a monstrous creature named Charon who demanded advance payment from his passengers in exchange for the labor of his services.

Of course, these souls were no longer of the physical world and could not make payment themselves, so it was up to their living relatives or friends to buy safe passage for them. They did this by placing a coin in the mouth of the departed. Charon extracted the coin and allowed the soul to board his boat, which he then steered through the roiling waters of the Styx to the other side.

Making it to the other side wasn't quite the end of the journey for the soul, however. Once across the river, there was a gate that blocked passage to the world of eternity. Cerberus, the three-headed dog with a voracious appetite, guarded the gate and could only be distracted from his duties by being fed. So, the living relatives of the departed put a cake of honey with the body as payment to Cerberus for entry into the Underworld. Only then could the soul pass through the gate to be reunited for all eternity with the loved ones who had already made their passages.

Only Charon could navigate the perilous river, and because there was no way to pay the fare for the return passage, he never brought anyone back. Although the physical person couldn't return to the world of the living, the spirit, however, could. Ghosts, visible images of the departed, often appeared to the living and engaged freely in communication with those in the physical world. After taking up residence in the Underworld, the soul could appear as a vision and speak with the living. Soldiers often called on the souls of great warriors who had passed on to be by their sides in battle and help them to great victory. (Does this sound familiar? If you're an *Outlander* fan, it instantly calls to mind a vision of James Alexander Malcolm Mackenzie Fraser calling on the spirit of his uncle, clan war chief Dougal, before the Battle of Alamance in the American colonies.) If survival of the battle were not to be, the departed souls of the great warriors would guide them to the shores of the river Styx for their own journeys to the palace of Hades and to eternal life.

Ancient Roman beliefs and practices were similar to those of the Greeks. Some of the names were different—the river the Romans crossed was the Acheron, for example. Of course, we are still retelling these mythological stories in our own time, making use of ancient metaphors to navigate a universal passage. British author Kazuo Ishiguro, winner of the Booker Prize for his beloved novel *The Remains of the Day* and the 2017 Nobel Prize for Literature, is also the author of *The Buried Giant*. Here, the story borrows Celtic and old Briton traditions to explore the quest to the river and the hope of life after life. With the help of the boatman, the elderly Axl will be ferried across the river to reunite with his beloved wife, Beatrice. (Beatrice was also the goal of Dante's quest through the afterlife in the magnificent classic *The Divine Comedy*—from losing his way in the Dark Wood to Hell's Inferno, Dante always strove upward for celestial bliss … and Beatrice. In this fourteenth-century epic poem, the ancient poet Virgil leads Dante's journey through the Underworld.)

Determining death in ancient times was less than precise. It was so common for a person to "come back to life" that Greek law required a waiting period of three days between the declaration of death and the burial of the body. The many "awakenings" that took place during the three-day waiting period no doubt reinforced the belief in the continuation of life.

In our time, viral infectious diseases such as SARS, Ebola, and COVID-19 are disrupting the personal and social process of dying and are making it difficult for loved ones to validate their loss first-hand. In African nations, burial customs traditionally involve handling the body of the deceased to bathe and dress it for burial. Continuing such traditions during Ebola outbreaks proved impossible without spreading the virus throughout the community. During the global pandemic of COVID-19, hundreds of thousands in the United States died alone without their families present at their bedsides and were interred, often with no family permitted to attend. The stress of so many people passing in this manner has caused breakdowns in the emotional health of loved ones. The health professionals' emotional health has also broken down because they must witness the anguish of the dying, as well as that of their loved ones.

The need to embrace a dying loved one and assist in easing their passage to the Spirit plane is an essential human desire. When that process is impeded, grief becomes overwhelming. Families need to know their loved ones died well and that they have their blessing for the journey beyond. Communicating with spirits performs a vital function in helping loved ones make that essential connection, to restore dignity, and to provide closure to the dying process. Even for those who do not believe, meditating on the essence of a loved one and asking for the best and highest for their journey to the light can bring about a beginning, a movement toward peace and comfort.

Embalming and the Circle of Necessity

The ancient Egyptians were the first to systematically preserve the physical body after death to prevent its decay and deterioration by using the process of embalming. The term originally meant, "to apply balm," a reference to the early practice of covering a dead body in fragrant oils and spices. The ancient Egyptians believed that once the soul left the body, it embarked on a long spiritual journey, called the "circle of necessity," after which it would seek to return to the body it had left behind in the physical world. This made it necessary to preserve the body for the duration of the soul's expedition, typically identified as 3,000 years, so the soul would be able to return to its body and live again.

Because a properly prepared and preserved body was so essential for the soul to complete its journey through the circle of necessity, only priests could perform embalming. This preparation for the soul's journey was so important that it took place behind the walls of the Necropolis … "death city."

The typical embalming procedure involved removing and carefully storing the body's organs, including the brain, in special urns called canopic jars. Resin was then poured into the jars to prevent the organs from deteriorating. After soaking in a salt solution called natron for as long as 70 days, the body was dried and wrapped in long, resin-soaked strips of cloth—creating what we call a mummy.

What we think of as traditional mummification was actually a service available only to ancient Egyptians who could afford it. The poor received a much less sophisticated embalming process, which involved soaking the body in the salt solution and then placing it in a common burial chamber.

The mummified body was then placed in a coffin or crypt of some sort, with the urns containing its organs surrounding it. The crypt was then carefully sealed; after all, it had to preserve its contents for 3,000 years so the soul could return to claim its body when the journey was complete. Without a body to return to, the soul was destined to travel endlessly, unable to come full circle into its new life.

While the soul was on its 3,000-year journey, it was not possible to communicate with it. It was common, however, to offer prayers for its safe travels and happy return. And of course, only through legend was there any "evidence" of a spirit returning to claim its well-preserved body. No one lived long enough to provide eyewitness proof!

The concept of the circle of necessity was common in other ancient cultures as well, such as the Celts and some tribes in Peru. And today it is an element of belief systems, such as some forms of Hinduism, although preservation of the body is no longer essential. The soul's journey is one of spiritual growth and enlightenment that leads to a higher spiritual existence, rather than a return to a physical life.

Spirits Among the Living

You might feel, see, and hear the presence of loved ones who have passed. This might happen during times of crisis, or it might be a normal part of your everyday life. If you're accustomed to these visitors, you probably find them comforting, as did the ancient Japanese. They believed that when the spirit left the body at death, it entered into existence as a *kami*, a spirit entity or supernatural being. Death was not a process of leaving but rather a transition into another form. A kami is the spirit of a departed family member that remains among the family and community. It comes from the Japanese word for "divine." As an element of the Shintō religion, kamis can also be the spirits of deities and of things from nature.

As a part of the family and the community, a kami remained to participate in important decisions and offer guidance. People who were good and helpful in life become benefactors and protectors as kamis; people who were not so good in life become troublesome kamis. Just as in physical life, the good and the bad were simply part of the mix. Kamis who had been leaders and heroes in physical life were more powerful spirit entities than those who had been ordinary citizens. A few, like kings and rulers, became god-like as kamis.

The belief in kamis became the foundation for Shintō, Japan's indigenous, or native, religion. Within Shintō, kamis could be deities (gods and goddesses), ancestral spirits (family members), animals, and even other natural things such as trees. Despite their presence in everyday life, kamis remained unseen and unheard except to those with special powers to communicate with them. Today, we would call such people mediums—those who could intervene to halt a disruptive kami's actions or to encourage help from a benevolent kami. Many of these interventions, according to legend, had to do with healing, either to rid a family or village of illness or to bring health to an individual.

Otherwise, communication with kamis came in the guise of actions and events. Fortune, good or bad, was considered the work of kamis. Every family's home had a shrine to honor its kamis, and throughout the countryside there were (and in many places still are) shrines to honor important kamis, typically deities and heroes. Through these shrines, people could share messages with kamis. Buddhism eventually incorporated some elements of Shintō, among them the concept of kamis, which spread the belief into other cultures and societies, including China and India.

Contemporary Belief in the Continuity of Spirit

Celebrations of Spirit exist in many cultures. Most had their roots in belief systems of some sort and now have migrated into popular culture. There must be something about the end of autumn as it transitions into winter that makes it an apparent window between the physical world and the Spirit world. Celebrations and festivals had their origins in pagan religious practices that have made their way into various faith systems. (Pagan beliefs allow the worship of multiple deities, gods, goddesses, and natural events such as the changing of the seasons. They are typically contrasted to belief systems based on worship of a single, omnipotent God, such as in Christianity and Judaism.) The Festival of Samhain, for example, has become the Christian celebrations All Hallow's Eve (falling on October 31) and All Saint's Day (falling on November 1).

Awaken, Spirits!

October 31 was the last day of the ancient Celtic year and the Festival of Samhain, the Celtic god of the dead. As one year became another, the Celts believed the spirits of the dead could return from the beyond to share joy and happiness with their living loved ones. Feasting, dancing, and singing celebrated this opportunity. Enormous bonfires lit the night sky, welcoming revelers and spirits alike.

But fearing that some of the returning spirits might have less than honorable intentions, people often donned masks and costumes to hide their true identities. Of course, the good spirits of departed friends and relatives knew those behind the masks and could make contact for a joyous reunion. The light of dawn, marking the start of the Celtic New Year, recalled the spirits to the Spirit world.

Today, we know this festival as Halloween, and its modern celebration has little to do with its Celtic origins. For most people, it is nothing more than an excuse to dress up in costumes (and perhaps behave in ways that cause them to be grateful their identities are hidden) and for children, to acquire enough candy to keep dentists very busy for yet another year!

Do you feel a little extra energy in the air on All Hallow's Eve? Do you have a sense that there is a presence around you that you don't ordinarily feel? Perhaps it is the spirits of your loved ones taking the opportunity of heightened awareness to attempt a connection with you. Many people experience such contacts around this time of the year, as well as throughout the year.

A Communion of Spirits

In 835, Pope Gregory IV proclaimed that the last day in October was to be known within the Catholic Church as All Hallow's Eve, or "All Holy Evening." On this date, the pontiff decreed that Catholics everywhere were to gather and remember those who had given their lives in the name of their faith. The next day, November 1, became All Saint's Day (also called All Soul's Day), a time to remember all who had passed on.

The Catholic Church views this time it has named a Communion of Spirits as a reminder that there is a continuous link between the souls of the living and the souls of the dead. Says the Catechism of the Catholic Church, the Church's official teachings, "Between them there is an abundant exchange of all good things." Various Protestant religions also observe these celebrations.

Day of the Dead

Day of the Dead doesn't sound like a very joyous celebration, but the tradition is quite festive. Day of the Dead started long ago with the Aztecs, who once inhabited the land we now know as Mexico, to honor the Aztec goddess Mictecacihuatl, who ruled the dead. Even in Aztec times, this was a happy celebration, praising Mictecacihuatl for watching over the souls of those who had passed into her realm. There were several days of dancing, singing, and feasting, during which the spirits of the departed also joined in the festivities.

Through the centuries, the influences of other cultures and belief systems realigned the Day of the Dead to take place during Christian celebrations of All Saint's Day during the last days of October and first days of November. Today, the official celebration of the Mexican Day of the Dead takes place on November 2. Families and friends gather at the gravesites of loved ones or establish shrines in their homes to tell stories and remember those who have passed.

It is said that you can feel the spirits reveling right alongside their living relatives! There is also much feasting and drinking, with small offerings of the departed's favorite foods and drinks (and even tobacco if the person was a smoker) at the graveside or on the shrine's altar.

Creating your own Day of the Dead celebration can be a cathartic and intimate experience. Think about assembling a shrine with an altar to your loved one, including photos, video, tokens, candles, food, remembrances; gathering whatever objects honor the deceased and your relationship. Is it too much to have a permanent shrine to your loved one? Probably, it is. But surely enjoying a celebration evoking the joyous vitality of the spirit of someone you have loved is a good way to lighten a special day of remembrance.

Finding Your Own Divine Purpose

We all have our reasons for wanting to establish and maintain a personal Communion of Spirits. Yours might be linked to your faith system or religious practices, or it might be the result of an independent belief in the continuity of the spirit, a curiosity about your ancestors, or simply the desire to heal the dying process through spiritual union. Traditions through the history of humankind and formalized celebrations within today's organized religions affirm that such desires are nearly universal. And these desires are positive. They are rooted in love and in goodness—truly what we would consider Divine purpose, connections for a greater good. This is the essence of communicating with spirits.

Spiritualism: Continuity of the Spirit

Many of the world's faith systems incorporate some concept of a soul's continuing existence after the death of the physical body. But just one, Spiritualism, is actually founded on these concepts. Spiritualism accepts that spirit communication is a natural and common occurrence in the physical world that has been taking place throughout the history of human existence and that much healing and good can come from it.

Like all belief systems, Spiritualism comes with its own traditions—the stories and experiences that make up its history and heritage. Some are entertaining, while some are inspiring. Collectively, they reflect the evolution of Spiritualist thinking from random communication with spirits to the purposeful connections that modern Spiritualist mediums, such as Rita, make in their teaching and practice. Spiritualism today has much to offer to those seeking to understand our human spiritual resources and the many ways in which spirits, in and out of the human body, interact and evolve.

Let's time travel through the evolution of Spiritualism. It's time to meet the characters and circumstances that have taken Spiritualism through its rise, its near-fall, and its revival in the world today.

Two Sisters and a Ghost

Modern Spiritualism came into popular practice in 1848 when two sisters—Catherine and Margaretta Fox—moved with their parents into a small house in Hydesville, New York. Their story is well documented through an affidavit Mrs. Fox wrote about the family's experiences, as well as through numerous anecdotes from those who heard about the strange communication that the Fox sisters established with a ghost who already resided—unwillingly and unhappily—in the house.

On December 11, 1847, the Fox family moved into its Hydesville home, which was to be a temporary residence while the family's new house was being built. Almost immediately, they heard noises in the night. Not being familiar with the history of the house, they tried to ignore the strange sounds that kept them awake. But on March 4, 1848, the bangs and rappings became particularly loud. Catherine and Margaretta were very frightened and ran to their parents' bedroom. The parents, too, were awake and listening, and walked through the rest of the house trying to find the cause of all the racket.

There were knocks on the pantry door and footsteps in the hallway. Windows and doors were closed tight; nothing appeared out of the ordinary. Yet the rapping, banging, and thumping continued even as the Foxes searched the house. "I then concluded that the house must be haunted by some unhappy restless spirit," Mrs. Fox later wrote in her affidavit about the family's experiences.

The frightened sisters decided they were going to sleep in their parents' room until the noises ceased. After a week or so, they began to feel more comfortable. One night, Catherine, feeling brave in the safety of her parents' bed, said, "Mr. Splitfoot, do as I do!" and she clapped her hands. To her amazement, she heard clapping in response. Then Margaretta clapped one, two, three, four … and heard back one, two, three four raps!

The girls called for their mother. Mrs. Fox took over the questioning, determined to get to the bottom of the situation. She tested the visitor's knowledge by asking it to rap the number of children she had. Seven raps. She asked again; she had just six children. Seven raps again. Puzzled at first, Mrs. Fox then asked how many of those children were living. Six raps. No one outside the family knew that the youngest Fox child, little Emily, had passed as an infant some years earlier.

With a simple code—two raps for "yes"—and more counting, Mrs. Fox extracted the information that this was indeed a ghost, a man who had been murdered in the house by a man who had once lived there. Not knowing the history of the house's residents, Mrs. Fox asked her neighbors, the Redfields, who had lived in the area all of their lives, to come over. As it turned out, the Redfields had once lived in the house and knew of the other families who had also called it home. Again, there was an exchange of names and raps. Mr. Redfield went through the list of names of the house's former residents until one name—Bell—returned two raps, the signal for "yes." Frustratingly, however, the neighbor wasn't able to identify the ghost. Finally,

Mrs. Fox hit upon the solution. She worked out a code to identify the letters of the alphabet, and instructed the spirit to rap once for each letter of his name. The questioning eventually elicited the name of one Charles Rosna, who, other neighbors later recalled, had been a traveling peddler who had disappeared six years earlier.

Further questioning brought forth the claim that Rosna's body was buried in the cellar. Neighbors who rushed to dig for the body were unable to locate anything because a high water table just a few feet beneath the basement's earthen floor flooded into the basement as soon as they dug into it, leaving Rosna's fate unproven. Or was it? In the summer of 1848, when the weather became dry, the Foxes and some of their curious neighbors went back into the basement. This time, they were able to dig deeper, unearthing bone fragments and a peddler's bag.

It was evidence enough to launch the Fox sisters into careers as mediums. They soon discovered that it wasn't only their resident spirit with whom they could communicate. It seemed they could summon spirits of all sorts, spirits eager to make contact with loved ones in the physical world.

The sisters quickly became well known even beyond their local community. Hundreds of people flocked to their home for spirit communication. In 1849, Margaretta Fox gave a demonstration of her mediumship abilities in New York City, which sealed her fame. Much of the time, the famous were among those who came to her during her career as a medium, including author James Fennimore Cooper (who penned *The Last of the Mohicans,* among other stories) and William Cullen Bryant, poet, attorney, and editor of New York's *Evening Post.* The media dubbed the sisters and those who believed in their abilities "Spiritualists"—and a movement was born.

The November 23, 1904, edition of the Boston *Journal* carried an article that claimed a skeleton had finally been discovered in the basement of the old Fox house. Children playing in the basement discovered a false wall, behind which the bones apparently belonging to Charles Rosna rested. The wall had been constructed directly beneath the kitchen and pantry, the location where the Foxes had heard all the knocking, rapping, and footsteps.

The Poughkeepsie Seer

The events that catapulted the Fox sisters to fame as mediums and established Spiritualism as a movement did not just happen out of the blue, of course. Others had been exploring the relationship between body and Spirit, some from within the context of religion and others from the framework of science. Just before the Foxes moved to Hydesville, another New Yorker, Andrew Jackson Davis (1826–1910), published what was to become a breakthrough work for him and for Spiritualism: *The Principles of Nature, Her Divine Revelations, and a Voice to Mankind.*

As a young child, Davis showed strong psychic abilities. When the family moved to Poughkeepsie, Davis encountered a tailor who detected these abilities and discovered that Davis could use them for medical diagnosis. At the age of 18, Davis had a metaphysical experience that changed the course of his life. In what seemed both a *trance* state and a *visitation*, Davis met the spirit of famed theologian and scientist Emanuel Swedenborg (1688–1722), who had died more than 100 years before Davis was born. A trance is a state of altered consciousness in which the medium allows a spirit to speak through them with information to be received. A visitation is when a spirit speaks directly *to* you rather than *through* a medium.

It was this "trance visitation" that produced the book *The Principles of Nature, Her Divine Revelations, and a Voice to Mankind,* which Davis dictated over the course of more than a year. In the book, he predicted the discovery of the eighth and ninth planets (Neptune and Pluto, respectively), at the direction of Swedenborg. Under Swedenborg's direction, Davis also wrote *Univericoelum (The Spiritual Philosopher).* Himself an uneducated man, Davis wrote these and other manuscripts in a ponderous, scholarly, and complex style similar to that of Swedenborg.

When published in 1847, *The Principles of Nature* met with intense interest among those already interested in the concept of the continuing the life of the spirit. It wasn't until after the events of Hydesville, however, that Davis's book gained popular attention. Although somewhat cumbersome to comprehend, *The Principles of Nature* outlined in great detail the interrelationships among human physical existence, the mind, and the spirit (personal spirit as well as Divine Spirit). The language was complex and technical, making it difficult for the average person to read but affirming the manuscript's connection to Swedenborg, who wrote in the same style.

Spiritualism's Most Famous Advocate: No Mystery Here

In its relatively short existence, Spiritualism has drawn interest and support from a number of famous people. Few were better known than Sir Arthur Conan Doyle (1859–1930). You might know of him as the creator of the great fictional detective Sherlock Holmes. But did you know this renowned writer was also a physician … and a prominent investigator of psychic phenomena, as well as one of Spiritualism's most zealous supporters? Although better known as a writer of mystery novels and stories, Doyle was trained and practiced as a physician. He was knighted in 1902 for his work with military field hospitals in South Africa during the Boer War.

As it turns out, 1902 was a fortuitous year for the good doctor. That was also when he met Sir Oliver Lodge, a renowned physicist of the time who was intrigued by the relationship between the physical world and the realm of human consciousness. He was particularly fascinated with the concept of thought transference—the process of being able to communicate one's thoughts without physical means, such as speaking or writing. Doyle was also interested in this area and had engaged in some informal research of his own. He respected Lodge and his studies and found the other scientist's methods compelling.

After establishing a literary career of writing detective and romance novels, Doyle's interest in thought transference led him to further exploration and to understand the notion of communication between spirits in this world and in the Spirit world. Doyle turned his full attention to that cause and joined the Society for Psychical Research, a prominent and well-respected organization of the time. He also attended mediumistic readings at his friends' homes, which so intrigued him that he began his own studies with a medium.

In midlife, Doyle published a number of books that were a considerable departure from the fiction that had made him famous: *The New Revelation, The Vital Message, Wanderings of a Spiritualist*, and the two-volume *The History of Spiritualism*. These books discussed his research, his conclusions, and his beliefs, all of which strongly advocated Spiritualism.

In his own spirit communication through mediums, Doyle was able to make contact with his son, who was wounded and died during World War I, as well as his mother and other relatives. These experiences were both comforting and validating for him and gave a depth to his insights that could only come from such deeply personal contacts. Unfortunately, they also gave rise to criticism from skeptics who felt that Doyle's personal grief dulled his scientific senses. But these criticisms only strengthened Doyle's commitment to Spiritualism.

Doyle concluded his literary career in 1930, not with a final Sherlock Holmes adventure but with what he considered a work of enlightenment, *The Edge of the Unknown*. This book, his last, presented Doyle's observations and insights about 15 famous mysterious events, such as magician Harry Houdini's apparent dematerializations and writings from the Higher side by a number of deceased authors, including Charles Dickens and Jack London.

Despite their opposing beliefs about Spiritualism, Sir Arthur Conan Doyle and magician Harry Houdini (whose real name was Erich Wiess) were good friends. In his book *The Edge of the Unknown*, Doyle writes of his belief that Houdini had significant psychic abilities, which Houdini denied. Houdini believed mediums were, as he was, simply masters of deception. However, when Houdini's mother died, he went to a medium who was able to bring her spirit through and convey what she and Houdini had established as the secret message they would use as evidence that life continued beyond death of the physical body.

Doubters, Challengers, and, Sadly, Frauds

Of course, there have always been—and always will be—those who doubt the authenticity of spirit contact and spirit communication. On the one hand, it's perfectly natural to expect proof or evidence that a spirit communication is authentic. (We discuss this in more detail later in this chapter.). But there are those who are never satisfied with the evidence as proof.

In the late decades of the nineteenth century, the Spiritualist Church became a formal entity with congregations throughout the Western world. This organization gave a level of credibility to Spiritualism and established it as a process inextricably linked to the Divine. (More on this later in this chapter.) Spirit contacts were not late-night parlor games but rather integral elements of a religious institution. This gave increased credibility to Spiritualism. Many of the movement's early detractors became its most ardent supporters (including Sir Arthur Conan Doyle, who started his explorations of psychic phenomena from the scientific platform of evidentiary proof).

Spiritualism as an institution has endured its share of scandal through the years, typically the result of fraudulent actions on the part of people acting as mediums. Tragically, those seeking insight and understanding, particularly when driven by unassuaged grief and desperation, are vulnerable to manipulation. By the 1930s, England had passed the Fraudulent Medium Act and other legislation intended to protect the public from cheats and hoaxers, which of course, didn't prevent them from proceeding to scam the unsuspecting. Over the next few decades, Spiritualism lost popular favor and entered a period of decline. Although this could do nothing to diminish the authenticity of true spirit communication (and the true practice of Spiritualism), the void left by charlatans did leave people somewhat floundering for trustworthy ways to address their spiritual needs.

Since the 1970s, however, interest in spirit communication and a sincere practice of Spiritualism has been on the rise. This is partly the result of a more open environment with regard to personal freedom and expression and partly the re-emergence of interest in self-healing. The surge of interest in "New Age" concepts that swept through the United States and other parts of the Western world in the 1980s broadened the appeal and acceptance of spirit contact and communication. As the decades went by, advances in science revealing the mysteries and capabilities of human consciousness have led many researchers and laypeople alike to reconsider exploring the rich possibilities of spirit communication. Although the exact numbers are hard to come by, it's safe to say that more people practice Spiritualism today than ever in its history.

Mediumship and Spiritualism

Mediumship is an integral part of Spiritualism. Through mediums, spirits communicate with those in the physical world. Mediums who are certified in the Spiritualist Church (as is Rita) undergo extensive training and must pass a series of qualifying examinations (including doing a complete church service with spirit communication to the satisfaction of a board of ordained spiritualist ministers and certified mediums).

All mediums have psychic abilities, but not all psychics have mediumistic abilities. (There's more on this in Chapter 14.) It takes time, focus, and training to develop skill as a medium. It is a Spiritualist medium's responsibility to prove the continuity of life beyond a shadow of a doubt. This means that when the Spiritualist medium finally begins talking to you with messages from spirits that are present, they have a clear sense of what the spirit looks or sounds like, why the spirit is present, and even who the spirit is. This doesn't mean the medium knows all of this for certain; it only means that they have a good sensibility surrounding it.

Before your first visit with a medium, or at least before the reading begins, ask about the medium's qualifications and training. Expect to hear where the medium received training and certification, how long the medium has been practicing, which kind of mediumship the medium practices, and also what other relevant background they have. Even though it is the mediumistic abilities that make spirit communication possible, it is the medium's life experiences that filter and inform the information coming through.

Spiritualism holds that every human being has at least limited mediumistic capacity. Each of us has the ability to communicate with spirits on the Higher side, if we pay attention to the signals we receive. As is the case with any human ability, some people are more innately skilled than others.

Mental Phenomena

Do you ever think something really obscure and specific, then have a friend text and repeat it almost exactly? It could be that great minds think alike, or it must be *telepathy!* Telepathy is a process of thought transference. Such events happen often, yet we usually don't give them too much additional thought. But have you ever struggled with a problem, then "heard" a voice (sounding, to the ear of your mind, suspiciously like your grandmother who passed away not long ago) giving you encouragement and words of advice and support? If you're tuned into your psychic senses, you might notice and acknowledge this message from your ancestor. If you're oblivious to your psychic senses, you might act on the message without understanding its origin from Spirit. Or, you might dismiss the message from your mind because a message from your grandmother who's passed doesn't register as being logical—because it *couldn't* have happened, right?

Such experiences are often mental mediumistic phenomena; that is, a spirit has activated your mediumistic abilities in an attempt to convey a message to you. Of course, that was your grandmother's voice speaking to you from beyond the physical world! You know, as she does, that only she would call you by the childhood nickname she gave you when you spent summers with her way back when, a name that'd nearly fallen from memory until you heard her voice say it again.

When a trained medium receives mental phenomena, they can be quite spectacular. There is countless documentation of mediums delivering messages of detailed instruction for carrying out tasks that the medium knows nothing about. Complicated endeavors, such as writing a book, preparing a seven-course meal, or creating an invention!

Physical Phenomena

Physical mediumship is more advanced and more complex. Not everyone has the mediumistic abilities necessary to receive physical phenomena. Such phenomena might include levitation, materialization, transfiguration—all of which involve the spirit using the medium's energy to convey its message. Rapping and table-tipping are also physical phenomena (see Chapter 11).

Sometimes physical phenomena are quite specialized, putting to use the medium's special talents. Rita receives physical phenomena in the form of Spirit drawing or Spirit painting; you'll see her artwork throughout this book. Other mediums might receive spirit communication through spirit photography or automatic writing (which we'll talk more about in Chapter 10).

Carolyn came to Rita for a sitting and Spirit drawing, and a great uncle who was a minister came through. Carolyn said she knew she had a great uncle in the family who wore a clerical collar, but she didn't know what he looked like. Three months later, her husband was looking through a box of old photos and called out, "I think I found a photo of the man Rita drew for you." Indeed, it was a match.

Spiritualism and the Divine

One important key to Spiritualism is the conviction that human existence consists of the body, mind, and spirit. The body, made of matter, is the outer, physical shell that contains both the mind and the spirit. The mind, also made of matter but of a different sort, houses the spirit, made of energy. This energy is what links spirits across the border of the physical world and makes spirit communication possible.

Another key to Spiritualism is the conviction that this energy is Light, in that it represents the presence and the power of the Divine. As a result, it is good, and it is for help and healing. Likewise, spirit communication is for good and for healing. Spiritualist mediums always begin their readings with a prayer to welcome the Light, the Divine, and request its guidance in keeping the reading focused on its intent—which is always to heal in some way.

Although its details change with each reading to be specific to the circumstances, purpose, and person, this is the general prayer Rita uses:

> Infinite Spirit, I ask that you be with me during this reading. I ask that you surround us with white light. I ask that this be healing, helpful, and evidential, to prove the continuity of life. I ask that this reading be blessed and that it help this person on their path of life. I give thanks for what we are about to receive. Amen.

The Power of Intent

To have a mediumistic reading without purpose is like driving without a destination. You certainly *could* end up someplace interesting and enjoyable, especially if you travel by car a lot and instinctively make the right choices about which direction to go. When the journey is spiritual rather than physical, most people have specific reasons for seeking spirit contact. Many desire contact with specific loved ones in the Spirit world. This is one part of intent. It doesn't always turn out that you get who you want; calling on the Divine places the communication direction in a Higher Power.

In seeking, the Divine will give you what you need but not always what you request. People sometimes make promises before they pass, but they can't always keep those promises because the choice might not be theirs. Know that whoever comes through to speak to you in a reading has a message for you that the Divine Spirit knows you must hear. It is for the highest and best purpose. So do not be disappointed if a medium is not able to contact a specific person from Spirit for you during a reading. Rather, open your mind, heart, and soul to welcome the spirit communication you receive and to examine its message, as well as feel the depth and breadth of its love.

Help and Healing

We've emphasized that the primary purpose of spirit communication is help and healing. What this means for you is unique and personal. Perhaps healing is closure to help you move on in your life following a loved one's sudden and unexpected passing. You could desire understanding of someone's behaviors that have affected you in some way. Or you might simply want to feel the presence of a beloved once more. You might just want proof that the spirit does continue after physical death and to give meaning and direction to your life's purpose.

Prove It!

It is human nature to want PROOF, especially of things that are deeply important to us on a personal level. For the Spiritualist medium, establishing proof of the continuity of life is essential with any spirit contact. This is usually not the kind of tangible proof in terms of something you can see or touch. Rather, it is evidence in the form of knowledge that only you and the spirit could share. Perhaps this is the spirit referring to you by a childhood nickname only one person would know. Or perhaps it is reminding you of a long-forgotten event or giving you the answer to a question you didn't know you were asking. Understanding and insight become clearer, which is how spirits are able to help those of us on the Earth plane.

The Appeal of Spiritualism

Spiritualism encourages self-exploration and learning. It fits within the context of just about any religious framework, and perhaps as importantly as any other function, it dispels fear. It is nothing more than the function of being spiritual—which we all are, regardless of our belief systems, simply because we are human beings with physical and spiritual selves.

Many of those attracted to the Spiritualist movement as it rose to prominence in the fifty years or so following the Fox sisters were people who challenged and probed the meaning of life from various contexts. They were physicians, scientists, writers, poets, and artists, but the early Spiritualists were also just ordinary people seeking answers to questions everyone has. The enduring appeal of Spiritualism speaks to the universal human desire to affirm the continuity of life through spirit communication. As an ordained minister in the Spiritualist Church and pastor of the First Spiritualist Church of Quincy, Massachusetts, Rita offers a healing ministry to those seeking comfort and catharsis through connecting to the Higher side of Spirit.

Spiritualist Declaration of Principles

Churches of many denominations offer services accessible by Internet streaming or video conferencing, allowing people the opportunity to participate remotely from any location.

Here is the Spiritualist Church's *Declaration of Principles:*

1. We believe in Infinite Spirit and that God is Infinite Spirit.
2. We believe that the phenomena of Nature, both physical and spiritual, are the expression of Infinite Spirit.
3. We affirm that living in harmony with one's understanding of Natural Law constitutes true religion.
4. We affirm that the existence and personal identity of the individual continues after the change called death.
5. We affirm that communication with the so-called dead is a fact, proven by the phenomena of Spiritualism.
6. We believe that the highest morality is contained in the Golden Rule: "Whatsoever ye would that others should do unto you do ye also unto them."
7. We affirm the moral responsibility of the individual and that we create our own happiness or unhappiness by choosing to live in harmony with Nature's physical and spiritual laws.
8. We affirm the doorway to reformation is never closed against any human soul here or hereafter.
9. We affirm that the precepts of Prophecy and Healing are Divine attributes proven through Mediumship.

If you are curious about the Spiritualist Church as a formal expression of the continuity of life, consider attending a service online. Video conferencing platforms allow for shared social relations. In the presence of others questing for Spirit, you confirm that you are not alone in your desire for connection to Spirit.

Spiritual Healing

Throughout this book, Rita guides you on a journey within that leads you from your deepest and highest expression of self to nurture a personal connection with Divine Spirit. In opening to the Divine, you allow yourself to welcome spirits to come through, for the purpose of comfort, healing, and holding onto the love that endures all things.

As you begin, Rita offers this prayer for spiritual healing:

> I ask the great, unseen healing force to remove all obstructions from my mind and body and restore me to perfect health. I ask this in all sincerity and honesty, and I will do my part.

I ask this great, unseen healing force to assist present and absent ones who are in need of help and to restore them to perfect health. I put my trust in the love and power of Infinite Spirit.

Remember—it bears repeating—*you are not alone*. Moreover, *your loved ones who have passed are not alone*. Spirit is everywhere around you. Let's begin the work of making contact.

Why Make Contact
with Spirit?

Does the soul's journey end with the death of the physical body? Neither science nor poetry, nor art's colors or music's fleeting notes have yet succeeded in revealing and validating the truth of human passage to the Higher side. However, the effort to do so is ingrained in the human psyche. There is a universal human need to understand the soul force that animates the human mind and body and to explore its eternal Spirit. Validation of continuity of life beyond death of the physical body means that we gain the knowledge that our spirits will continue on. In your life, what drives your interest in communicating with spirits? What do you want to learn and understand? Whom do you want to contact? Although most of the time it's usually those of us people in the physical world who wish to contact the spirits of loved ones who have passed on, sometimes it's a spirit on the Higher side that initiates communication. What could a spirit possibly need from us on this Earthly plane of life? You might be surprised!

Inquiring Minds Just Want to Know!

You're curious. You yearn to know that there *is* something beyond this physical life for you and for those you love. And you wouldn't mind knowing a bit about what that something might be like. This desire to prove for ourselves what has yet to be empirically proven is a normal impulse. The desire to prove the continuity of life is among the most basic of human curiosities.

We think, therefore we anticipate and we question. To validate for ourselves, in our own knowing, the continuity of life is also to validate something essential in the act of living itself. Such knowing gives our lives meaning both individually and collectively. So, to know there is life beyond life—that our identity as human beings continues after the physical life is over, gives meaning to the nature of life itself.

Spirit phenomena comes in many forms—voices, visions, and sensations. Being able to validate or authenticate these messages is what establishes them as intentional. This happens when all of the bits and pieces of received information that you gather build images from Spirit that will prove familiar to you. Sometimes the Spirit images aren't what you expect, and sometimes they aren't even recognizable until you do a little research and analysis.

The very first spirit message that Rita received in a reading was from a great-aunt she didn't know she had. After the reading, Rita called her mother, who verified and deciphered the meaning of the spirit's message. Also, her mother was able to tell Rita about this wonderful great-aunt who had passed to the Higher side quite a few years before.

Currently, there are also many excellent digitized genealogy resources available, in addition to conferring with other family members, which can be helpful in uncovering personal family lineage. Rita's experience of discovery with her great-aunt was compelling enough to demonstrate the continuity of life, and it also convinced Rita to investigate communication with spirits.

Spirit contact is not random. Communicating with spirits can be a profound and life-changing experience. The spirits who come through have some *connection to you*. You might not be aware of the connection at first. They could be spirits who passed over long ago or people you don't remember or didn't even know about (such as Rita's great-aunt). You might need to go away from a reading and do some research. Family interviews could reveal specific details of character and clues about your extended family lineage that allow you to do further genealogical research. You might discover details about military service, occupation (a school teacher or a tailor, for example), or a place of residence (including information about the country or region of origin). Spirit communication has much it can teach you about the history of your family, as well as about family relationships.

The spirit connecting to you could also be someone you know quite well, who was close to you in life, and who may have recently passed over. Often, we carry the pain of loss through the years along with the joy of love. But remember that the spirit you are yearning to connect to might not be the spirit that comes through in a reading. It could be that the spirit has internal healing work to do before returning. Know that the spirit coming through offers a healing ministry *for you* if you are open to hearing the message. Such messages can bring comfort and give much-needed context for alleviating the grief you experience.

The spirit coming through in a reading may not be a spirit you know or have had some relationship to on the Earth plane. It could be that you are connecting to a Spirit guide, one of many spirits entrusted with being accessible to help you throughout your life. When you connect to a Spirit guide, know that there is a reason the spirit reveals its nature to you. Whether you feel the presence of Spirit guides as you go about your daily life or whether you are unaware of their presence, it is a comfort to know that Spirit is everywhere around you. Your Spirit guides have only your highest good as their intent, and they have a desire for you to have your best experience of life.

Most of all, understand that the spirits who come through are *important to you*. The spirit(s) are willing to establish contact, and they have something to say *to you*. Before any reading with a certified medium, set a conscious intention to meet with Spirit. Ask your guides and loved ones to be with you during your reading and be open to what comes through *for you*.

A Time for Healing

Every spirit communication should be a healing experience and should always be looked at in that way. When you first embark on a contact experience with Spirit, you might not know what healing you need. You might need closure or help getting through a difficult time. Much of the hurt people carry around is buried so deep within that they are no longer consciously aware of its source. Communication with a spirit who knows exactly what the wound is and what caused it can bring that hurt to the surface, at which point, the healing process can begin.

If it seems that we keep stressing the point about healing, you're right. Spirit contact always comes in healing and light, which is so important that we can't stress it *enough*. Even when the messages you receive aren't what you expected or what you *want* to get, you must know they are meant to be positive and helpful. If you have any sense that the situation in your reading becomes dark or negative, end it immediately. This is not spirit contact. It might be manipulation (from this side, not the Higher side!), it might be your fears, or it might be a matter for which you should seek psychological counseling. But it is not from Spirit if it's not happening with goodness and light.

Mission: Unknown

Your life—your existence in this physical world of the Earth place—has purpose. You, particularly and uniquely *you*, are here for a reason. Your soul has a mission to complete during its time on Earth. One of the most exciting (and at the same time most frustrating) aspects of this Earthly life is the mystery of it all. You don't know what your soul's mission is; you don't know the grander scheme of why you are living your life. Yet still, you must find your way. You make the choices you hope and believe will take you in the right direction. Each soul's lessons are unique. The path of your life, the journey of your soul, matters to your individual existence and beyond. You may come to intuit the truth of the nature of your path as you live, as you come to know in the essence of your being.

The freedom and opportunity offered by life's mystery means you are not compelled to follow any particular path. Your life is not predetermined; your destiny is not a stationary target. Instead, it is a dynamic and ever-changing journey. *You* make the choices and decisions that become your life's—and your soul's—path. With this freedom comes accountability, of course. You, and you alone, are responsible for the choices you make and the outcomes that are the consequences of your decisions.

This is the growth element of your spirit's journey through physical life on the Earth plane. As we all know, growth is not easy. It often involves starts and stops, and sometimes even backsliding to repeat the lessons we didn't quite get the first time around. It might seem that your decisions always end up leading you in directions you don't want to follow but find yourself headed toward nonetheless. Rather than making choices, you are following patterns. And rather than spiraling upward to higher levels of understanding and insight, you end up running in circles!

Many people believe that their fates are absolutely predetermined. An in-depth study of religions, however, will show that free choice is always given to us. We make our own decisions about how we live. As a Spiritualist minister, Rita preaches personal responsibility, that each of us is responsible for our own decisions in life, and that we create our happiness and inner peace by living according to natural law.

Many of us want to know more about *why* we are here, what lessons we need to learn during our physical lives, and how we can leave the Earth plane a better place, however slightly, than it was when we arrived. With knowledge comes an increased ability to make appropriate and directed choices and decisions.

And wouldn't it be nice if you could get a little help and guidance from Spirit to bump you off a familiar but perhaps uninspired track and onto the path to the life you *want* to live, the life you feel could or should be yours, and the life that will make a difference? Well, you can. Although *your life is yours and yours alone* to shape and direct, there's no rule that you have to go it alone. Those who have passed this way before you and moved on to Spirit are more than willing to reach out a helping hand … figuratively speaking.

A Self-Exploration

Why do *you* seek contact with Spirit? The more clearly you can establish your intent for seeking contact, the more likely it is you'll obtain specific, and useful, information. This is not to say that you'll then get the answers from Spirit that you want. But you will receive the answers you need. The following questions can help you clarify what contact you are seeking and what it is that you hope to find out. This is not a test; there are no right or wrong answers. This self-exploration exercise is just a process to get you thinking about how communication with spirits can help *you*.

Personal Reasons for Contacting Spirit

1. Are you presently grieving the loss of a loved one? If so, whom, and what were the circumstances of their passing?

   _____

   _____

   _____

2. What unresolved issues have been left unsorted or unaddressed in your life by the passing of a loved one?

   _____

   _____

   _____

3. Are there particular people you want to contact in Spirit? What are your reasons?

   _____

   _____

   _____

4. What changes would you like to see happen in your life as a result of spirit communication?

   _____

   _____

   _____

5. Do you have a message to convey to a loved one who has passed on? If so, what is your message, and what is the intent behind it? What change do you hope will be effected by your message?

   _____

   _____

   _____

6. If you had particular moments or experiences to relive with a loved one(s) who passed, what would they be?

   _____

   _____

   _____

7. What expectations do you have about working with a medium to connect with the Spirit plane?

    _____

    _____

    _____

8. Who might come through from Spirit that would be a complete surprise for you?

    _____

    _____

    _____

9. What fears or apprehensions do you have about spirit contact? Once connection is established, do you have fears or apprehensions surrounding what might be communicated? Why do you think that might be?

    _____

    _____

    _____

10. What do you most want to know or to have happen through a spirit contact? How enduring do you want the spirit contact to be?

    _____

    _____

    _____

If other questions about your reasons for contacting the Spirit world occur to you, make note of them here.

_____

_____

_____

_____

_____

_____

The idea behind completing the self-exploration exercise is to help prepare you for spirit communication. Also, if you do have access to a family genealogy chart, it may be helpful to study your family's history before having a medium do a spirit reading. This gives you a broader sense of who might come through, and provides potential clues for understanding your message from

Spirit. And remember that contact with spirits is not limited to relatives. Friends or friends of the family who have passed to the Higher side also have connections with you, as do your Spirit guides, and they are just as likely to come through for you during a reading, depending on the messages they bring.

Identifying Spirit Contact

How do you locate a loved one in a crowd? Do you look for someone who is six-foot-two, who has brown hair and hazel eyes, and who wears a New York Yankees cap? It's a good place to start. Do you listen for that special laugh that quickens your pulse? Do you try to capture the essence of a familiar scent as it lingers in the air? Or, do you watch closely on the alert for certain movements and gestures? Details help!

Once, when Rita initiated spirit contact during a Spiritualist Church service, a young man came through for a woman in the congregation. Rita gave the young man's physical description and then said, "… and he's *extremely* strong in personality." Rita stood up and demonstrated the young man's walk and shared some of the colorful language he was using. The woman for whom this spirit was coming through laughed; she recognized the young man immediately. The details Rita received through her mediumship led the woman in the congregation to acknowledge a *knowing* of the young man as the spirit coming through!

We tend to identify people who are important to us by their characteristics that matter most to us. This is how we establish a sense of familiarity and recognition. Physical traits alone, although they are helpful in making preliminary assessments, are often too general to make conclusive identification. You might think of those gorgeous hazel eyes when you picture your loved one. However, it is your loved one's unique personality traits surrounding those lovely eyes, patented eye roll and accompanying shoulder shrug, or that upturned gaze that penetrates to your heart and make the case.

Recognizing a spirit's identity is a similar process, one of connecting to familiar personality traits. After all, you don't get a set of wings and a golden harp when you pass over and then instantly become something you never were in physical life. (Really, you don't!) The personality that was the essence of your identity as a physical being on the Earth plane survives to remain the essence of your identity as a being in Spirit. Just as in our physical world, it is the minutiae of the person that lets you know it is irrefutably that person and no other.

Physical characteristics, although helpful, are sometimes too vague or general, depending on the depth of the description, to provide conclusive identification. A spirit can come through at any age, even older than at passing. This is particularly true for those who pass from their physical lives as children or young adults whose bodies haven't yet reached physical prime. Generally, there are some features that make the spirit identifiable, but they might not be what you expect or anticipate.

The character traits that come through during a spirit contact make it possible for you to establish a spirit's identity. These traits comprise the evidence that proves the continuity of life, because they are the bits and pieces *of* life. Sometimes the confirmation of identity happens almost immediately; there is something the spirit does or says that lets you know without a doubt this is your Aunt Margaret or your great-grandfather from the old country. Sometimes the clues are subtle, and the spirit's identity remains uncertain until you have time to think about the messages, or to do research that provides new information or context.

It's important to separate spirit communicating from what could be psychic. Sometimes, what you don't know turns out to be more evidential than what you *do* know. This happens when relatives you didn't know you had come through or you receive information about them that you didn't know. Sometimes, a spirit comes through with a message it intends for you to pass on to someone else, though that may not be readily apparent during the reading. It may take further conversation and research within your family to uncover the true recipient and import of the spirit message—and the reason why you have been chosen by the spirit to receive it.

When Rita was doing spirit contact during a church service, a man came through who kept showing an amazing array of Italian pastries. Sitting in the congregation was his daughter, who recognized her father but was puzzled by the Italian pastries. Her father, she said, had been a baker by profession but he baked only bread. The woman went home and talked with her uncle, her father's brother. Her uncle said that although his brother had established his career baking bread, he had originally trained as a pastry chef. This is how doing your research and exploring the information you receive gives you the full message.

During another of Rita's readings, a woman's mother came through from Spirit for her daughter. Rita described the mother as holding a small fluffy white animal, perhaps a stuffed animal? It was important for the daughter to know the mother had it with her. The daughter, who had received a white Maltese dog for a teenage birthday, knew the spirit as her mother immediately and marveled that the tiny spirit of the family dog whose life had become so important to her mother should be with her in the Spirit world.

At another point in the reading, the mother revealed to her daughter that someone close to her had recently experienced the pain and distress of a miscarriage. This proved puzzling and unanswerable until sometime later when the daughter visited her brother and his wife who lived across the country. Her brother revealed that his wife indeed had experienced a miscarriage some years before. Consequently, the woman and her sister-in-law began to maintain a close relationship, and her sister-in-law's role as auntie to her niece became an important bond for the women of the extended family.

So, as often may occur during a reading, Rita received a detail of personality that confirmed the spirit's identity. With identity firmly established, a powerful family message could be delivered, shared, and honored among these women on a shared and multi-generational life path.

Janice came to Rita for a spirit drawing. As Rita began to draw the spirit image that presented, Rita felt an overwhelming desire to draw a knot of hair on the top of the spirit's head, rather than at the nape of her neck, as was the style of the time. Rita tried several times to move the knot to a more conventional placement but kept redrawing it on the top. Janice recognized the woman as her beloved great-grandmother, and she came back a week later to share two photos with Rita, each showing the knot centered on the top of her great-grandmother's head—just as Rita had been guided to draw it.

The Communication Challenge

Effective communication certainly ranks right at the top of the list when it comes to human challenges. Even among those of us on the Earth plane, communication problems have made *"I'm sorry"* our most common words! Even when we stand face to face, make eye contact, and observe body language, we can misunderstand one another. We confuse meanings and intent, say things we don't mean, and misinterpret the words of others. Add differences in language and culture to the mix, and a translator becomes necessary.

Imagine the challenges, then, of communicating across the planes of spirit existence! The most amazing aspect of the Fox sisters' contact with the spirit of Charles Rosna in their Hydesville home was not the contact itself but that they worked out a code through which they were able to exchange information (see Chapter 3).

Just as existence on the Spirit plane transcends the physical body, spirit communication transcends language. Spirit beings don't require speech in words as we know it to communicate with each other. So, when beings from Spirit make contact with those of us still bound to dwell on the Earth plane, it is sometimes difficult to find ways to communicate their spirit messages. This is particularly true when those messages are about learning that has happened for them on the Higher side. Spirit messages seem to defy the powers of human description. Spirits can often struggle to convey on the Earth plane the knowledge they've gained on the Higher side. Our human minds are made for Earth plane learning.

What Does That Mean?

A medium's consciousness interprets the messages that come through from Spirit, translating them into concepts and ideas that those of us on the Earth plane can understand. A spirit must work within the capabilities of the medium's interpretations. Most mediums acquire a *psychical vocabulary of symbolism* that allows them to have consistent communication with spirit entities. It's another language of sorts, a dictionary of symbols and representations that a medium acquires to make communication with spirits possible. It's related to the medium's level of development, and it becomes the standard that spirits use in working with the medium. Different mediums receive information differently, so the dictionary is unique to that medium, their skills, and their innate abilities.

Colors, feelings, numbers, and an array of sensory experiences (representations of sight, sound, scent, taste, and touch) often become part of a medium's psychical vocabulary of symbolism. A medium might typically see the color blue, for example, when a spirit is attempting to communicate about an event that caused sadness. The logic of the connection might not be apparent to the medium; what matters is that the medium knows the connection is surrounded by sadness and uses that knowledge to clarify and express the spirit's message.

We'll say it again. If you hear voices that are dark or negative or that are telling you to do things you know are wrong, these are not the voices of spirits. Spirits always come through in goodness. They will not come through to approach you or those you love in a negative way. If the voices that are coming through are negative or potentially harmful, you need to seek guidance from a certified medium or a credentialed mental health professional.

Also, don't let your curiosity about spirit communication suppress your normal good judgment. Unfortunately, wherever there is need, there is someone waiting to take advantage of it. Spirit contact is certainly no exception. Let the detail of any reading speak for itself. Take what you experience with a great grain of salt; information that comes through a medium can be colored by the medium's perceptions, which aren't always accurate when applied to your situation. Also, someone who wasn't especially insightful in physical life doesn't become All-Knowing in the Spirit world! If the experience of a reading doesn't feel right to you in any way, don't feel compelled to stay or continue working with that medium.

Like a Good Book …

We call spirit communication a "reading" because the medium reads (or interprets) all of the fragments (all the signs) of information and organizes them into a presentation that makes sense to the person desiring contact. As with books, there are varying degrees of complexity in such a presentation. Sometimes, it's simple, and straightforward, and the key points are clear and unmistakable. Other times, the medium must work with the spirit, and also with you, to get the translation of the message right. And sometimes, you need to take the information home with you, to think about it, and try to understand its multiple layers and meanings.

When a Spirit Reaches Out to You

Many times, spirits initiate contact to be helpful, to make amends, to say, *"I love you and I'm still with you,"* or even, *"I'll be waiting for you, to reach out to you when it's your time to cross."* Remember, the essence of an individual's personality as it was here on the Earth plane extends into the spirit's existence on the Higher side. Someone who was compassionate and helpful in the physical world will still want to reach out to help others. And those who maybe were not quite so understanding and interested in others when they were on the Earth plane often become more understanding and outwardly interested as they move forward on their spiritual journeys.

As one illustration of the soul's evolution and progression after passing, Rita shares an experience from her own life. Rita and her father had a difficult relationship. The medium who first brought him through in a reading said, *"He's saying he's sorry because someone told him he had to."* Rita made a joke about there being a 12-step program on the Higher side, and the medium said that, for many spirits, it truly was something quite like that. A year later, a different medium brought Rita's father through, and that medium said, *"He's saying he wants to say he's sorry, but he says that you wouldn't recognize him as saying that."*

Can I Help You?

Spirits don't suddenly know everything, see everything, and hear everything. Passing to the Higher side doesn't make a spirit omniscient or All-Knowing! Although many spirits do acquire heightened insight, understanding, and knowledge, this results from the growth and evolution that takes place as the spirit continues its mission.

The spirit that has learned a lesson sometimes wants to share the learning with others who are struggling with the same issues. Perhaps the situation doesn't need to be as difficult as you are making it, or you are overlooking an important piece of information. Maybe the answer is right there in front of you, but you just can't see it. Just as family and friends on the Earth plane might try to help you with such matters, those who have passed to the Spirit plane might want to reach back and offer a helping hand. Accept, use, and enjoy this help! It comes to you in goodness and healing.

Making Amends

One of the most common reasons spirits seek contact with their loved ones on the Earth plane is to make amends for mistakes they made during their physical lives. This can be as healing for the spirit as for the person on the Earth plane. Mary, a woman at the start of her middle years, came to Rita desperately wanting to contact the spirit of her stepfather who had raised her. The stepfather had been a tall, slender man during the prime of his life, but in old age, he had developed the Alzheimer's disease that ultimately resulted in his death.

What came through to Rita, however, was the image of a husky, short man who had died of a heart attack. Rita drew the image that came through, and when Mary saw the Spirit drawing, she gasped in disbelief: The spirit visitor was Mary's natural father who had abandoned the family when Mary was a child! Mary had spent most of her life hating this man for what he did to her family, and now here he was, reappearing from beyond the physical world. To do what? More damage?

As Rita continued the reading, it became clear that Mary's father had come through to say he was sorry for having deserted the family so many years before his death. There were circumstances Mary didn't know about, but the bottom line was that her father made decisions that hurt his family, and he wanted Mary to know he understood how hard her life had been as a result. Although this was not the contact Mary wanted, it provided the answers to many questions she had and ended up being a tremendous healing experience for Mary, as well as for her father's spirit.

When Crisis Strikes

It's common for spirit contacts to come through in times of crisis, either personal or large-scale (such as the tragic losses of war or of global pandemic). People who become critically ill and spend days or weeks in the hospital hovering between life and death often report that when they recover, loved ones who had passed were with them the whole time. These contacts are comforting and let you know that no matter what the situation, *you are never alone.*

Easing the Pain of Grief

No matter how strongly you believe that you and your loved ones will reunite on the Higher side, there is grief when a loved one passes before you do. The emptiness that you feel can be overwhelming. Sometimes a spirit can reach back from the Higher side to offer comfort and solace, to say, *"I'll always be with you."* These contacts can come through a medium or through direct experiences. A familiar fragrance that floats seemingly from nowhere. The sense of a laugh, distant and not quite audible, over something your loved one would have found hilarious. Being guided without fail to the best bargains offered during a sale. Knowing the bus or the train will arrive precisely when you set foot on the platform, as it always seemed to for your partner. A recurring dream in which your loved one appears. In reality, these contacts are probably much more commonplace than most of us recognize. Because they are often so subtle, and because grief is such an overwhelming emotion, we just don't pick up on the gentle signals. But the messages from Spirit are there, and they can be a source of great comfort.

When It's Your Time to Make the Crossing

If there is only one message you get from Spirit, let it be this: *You are not alone!* When it is time for your spirit to cross from the Earth plane to the Spirit plane, there will be a gathering of spirits waiting to welcome you. This can be a great source of comfort for those who know passing is imminent, such as people who are terminally ill, as well as for family and friends who remain on the Earth plane and are grieving.

Even Spirits Have Needs

The Spirit plane is a busy and dynamic existence. Spirits are not just floating around. The soul's mission continues, and the spirit often experiences significant understanding and insight as its mission continues to unfold. A loved one who has passed to the Higher side might need help from you for this to happen or might want to let you know that you are providing help even though you don't know it. When you accept the amends offered by a spirit from the Higher side, it allows that spirit to move forward.

Keeping the Connection

You might experience a range of emotions and feelings as you begin thinking about spirit communication and all that it might mean in your life. The opportunities are nearly endless, and what you make of them can change your life in ways you can't now imagine. Yes, there is often sadness, regret, hurt, or loneliness when a loved one passes, but the connections with Spirit are still there; the existence continues. You don't ever really lose someone you love. Spirit communication holds within it love and light. It's all in the details—validation of continuity of life during a reading comes down to recognizing and acknowledging bits and fragments of a life lived, as well as sometimes learning new information about a loved one's life or about your family. Life is a journey, a journey that continues in Spirit after life on the Earth plane.

Now, let's take a closer look at existence on the Higher side, and what we might find there.

PART
2

What's on the Other Side?

From the sacred texts of religious writings to the myriad stories told in the popular culture of books and movies, and to the explorative internet platforms of podcasts and social media, there are many expressions of the Higher side and what it is like to be there. Is it Heaven? Is it a void? Is the Higher side another dimension of existence?

Time and space are boundaries that apply to the Earth plane. The Spirit plane is without such boundaries or limitations. The two defining transitions of physical life are birth to the Earth plane and the release of the spirit through death to the Spirit plane. During our lives on Earth, Spirit guides join us to share their wisdom and knowledge and to help us with the lessons of our lives. Some spirits do stay behind, reluctant to make the passage to the Higher side. They might have unfinished business or need a little help to make the crossing.

Let's investigate what existence on the Higher Side might be like, as well as some of the ways spirits communicate across the veil between life and what's beyond it to bring messages of love and healing.

CHAPTER

5

Spirit Geography: Planes of Existence

In this physical world, on our Earth plane, we define nearly everything in terms of time, space, and distance. We all learned the equation in school: Distance = Speed × Time. Remember the speeding train in school word problems? This is a simple way to orient our bodies, and/or objects (such as a speeding train), as we and they move. Consider this formula for Newton's Second Law of Motion: Force = Mass × Acceleration (velocity/time). Pretty soon, we're moving toward Einstein's Theory of Relativity and traveling the space-time continuum. Physicists explain that space-time creates relativistic changes when accelerating close to the speed of light and in the motion of massive objects in the Universe. The further our human awareness expands into the far reaches of the Universe and into the exquisite relationships of particles in an atom's microcosm, the closer we come to exploring the infinite realm of the Spirit plane, and the closer we come to understanding the Divine motion of existence and the essence of animating Spirit.

The first time Rita's father showed himself to Rita from Spirit, he presented himself at the age of 27 with a full head of golden hair, a pier 49 T-shirt, and a muscular physique. When Rita took notice of him, she actually questioned whom he could be. He had been 41 when she was born, so she never had seen him in life as a young man. Other times after that, he showed himself at age 50 or so, although he was almost 81 when he passed to the world of Spirit. While we all have the ability to access the Spirit plane, mediums like Rita have developed their senses to intuit and connect directly to Spirit. Does Rita know the equation for how she (or we) can connect? No, not at present. Mediums do have knowledge about the Spirit plane through their experiences, prayers, and intuitions.

On the Spirit plane, there is no time and space or distance as we understand them. There are different levels of existence, but there is no sense of linear time or structured space as we know those limitations here in the physical world on the Earth plane. Spirits do not age chronologically (at least not in any sense we humans can understand). When they come through in communication with us, spirits might appear at any age from before or after their physical lives on Earth ended. The spirit *embodies* its image of ideal presentation (in human terms of space, time, and distance), whatever that might be, which might change as the spirit evolves.

"Stay in the harsh world long enough to tell my story..."

As humans, we spend a lot of time and energy trying to understand, to define and explain life beyond death, and trying to tell the story. From the spooky to the sentimental, from the profound to the ridiculous, we've created views of the hereafter in books and movies. Here are just a few:

- William Shakespeare's *Hamlet* (1603), a tragedy in five acts, is one of the earliest works in which the plot revolves entirely around interaction between a spirit and a person in the physical world. Hamlet, the young prince of Denmark, receives visits from the spirit of his recently murdered father, the king, who tells Hamlet the murderer was none other than Claudius, the king's brother who has since assumed the throne (and married his mother). To authenticate the spirit's claims, Hamlet has his father's murder re-enacted according to the spirit's description of the events and finds Claudius's reactions convincing proof of guilt. Four hundred years after it was originally written, Shakespeare's play still appears on stages across the globe. In 2021, the New York Met premiere of Australian composer Brett Dean's opera based upon Shakespeare's play first produced in 2017, keeps the classic masterpiece alive with an exciting interpretation for modern audiences.

- Charles Dickens's holiday classic, *A Christmas Carol* (1843), immortalizes the tale of the ignominious Mr. Scrooge and his Christmas Eve visitation by three spirits—the spirits of Christmas Past, Present, and Future. As the story begins, Mr. Scrooge—a miserable, miserly financier is first visited by the spirit of Jacob Marley, Scrooge's former business partner. Marley is wrapped head to toe and bound by loop upon loop of heavy chain and he declares to Scrooge "I wear the chain I forged in life. I made it link by link and yard by yard; I girded it on of my own free will, and of my own free will I wore it." Most of us remember what happens next. Marley tells Scrooge that he is to be visited by three separate spirits during the night's wee hours; each one tasked with guiding his soul's restoration. Should Scrooge fail to take heed, his chain in the Spirit realm will be far heavier to bear than the weight of Marley's own bonds. *A Christmas Carol* is the testimony of a soul's peril and it's spiritual redemption. By the light of dawn, Scrooge has accepted the true meaning of keeping Christmas, and agrees with Tiny Tim as he carves the Christmas goose, "God Bless Us, Every One." Dickens meant his book to be a social commentary of his time and to underline the need for good works, as well as good will toward men, all the year round. The author wrote the manuscript in a brief six weeks—to keep his own creditors away, not realizing he'd written a masterpiece to be beloved by generations. Printed in countless editions and dramatized in plays and films up to our own twenty-first century, *A Christmas Carol* represents the true Spirit of Christmas.

○ Another Christmas classic, Frank Capra's film *It's a Wonderful Life* (1946) starring James Stewart, Donna Reed, Lionel Barrymore, and Henry Travers as Clarence Odbody, AS2 (Angel Second Class), tells another redemptive story. This time, the redemption is a faith in life itself, as well as a faith in human goodness and the Holy Spirit. As our hero, George Bailey, contemplates suicide (for the value his life insurance policy holds to save his family's well-being), Clarence is summoned by the angel Joseph and tasked to save George, body and soul. Should Clarence succeed, he will gain his angel's wings. As mayhem and a sweet comedy of errors ensue, the film underscores a deep bond of trust between human beings and their Guardian Angels. Even though, upon introduction, George declares to Clarence "Well, you look about the kind of angel I'd get…." Each human being is watched, cared for, and protected by entities and spirits on the Spirit Realm. For many, the sense of this relationship follows them throughout their lives, providing solace, direction, and company. Through the ministrations of Clarence, George Bailey discovers he is "the richest man in town."

○ *Ghostbusters* (1984) and *Ghostbusters II* (1989) combine surprising compassion with comedy and action as these films follow the adventures of a team of "scientists" that lure and capture ghosts and entities to release them later to the Higher existence they can't seem to find on their own (or hold them captive if they aren't willing to go willingly toward that Light). The original 1984 cast included Bill Murray, Dan Ackroyd, Ernie Hudson, Howard Ramus, Sigourney Weaver, and Annie Potts. Released in 2016 with an all-female leading cast of Kristen Wiig, Kate McKinnon, Melissa McCarthy, and Leslie Jones, along with male co-star Chris Hemsworth, *Ghostbusters: Answer the Call* revisits the ghostbusters comedic story thirty years later, proving a curiosity about the Spirit realm is enduring—and that misbehaving ghosties can be funny.

- In the 1990 romantic thriller *Ghost* (Patrick Swayze, Demi Moore, Whoopi Goldberg), a husband refuses to move on to the Spirit realm until he saves his wife from the unscrupulous "friends" who murdered him. The film won Whoopi Goldberg a Best Supporting Actress Oscar for her role as Rita, the reluctant medium who connects Sam (Swayze) and Molly (Moore). And it contains the scene no movie lover can ever forget when Sam, in the Spirit realm, visits Molly while she is at work sculpting at her potter's wheel. Sam stands behind her, moving as she moves, communicating with his beloved, with all of his body and soul. *Ghost* raises the question of good versus evil and where we "go" after death: to Heaven or to Hell. As our medium Rita (Berkowitz, that is) believes, Spirit is a realm of healing, goodness, redemption, and spiritual growth. The soul does not need to choose between Heaven and Hell, but the soul *does* need to move into the Light to accept its path toward Enlightenment. Devils and hell fires might make for a shocking thriller (and a satisfying fate for the "bad guy") but embracing the highest and best for the good is where life and Spirit lead.

- While inattentively fiddling with the radio, Daniel Miller (Albert Brooks) drives his sports car into the path of a bus in the 1991 movie *Defending Your Life*. He finds himself in Judgment City, where a panel reviews the key points of his life to determine what existence Daniel goes to next. Along the way, he meets a kindred spirit (Meryl Streep), with whom he falls in love and who inspires him to reach for the highest and best within himself to be allowed to accompany her on their souls' journey together. The film's message declares that love truly hopes all things, believes all things, and endures all things. The greatest power, on Earth and in Spirit, is the power of love.

- Young actor Haley Joel Osment captivated audiences in the 1999 film *The Sixth Sense*, with his character Cole's somber assertion: "I see dead people." Among them is child psychologist Malcolm Crowe (Bruce Willis), who is not yet aware that he no longer inhabits the Earth plane. Cole's paranormal ability exists to help those, like Crowe, who are stymied by trauma from understanding their passage from life through death to spirit. Cole helps them realize they have died and obtain the clarity to move forward in their souls' evolution. While the film makes for a great thriller and emphasizes the healing nature of Spirit, Rita stresses that spirits do not appear in threatening or traumatic form. Spirits do their own healing work in the Spirit realm and appear to human beings only with messages that support the highest and best for all. Should you find yourself having violent dreams or frightening visions, consult a physician or medical health professional who can help you sort through what you see and feel.

- Diana Gabaldon's best-selling book series *Outlander* was launched in 1991 with the novel of the same name and is so popular it was chosen as #2 of 100 best-loved books in PBS's The Great American Read—second only to Harper Lee's classic novel *To Kill a Mockingbird*. The *Outlander* books tell the story of WWII nurse Claire Beauchamp Randall and her husband, historian Frank Randall. After falling through time while exploring a group of standing stones near Inverness, Scotland, Claire finds herself waking up in 1743. The story follows Claire's adventures, passionate romance, and marriage to red-headed Highlander James Alexander Malcolm MacKenzie Fraser. Caught between two times and married to two men, Claire grapples with the meaning of time itself and holds onto the enduring bonds of love. As a doctor—a surgeon in the 1960s and by turns called a conjure woman, a witch, and even a druid—Claire prefers to call herself a *healer*, and she explores the reaches of the human body and soul with the tools of the times at hand. Her daughter Brianna's husband Roger Mac ponders Claire's calling in *A Breathe of Snow and Ashes*: "Did Claire see the touch of beauty in the bodies beneath her hands? Was that perhaps how—and why—she was a healer?" As the stories begin to accumulate time travelers, the whole nature of time, space, and distance blurs and characters face the true meaning of embodiment and the direct effect of a soul's purpose. Time travelers may be spirits only by a technicality of the space-time continuum, but *Outlander* is also full of spirits and entities—faeries and kelpies, piskies, riders of the Wild Hunt, and everywhere, the spirits of the dead. Honoring the spirits of the dead is a big theme in *Outlander*, most controversially, the spirit of Jamie Fraser himself. Did he die at the Battle of Culloden in 1743 to travel from the Spirit realm to Claire? Is it Jamie's spirit that appears as a Highlander under Claire's window in 1946 and sets the whole saga in motion? Does Claire's spirit heal Jamie and restore him to life after Culloden? For those of us who want to feel the restorative power of life and death; of bursting through the limits of time, space, and distance; and of healing Spirit, *Outlander* is a gripping story and a great quest for enduring love, body and soul. The *Outlander* books are also the basis for a television series that brings the characters and times to life with unerring devotion and detail, through war and peace and across centuries.

These, of course, are but a very few of the great stories that investigate the "Is there life after death?" question. Feel free to add your favorites to the list, which truly is so extensive it could be the topic of a web database itself! Indeed, it seems that storytellers, whether on the page or the screen, bring us new and varied presentations of life beyond physical death each year. How close to the truth are their stories? Stories entertain us, but within them, always lay the essence of a human need or longing. When we humans don't understand, we embark on a quest for knowledge, edging closer and closer until true meaning is understood. Stories of the Spirit realm charm and fascinate us, frighten and call to us, and fill us with yearning for love lost in life that endures in our hearts and in memory. The best story always holds the element of human truth of spiritual essence. Exploring stories can help us understand our own thoughts and feelings about the nature of the Earth plane and the Spirit plane and what it might be to cross over their boundaries. For as long as humanity continues, human beings will tell stories, listen, and watch for Spirit. Spirits come through on the Earth plane as they want us to perceive them and in ways that affirm their identities to prove the continuity of life. Spirit communication, we say again, *is always about goodness and healing.* When we seek genuine Spirit communication in real life and real-time, the drama of that connection is what keeps our attention—often for long after the experience of the connection draws to a close.

Heaven and Hell, Reward and Punishment

Many Western faith systems present a view of life, death, and what happens beyond death as a structure of good and bad, reward and punishment, and Heaven and Hell. You live a good life here on the Earth plane, and then, as a reward, your soul goes to Heaven when your body dies. There is a process of judgment by an all-powerful God, with an immediate result. In some belief systems, the decision is final, while in others, there are ways the spirit can "earn" its way to a better place in the hierarchy of the hereafter, either through its own actions (penitence) or through the prayers and penitence of those on the Earth plane.

The soul's destination after physical death—Heaven, Hell, or Purgatory (in the Catholic faith)—is a place described by physical attributes. Heaven is generally portrayed as a location beyond the sky that exists above the Earth, far beyond our human ability of sight to perceive it. In many Christian faiths, Heaven is the home of God and the ultimate blissful destination for "good" souls. Hell, by contrast, is generally portrayed as deep within Earth's core, a place of fire, lamentation, and eternal burning. It is the domain of demons and devils, the ultimate evil, and the ultimate destination for "bad" souls. The concept of judging a life to determine the soul's destination and journey beyond physical death did not come into existence until the Middle Ages (800 C.E. or so). Roman Catholic's Purgatory, a colorless, nondescript place, is a waystation of transition where the soul goes to pray (and be prayed for) and atone for the sins committed during its physical life, thus earning its entrance into the eternal existence of Heaven.

The role of such representations is often more to enforce codes of morality and behavior here on Earth than to advance an understanding of the soul's continuing existence after death. Rewards encourage one set of behaviors, while punishments discourage another. Strict reward and punishment structures leave little room for learning or changing. An action receives a judgment for which there is then either a beneficial or detrimental consequence. A more acceptable, and certainly more positive, approach for many people is one that requires spiritual accountability within the context of a soul's learning, growth, and evolution.

Eternal Existence with the Gods

The premise of Heaven and Hell predates Christianity and other modern faith systems, existing in the mythology of many ancient cultures whose faith systems embraced multiple gods, including the Greeks, Romans, Egyptians, Hindus, Celts, and Mayans. In these systems, Heaven was the home of the gods from whom came the light and warmth that made life on Earth possible. This Heaven arched through the sky above the Earth, with the movements of the sun the visual evidence of its existence. In Greek and Roman mythology, Hades ruled the underworld from his palace within the underworld, and various other gods did so in other cultures (see Chapter 2).

Neither Heaven nor the underworld in these ancient cultures were exclusively good or bad; the gods and goddesses who inhabited them had both good and bad characteristics. And everyone who died went to the underworld because this was where the dead "lived" after death. They didn't endure eternal suffering; to the contrary, theirs was an existence free from the pains and problems of physical life. There was no judgment to determine who ended up where; it seems that "life" pretty much went on as before death, but without the physical trappings.

Travel to the underworld often involved passage across a river, representing the physical separation of the land of the living from the land of the dead. Crossing the river was usually a one-way proposition, from life to death. Attempts to reverse the flow often resulted in catastrophe; just search for the story of Orpheus and Eurydice on Wikipedia. Nobel-prize-winning author Kazuo Ishiguro explores the nature of a fantasy Spirit quest through life across the river to the underworld in his novel *The Buried Giant* (2015). Author Haruki Murakami also writes about the Spirit quest through time, space, and distance—including crossing the river—in his exploration of Spirit in art and its creative manifestation in *Killing Commendatore* (2018).

Transcendence, Nirvana, and Beyond

The faith systems of the world are varied and diverse, and each has its own perspectives on life, death, and beyond. Here's what some of them are:

- Olam Ha-Ba, the "World to Come," is the belief in afterlife, as in some Jewish sects.
- The Muslim belief in the Oneness of God is the Divine possessing no body, gender, race, or children and is unaffected by the characteristics of human life.
- Reincarnation is the belief that the soul returns to another physical life; it is integral to faiths such as Hindu.
- Resurrection is the belief that the soul returns to its physical body in a whole and pure state, as in Christianity.
- Nirvana is the belief in transcendence of the self, as in Buddhism.

It's All About Energy

It is through energy that spirits are able to communicate across the boundary between the Earth and Spirit planes. Understanding different approaches to energy systems gives us insights into how spirit communication takes place.

Energy both separates and links the physical and Spirit worlds. It is the essence of all existence, although it takes many different forms. You are energy; the chair in which you are sitting is energy; and the book or tablet you are holding is energy. The principles of science—physics, specifically—substantiate this. All objects, tangible and intangible, visible and invisible, audible and inaudible, are matter. And all matter is comprised of energy structures—atoms, molecules, and electrons—particles that vibrate at certain frequencies. The rate, or speed, of the frequency determines the matter's tangibility.

The energy of matter that forms an object we consider solid, such as a chair or a book, vibrates so slowly that we are able to physically perceive its matter. The energy of matter we cannot see, such as the air we breathe, vibrates very fast. Your physical body vibrates slowly enough to have tangibility, while your spirit vibrates so fast that you cannot perceive its presence through your five physical senses. And energy on the Spirit plane vibrates so fast that it doesn't have an appearance or presence at all, as we might define that, unless a spirit chooses to represent itself in a tangible form.

Few people think of physicist Albert Einstein (1879–1955) as a mystic. But it was Einstein who, in his watershed work in physics, *Relativity: The Special and the General Theory* (first published in 1918), described, defined, and quantified all existence as energy that vibrates at different frequencies. Einstein said low-frequency vibrations produce tangible or visible representations, such as the objects of our everyday lives. High-frequency vibrations produce energy that does not have tangible or visible representations—we can't quantify with our physical senses.

The energy of the physical body is not capable of vibrating at a high enough rate to exist solely on the Spirit plane, so when there is a spirit contact, the spirit comes through to the Earth plane. To make its presence known, the spirit must slow its vibration as the medium raises their vibration so spirit and human can meet and communicate.

Your Body's Energy Centers: Chakras

As a structure comprised of energy, your body has dynamic energy centers called *chakras*, which means "wheel" in Sanskrit. Life energy, called *prana*, flows through them. Your *aura* is a final, outer layer of energy that surrounds the body.

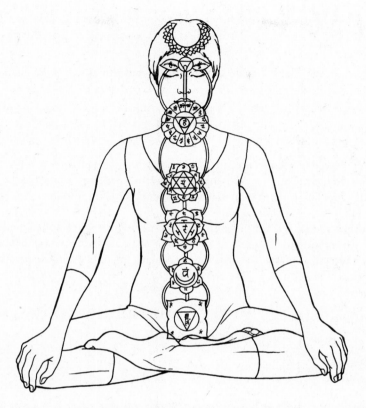

In yoga, the seven chakras are dynamic centers of energy that flow life force through the human body.

There are seven chakras, which roughly align with your body's physical nervous system:

- The first chakra, often called the root chakra, resides at the base of your spine. Its energy is the energy of survival, which relates to your security and wellbeing. Your root chakra connects you to your physical life. The color associated with this chakra is red.

- The second, or sacral chakra resides in your lower pelvis and is the energy of sexuality, relationships, creativity, and emotions. The color associated with this chakra is orange.

- The third, or solar plexus chakra, resides in your solar plexus or "gut"—the center of your abdomen just above your navel. Its energy relates to personal power and self-esteem. The color associated with this chakra is yellow.

- The fourth, or heart chakra, resides at the level of your heart and is the energy of emotional love, affection, and partnership. The color associated with this chakra is green.

- The fifth, or throat chakra, resides at the base of your throat and is the energy of expression and truth. The color associated with this chakra is blue.

- The sixth, or Third Eye chakra, resides in the center of your forehead. Its energy is the energy of inner vision and psychic perception. The color associated with this chakra is indigo.

- The seventh, or crown chakra, resides at the very top of your head. It is the energy portal that connects you to the Divine and the collective Spirit that exists beyond your individual being. The color associated with this chakra is violet.

The life force of prana that flows through your chakras connects your physical body with your spirit. Increasing the flow of prana to a particular chakra activates and enhances it. Yoga and meditation are two ways to awaken your chakras (more about these practices later in this chapter).

The Human Energy Field: Your Subtle Body

Your physical body is more than a container that carries you through your life. Your existence is a composite of seven layers of energy known as the human energy field. These layers are called the subtle bodies. They are simultaneously independent and interrelated, and they correlate to your chakras:

- Your etheric subtle body is like an energy shadow of your physical body. It is the energy element that connects you to physical life, and it correlates to your first, or root chakra.

- Your emotional subtle body is the energy of your feelings and emotions. It correlates to your second and third chakras—the sacral chakra and the solar plexus chakra.

- Your astral subtle body functions as a conduit between the physical energies and the spiritual energies of your existence. It correlates to your fourth, or heart chakra.

- Your mental or intellectual subtle body is the energy of your thoughts and intellect. It correlates to your fifth and sixth chakras—the throat chakra and the Third Eye chakra.

- Your causal subtle body is your connection to the Divine. It correlates to your seventh, or crown chakra. It is the most highly developed of your energy structures, and through it you are connected to a greater cosmic or spiritual existence.

Remember our discussion of energy vibration earlier in this chapter? The varying vibrational levels of these different energy layers, or subtle bodies, allows them to coexist with what you perceive to be your physical existence. They just vibrate at higher rates, so you are mostly unaware of them.

Energy flows between the human energy field that is beyond your individual existence and the chakras that are your personal existence. In this way, you are separate from, yet integrated with, the overall energy of all existence. It's as though your body "plugs in." Even though you reside on the Earth plane because your existence is physical, you remain connected to the Spirit plane because, after all, the essence of your existence is the energy that is your spirit.

Your Soul's Story: Your Akashic Record

An Akashic record is a cosmic collection of all that ever was, is, and will be, as documentation, so to speak, of the soul's existence, mission, and journey. It's not an actual document or book or even record as we might think of these; rather, it exists in the realm of Spirit as a Divine record. The content of the Akashic record is said to be deeply symbolic. An Akashic record documents all your soul's actions and travels—past, present, and future. The term comes from the ancient Sanskrit word *Akasha*, which means "primary or primordial substance." It is possible to connect with your Akashic record through meditation or through a good psychic counselor.

Psychic counselors who do past-life regressions believe this is made possible by accessing your Akashic record (see Chapters 21 and 22). And some people believe that your Spirit guides draw from your Akashic record as they provide you with guidance and assistance (see Chapter 7).

There are references or parallels to the concept of Akashic records in many faith systems, including the following:

- The Bible's Book of Revelation (the Book of Life) and recording angels, who document the soul's thoughts and deeds for God to review on Judgment Day

- Buddhism's Akasha or Akasa, the life essence that is present as a space around the physical and Spirit worlds and that contains all existence

- Psychoanalyst Carl Jung's collective unconscious, the premise that all people share certain symbolisms, thoughts, and beliefs through a connected unconsciousness (see Chapter 22)

- The cosmic consciousness or collective mind of metaphysics, which holds that all spirits on the Earth and Spirit planes are united on a deep level of consciousness

Connecting with Your Divine Energy

There are a number of ways you can connect with your Divine energy. Among the most common are prayer, meditation, and yoga. All combine the physical, mental, and spiritual dimensions of existence.

Prayer

Through prayer, humanity communicates directly with the Divine, however we perceive it. This can be as God, as god or goddess, as the Universe, or as the collective Spirit. Although it is a communication between an individual and their Divine, prayer can take place in groups. The collective power can be amazing, particularly when directed toward healing or releasing a spirit to continue on its journey.

Rita was once called to a house where a spirit whose physical life had been ended by murder was unable to complete its transition from the Earth plane to the Spirit plane. The house was filled with great sadness, and its new owners often saw moving objects and heard noises. They realized that this was an opportunity and wanted to help the spirit. Rita gathered a small group at the house to pray for and with the spirit, encouraging the spirit to accept the welcoming contact from friends and family already on the Higher side and asking for Divine assistance with the transition. Finally, the connection was made, and the spirit moved on. All who were praying could feel the sadness suddenly lift.

Prayer connects you with the Divine by activating your causal body and the energy of your seventh, or crown chakra. Many religions incorporate structured prayer into meditations for the soul's benefit. Roman Catholics pray the rosary using prayer beads that assist in saying prayers or perform novenas, which are prayerful devotions that spread over a series of days.

Meditation

Meditation connects you with the Divine by activating your mental subtle body and your sixth, or Third Eye chakra. A common meditative practice is to focus on a single thought until all other thoughts leave your mind. You then explore this single thought in total completeness. Through this process, you gain relaxation and clarity.

Other ways to begin a meditation practice include focusing on a simple mantra, a repeated phrase that creates healing tones that resonate in the body or gazing at a single fixed object, such as a candle flame. Many believe that meditation is the study of the breath. In meditation, if you feel your mind wandering or fall prey to distraction, call yourself to attention with a focus on the breath, feeling the movement of breath into and out from your body. If you like, repeat the following mantra as you breathe: "Breathing in, I calm my body. Breathing out, I smile. Dwelling in the present moment, I know this is the only moment." This mantra was created by renowned Vietnamese Buddhist monk Thich Nhat Hanh.

Yoga

Yoga postures, or *asanas* in Sanskrit, activate various chakras, which in turn access their correlating subtle bodies. Yoga combines activities of the physical body with meditation, providing a range of connections that can be quite basic, as with breathing exercises, or complex, as with postures that access the causal subtle body.

Yoga's Sun Salutation allows you to feel Spirit's life force move and flow within and without you. Rise to greet the Sun's energy and the warmth of each new day.

For more information on the movement of life force energy through the human body, including yoga and meditation, read *The Awakened Life: Chakra Healing* by Betsy Rippentrop, Ph.D., and Eve Adamson.

Spirit Evolution

Even though they don't age as we think of aging, spirits evolve as they acquire wisdom and insight. Here on the Earth plane, we tend to think of evolution as a scientific process defining the changes that a species of animal or plant experiences over the course of its known existence. This is the means by which the species adapts to changes in its environment. In a Darwinian view, which refers to the theories of evolution put forth by naturalist Charles Darwin, evolution is the means by which the species extends its life. In theory, a species can perpetuate its existence for as long as it is capable of changes that remain compatible with its environment.

Charles Darwin (1809–1882) was a physician, minister, and naturalist who studied the survival of plant and animal species in their natural habitats. Darwin observed that natural selection meant the strongest and most adaptive representatives of a species were the ones that survived and reproduced, but only if they were not able to practice the art of cooperation and proliferate in aggregate. Darwin published his findings in 1859, in what would become his defining work and most famous book, *On the Origin of Species by Means of Natural Selection, or the Preservation of Favoured Races in the Struggle for Life*.

When a species exceeds its capacity to adapt, it dies out—one by one—until finally there are no members of the species left. Prehistoric creatures, such as the dinosaur and the wooly mammoth, are now extinct; they were unable, as a species, to adapt to the changes in their environments. Scientists theorize that every species will ultimately reach the limits of its abilities to cooperate, to adapt, or to evolve, and will become extinct. But even in the finality of one ending is the beginning of a different existence. New species arrive with new capabilities for change and adaptation, and the cycle of life continues. Some scientists believe the Earth is in the process of a Sixth Great Extinction, such as the one that led to the demise of the dinosaur. With skill—and luck—humanity will need to adapt to the demands of such an overwhelming event or somehow prevent its occurrence.

Remember, though, that time, distance, and space define the cycle of life here on the Earth plane. These borders contain and define the spirit's physical existence here, as they do all living things. But on the Spirit plane, there are no such boundaries. Evolution is endless. A less common definition of evolution seems more applicable to the concept as it applies to spiritual growth: "unfolding; the action or instance of forming and giving something off; emission" (*Merriam-Webster's Collegiate Dictionary, Tenth Edition*, Merriam-Webster, Inc., 1993). Perhaps our unprecedented times will help humanity break the bounds between the Earth and Spirit planes in ways that will heal and restore the planet and secure the life of the species upon it.

The instant the physical body's death releases the spirit, the spirit's experience of its existence changes. (Think of a butterfly emerging from a cocoon.) The Higher side consists of many different levels of evolution, although these are not hierarchical or judgmental. The spirit, of course, evolves during its physical existence on the Earth plane, too. Your physical life is a dimension of your soul's mission and is a necessary (and, we hope, a most pleasant) journey that leads you to Spirit.

CHAPTER
6

Birth, Death, and Passing Over

In the year of this writing, 2021, the United States is the third most populous nation on the Earth—following only China (1.44 billion) and India (1.38 billion), with approximately 330 million souls out of the Earth's 7.8 billion souls … and counting. Global population is forecast to peak in 2064 at 9.7 billion. For all of humanity, regardless of place, our physical life holds two defining transitions: birth and death.

When giving birth, a woman and her partner usher new life into our world. This is a wondrous event, often considered miraculous by witnesses and rejoiced by extended family; a new birth presents a glorious time of welcome. Even complete strangers to the parents will smile and offer their congratulations at the news of a baby's arrival. But what does the spirit experience as it transitions from the Spirit plane to the Earth plane and so to the confines as well as the potential of a physical human body? Does the spirit welcome the journey as much as we welcome its arrival?

And what about the transition of death at the end of the soul's physical life? As a medium, Rita knows from communicating with those who have passed over that there are varying experiences of the transition, although crossings seem to share several common characteristics. Is this a solitary passage? Do the spirits of those who may be gathered around us on the Earth plane at life's end somehow send us off to a welcoming contingent waiting in Spirit on the Higher side? Spirit communications and near-death experiences suggest that a spirit is never alone in its passage from physical life to the Spirit realm. The transition between one world of existence to another is always met in Spirit with healing and grace.

In birth or in death, in life or in Spirit, we are *never alone.*

The Spirit Before Birth

During our lives, we all think over and talk about what might happen *after* death parts our spirits from our physical bodies. As soon as we become aware of our life's mortality, we begin to have opinions and theories, even to worry about its inevitable conclusion, when, as Shakespeare wrote for Hamlet to speak: "we shuffle off this mortal core." But what about what happens *before* our entry into this physical world? Where and what are we? When it comes to the soul's beginnings, we have far more questions than answers!

Soul: A Theological Perspective

Through the ages, theologians and religious scholars have debated the matter of the soul's beginnings, putting forth various theories. Some of these theories are decidedly Christian, while others either predate Christianity or appear in numerous faith systems, Christian and non-Christian. These are, of course, very complex concepts. We'll just briefly touch on a few of them to give a sense of their diversity and variation.

The prevailing, or at least most widely held, view of the soul's origin dodges the question of origin altogether by simply saying that the soul has always existed. This view shows up in various Western and Eastern faith systems, including certain Christian sects, Judaism, Hinduism, and Buddhism. It also exists in secular (nonreligious) views, such as the discourses of the ancient Greek philosopher Plato. Muslims believe that human beings are constantly in pursuit of self-knowledge in order to achieve the grace of self-improvement; they believe that as the animating method that gives life to the human body is the most sacred in the Universe, it cannot be known or understood by any but God.

Many Christian faiths, including Catholicism, hold the view that God creates a new soul each time a child is conceived. If for some reason that child is not born into a physical life, its soul goes directly to a spirit existence—in this context, to live in Heaven. Other faith systems believe that just as a child's parents create a new physical body from the joining of their bodies, their united spirits contribute equal parts to creating the new spirit that will inhabit that physical body.

And still other faith systems blend various theories and beliefs to come up with approaches that take a little of this and a little of that.

Soul: A Metaphysical Perspective

Within the framework of the metaphysical arts such as Numerology (the study of energy as expressed through numbers) and Astrology (the study of energy as expressed through the movements and relationships of stars, planets, and other celestial bodies), the soul chooses the moment and circumstances of its birth. This choice helps to define the soul's mission in its physical life and defines the energies of the Universe that will support the soul as it moves toward achieving its mission. This framework is not one of Destiny, but rather it is of the choices of Free Will that lead the soul either toward or away from its mission. The soul travels toward its mission for as long as that process takes and regardless of whatever detours the soul may encounter along the way. There is no predetermined path; the path unfolds according to the decisions and choices a person makes that fulfill the metaphysical blueprints of their soul's mission.

The Stars at the Moment of Your Birth

An astrological birth chart, with its planets, houses, and signs reveals your personal energy signature. As unique as a thumbprint, your astrological chart shows the heavens as they were positioned at the exact date, place, and time of your birth. At your birth, your astrological chart reflects basic knowledge about you and the energies within the Universe that will support or challenge your spirit's journey through this physical life.

Rather than pinpointing your soul's origin, astrology maps your spirit's travels. This reaches far beyond the traditional Sun sign astrology most people know from receiving texts on their phones for daily horoscopes! Birth chart astrology and the interpretation of astrological cycles are quite complex and exacting, requiring algorithms and computer formulas based on specific astronomical data to calculate. (In the "old days," calculating a birth chart involved so much tedious detail and special knowledge that very few except professional astrologers attempted it.) Today, anyone can obtain a reasonably accurate astrological birth chart from the many web sites designed to create and interpret them, including Co-Star and Sanctuary. You should be aware that many professional astrologers believe that while computer-generated birth charts may be accurate, computer-generated interpretations of them may be found to be sorely lacking. An in-person, one-on-one reading from a credentialed, flesh-and-blood astrologer makes a direct and valuable spiritual connection between two people where you can ask questions and receive answers in a personal flow of information designed exactly for and about *you*. Gaining a knowledge about astrology and an interpretation of your birth chart can help you explore your connection to the spirit of the Universe. These provide a unique way to connect the Earth plane and the Spirit plane, through steering by the great motion of the stars and heavens. To learn more, read the wonderful astrological primer, *The Awakened Life: Astrology* by Madeline Gerwick. Always remember the importance and role of Free Will in any metaphysical exploration. Every choice you make affects the course of your physical life on the Earth plane and your spirit's journey through its existence here. Even if you could look ahead, what you would see would be a future that flows precisely from the state of your existence at this very moment. Your birth chart is your astrological signature, which resonates uniquely to your spirit in the Universe. So, while the energy is uniquely yours, its expression of your soul's evolution is up to you, and you alone.

The Universe Vibrates to Your Number

Numerology assigns numeric values to all aspects of your existence. You already know some of your life's defining numbers—your date and time of birth, your age, the current date. Other dimensions of your life have numeric values as well, such as the names of people and places. Every number has a particular symbolic representation. Certain numbers are Master Numbers (such as 11, 13, 16, 22, and 33); that is, they are more powerful than other numbers.

The Greek mathematician Pythagoras, who lived in the sixth century B.C.E., established a correlation between mathematics and energy. He determined that certain numbers reflect a higher vibration of energy than others, leading to their interpretation as Master Numbers.

In numerology, the numbers associated with your physical life represent various characteristics of your spirit, from its mission to its challenges. You can look for the number that vibrates to your numerological personal year, month, and day by calculating, as follows (reducing the result if necessary until you reach a number between 1 and 9):

- **Personal Year:** Add birth month + birth day + current year
- **Personal Month:** Add calendar month + personal year
- **Personal Day:** Add personal month number + calendar day

Vibrational Energies of the Numbers	
1	Beginning of cycle, leadership, direction
2	Balance, harmony, cooperation
3	Joy, creativity, self-expression
4	Secure, hard work, master builder
5	Change, freedom/on the move, sexual
6	Marriage, family, home
7	Alone, intuitive, questioner
8	Success, money, authority
9	Compassion, spirituality, end of cycle

Understanding your personal numerology can give you additional insights into your spirit's journey.

Soul: A Spiritualist Perspective

Spiritualism teaches that the origin of the Universe and all that exists within it is unknown and really doesn't matter! What does matter is that we *do* exist and that our spirits continue across the spectrum of physical life and the Spirit world. The focus in Spiritualism is on advancing the spirit's mission as the spirit travels through the physical world.

Being with Someone at Birth or Death

At birth, we know there is a considerable contingent waiting on this side of the divide to welcome the new life. Doctors, nurses, partners, siblings, grandparents, friends, and even coworkers traditionally all gather to participate in the birth in some way or another. What we can't see is the contingent gathered on the Higher side, spirits surrounding the new life with love and ready to assist a spirit in its transition at birth into the physical world—although we must presume they are there. During spirit contacts, it is said that those in the Spirit world cry when a baby is born to the Earth plane, just as we cry when a person leaves their physical existence to enter the realm of Spirit.

The situation repeats itself at physical life's other transition: death. Loved ones and often health care professionals gather around the dying person to offer whatever comfort is possible. And although you cannot see them, the welcoming contingent from Spirit has gathered on the Higher side, waiting to greet the passing spirit in its return.

What's different, typically, is the mood and tone of these two events. A baby's birth inspires a great sense of joy and wonder. A person's impending death often fills us with sadness, loss, and even despair. This grief is, of course, normal. We mourn the loss of those we love, even when we believe they aren't really lost to us but are just moving into a different existence. Our point of focus is on the "different," and we know we will miss what we had. Knowing that there is life beyond the death of the physical body helps relieve some of the hurt. You know the life of the spirit continues, and this knowledge brings comfort and peace.

If you are with a loved one who is dying, let the person know you are there even if they appear to be unaware of what's happening. Touch, talk, cry, laugh, pray—do whatever comes naturally. The mind and body might be shutting down, but the spirit is expanding. As it often happens in spirit contact, the spirit wants loved ones to know that those final words and caresses were both noticed and helpful. And as your loved one's spirit achieves release, open yourself to feeling its joy and liberation.

Although you will feel loss and grief when you realize the passing has taken place, you will also have the comfort of knowing that you shared in the passage and that your loved one made the transition. This is one of the most intimate sharings you can have with someone. As a medium,

Rita has been with those who are about to pass and has seen the gathering of the ones, the family members and friends on the Higher side, reaching to welcome the one who is about to pass.

The experience is amazingly powerful and is often the resounding "Yes!" that you seek when asking the question (aloud or whispered in your mind), "Is there really life beyond death?"

At the start of 2021, nearly 500,000 Americans had died from COVID-19, with the pandemic still raging and vaccinations just taking off. For too many families, it was impossible to be present at their loved ones' deaths. This extra heartbreak has no words. If you are grieving the absence of a loved one lost to you without the caress of your touch and of your voice to ease their passage to Spirit, please know we are giving you virtual hugs and wishing you peace. While reality cannot be changed, know that your loved one was *never alone* in the process of dying and that your loved ones came to the embrace of Spirit with love and were greeted by the spirits of loved ones that went before. Know, too, that your loved ones were accompanied by the tireless and dedicated medical staff attending them, who share your grief and who also badly need our love and support to recover from their trauma of fighting for so many lives.

Now, if you are facing the death of a loved one you know you cannot be with at their time of death, there are things you can do. If you are at home, create an altar with pictures and reminders of your loved one. Let everyone in the family contribute something to the altar. Set aside a time for family devotion to honor your loved one through their passage to Spirit. Keep vigil, if you must, but remember to maintain balance and *always* remember that *you too, are not alone!* Spirit attends you always (in all ways!) and holds you with love and care. If you desire, choose a small prayer to recite as a mantra for the soul's passage, such as the one we suggested in the previous chapter composed by Vietnamese monk Thich Nhat Hanh. Repeat the following as you breathe: "Breathing in, I calm my body. Breathing out, I smile. Dwelling in the present moment, I know this is the only moment."

More than anything, know that we are *all* connected through Spirit.

Releasing Fear

Letting go is as important for the departing spirit as it is for those left on the Earth plane. The transition from physical life to spirit existence is both natural and inevitable. We on the Earth plane can assist a spirit to complete its transition, through spirit contact and prayer. This can provide the comfort and the encouragement the spirit needs to release its bonds with the Earth plane and allow those in the Spirit plane to welcome their loved one.

Releasing Love

Love is our most powerful emotion. It can enable us to do things that should be beyond our abilities, such as when a woman lifts a car to free a loved one trapped beneath in an accident. Love, we say poetically, transcends all. Because of this, we long for love; it is what makes our human existence meaningful. And when love enters our lives, we don't want to let it go. Because these words, no matter their source, are true: *Love hopes all things, believes all things, endures all things.*

Sometimes, the power of love can be strong enough that a loved one's spirit is unwilling to pass over after death releases it from its physical body. The spirit might want to stay as close to the Earth plane as possible for as long as possible to remain near the loved one who is still there. Or the spirit might feel unable to move away because the pull of love from the one remaining on the Earth plane is too strong to let it go.

There are ways for those in the physical world to help the spirit's transition between the Earth and Spirit planes. For example, spirit contact and prayer can help both the person remaining on the Earth plane and the spirit that needs to pass over. Love is like an incredibly fluid and flexible band of energy. It will always flow between and around the spirits on either side of the divide, maintaining the connection between them.

Completing Unfinished Business

Sometimes, a person's passing happens before the spirit feels it has finished its business on the Earth plane. This is especially the case if death is sudden, leaving behind tangible loose ends such as financial matters. Spirits might not become All-Knowing once they pass over to the Higher side, but they do know that loved ones who remain on the Earth plane often need help with these loose ends. So, the departing spirit stays close to the Earth plane to try to communicate the message while offering guidance and help from the Higher side.

Sometimes the loved one on the Earth plane can feel this presence. There might be a sense of being directed about what to do with certain bills, to look in the upper left-hand desk drawer for the check ledger, to contact the bank about joint accounts, to find the deed to the house, or to find the key to the safety deposit box. Sometimes another person comes in to handle these matters and seems to know just what to do even without any previous experience. Once these tasks are accomplished, the spirit is satisfied and moves on. Rita was doing some message work that those in the Spiritualist Church sometimes call the portion of the church service that presents spirit communicationand. She came to a woman whose significant other, the man with whom she shared her home, possessions, and life, had passed. After providing a full description of himself to Rita (and that the woman joyously recognized), the man said he wanted to talk to her about some papers that needed to be signed. "Tell her," he communicated to Rita, "to make her own decisions and not pay any attention to all the others who feel they have her best interests at heart, because only she knows the right thing to do."

The woman nodded and said nothing, and Rita concluded the service. Afterward, the woman came up to Rita and asked if they could talk for a moment. It had taken some time for the woman to absorb the communication and all that it implied, she said, but she wanted Rita to know how important and timely the message was. "I'm selling some property that we had owned together," she said. "Everybody has advice, but this is what I want to do. I'm signing the papers next week!"

Unfinished business is not always task-oriented, of course. Because the timing of death is more likely to be unexpected than anticipated, there are often dangling issues that get cut off before resolution. A father and a daughter might never quite acknowledge to each other that they respect and admire the other's achievements. Spouses or partners might not have the opportunity to apologize and make up after an argument. Siblings might find themselves grown apart, or even estranged, unwilling or unable to reconnect. Or maybe you weren't able to give that one second, or second hundredth, chance at reconciliation. No matter. It is okay to let it be. Love endures.

But if it can't be let be, loved ones remaining on the Earth plane, as well as the spirits who have passed, often feel a need to bring these matters to resolution. Sometimes the experience of this happens through a dream or visitation immediately following the death. Other times, it takes place months or years down the road and might require intervention from someone else, such as a medium like Rita.

People sometimes worry that reaching a level of completion has taken too long and that it must have interfered with the spirit's existence to the same extent it has disrupted their own. Although here in the physical world, a significant amount of time might have passed since the loved one's death, remember that on the Higher side, there is no time or space as we understand them. What feels like a long time to you is really no time at all for the loved one on the Spirit plane. All that matters is that the healing takes place, so both the incarnate and discarnate spirits can move on.

Reaching Across the Border

Spirits are busy on the Higher side. There are no spirit communications that suggest spirits are lolling around out in the ethereal heavens somewhere, plucking at stars and watching the Universe unfold before them. To the contrary, it appears that existence on the Higher side is quite active and even intense. The difficulty for us on the Earth plane is in trying to understand how this can be when the framework we use to measure it—time, distance, and space—does not exist.

So what do they do on the Higher side of life? To be sure, there is much learning and developing as each soul embarks on the next segment of its journey, but all is not serious! Part of the evolution for most spirits is having fun and enjoying things that perhaps they didn't get to do on the Earth plane.

Rita was doing a reading for a woman whose fiancé had passed. "I have someone here who is playing the trumpet," Rita said. "He's quite resoundingly playing 'When the Saints Go Marching In!'"

The woman burst into tears of joy. Her fiancé, she told Rita, had always wanted to learn to play the trumpet but had never had the time or the resources. Clearly, once those factors didn't matter, he was free to pursue this dream … and pursue it with vigor! Many, many spirits share with us the fun and wonderful experiences they are having.

It's hard for us to imagine being busy when there are no time, distance, and space constraints because these are the factors that define "busy" for us here on the Earth plane. It is hard not to think of the words of author Henry Miller: "Human beings make a strange fauna and flora. From a distance they appear negligible; close up they are apt to appear ugly and malicious. More than anything they need to be surrounded with sufficient space—space even more than time." But spirits certainly have plenty to do on the Higher side, and are likely busier than we can comprehend!

Do (Not) Disturb

We've been saying that each spirit has a mission. Part of this mission unfolds during the spirit's existence on the Earth plane, and part of it on the Spirit plane. When we attempt to make contact with the spirit of a loved one who has passed, are we interrupting anything?

Spirit contact sometimes comes without being summoned. Rita was at a wake for a friend's father who had passed when the father's spirit grabbed her by the psychic coattails and communicated that he wanted to convey a message to his daughter. Rita walked over to her friend, took her hand, and said, "Your father wants me to tell you he's dancing with your mother again!"

It's important to always keep in mind that a spirit who does not *want* to make contact will *not* make contact. You cannot force spirit contact or communication. You cannot demand that a spirit make itself available to you. (Well, you can demand all you want, but nothing compels a spirit to respond!) A spirit comes through because it wants to, because it desires to share a message with you. Your efforts to make contact will not disturb a spirit or keep it from what it needs to do. Just as you won't answer your doorbell if it rings when you are in the shower (if you even hear it), a spirit will not respond to communication attempts if it is otherwise occupied.

When a spirit chooses not to come through, it is likely because it is involved in something it does not want to interrupt. Just as there are activities here on the Earth plane requiring our intense concentration and participation from start to finish, there are such events on the Spirit plane, as well. After all, insight and enlightenment don't just happen! Spirits must *work* to understand and complete the lessons that are crucial to their soul missions on the Higher side, just as you must do the same during your existence in the physical world.

Death by Choice: Suicide

Suicide is a great moral and spiritual dilemma for us on the Earth plane. Nearly every faith system views suicide as an act contrary to the normal order of things, whether as an interference with the role of God in determining physical life and death or as a rift in the energy flow of the

Universe. After a loved one takes their own life, those who remain on the Earth plane are left not only with tremendous grief, pain, and guilt, but they are also left to wonder what consequences await their loved one on the Higher side.

Those remaining on the Earth plane worry tremendously about what happens to those who pass by taking their own lives. What spirits tell us is that when someone passes through suicide, the Higher side is a classroom of sorts where the spirit gets help thinking about and handling the issues that led to the suicide. Some souls, whether in their physical lives or on the Spirit plane, are just not able to work through their problems and issues. On the Higher side, there is help. There is always learning, and there is always a positive outcome to be found somewhere, sometime, somehow.

If you or someone you know are thinking about committing suicide, please seek professional help without delay. Suicide is *not* the answer to any question or problem. Nearly every community has a suicide hotline you can telephone for information and referral to an appropriate health care provider.

Violent Death

We know that the spirits of those whose lives are taken through violence or trauma are more likely to remain earthbound than spirits that don't experience such abrupt transitions. It is this circumstance, indeed, that resulted in the birth of modern Spiritualism when the spirit of a man murdered in their house inspired the Fox sisters to attempt communication with him (see Chapter 3). Such traumatic and unexpected death moves the spirit from its physical body so abruptly that it sometimes cannot complete the transition.

When this happens, we on the Earth plane can help, again through spirit contact and prayer. We can help send them to the Light! Visualize the person who has died moving toward the Light, helping them see the hands that are reaching out to them so they can make the transition. It is sometimes necessary to convince a spirit that their physical body is gone and there is no choice now but to move on. When done with love and compassion, this is greatly healing for the spirit and allows it to continue its transition. This is the positive message of the film *The Sixth Sense* that you read about in Chapter 5.

In many ways, the violent trauma is just as disruptive for loved ones who remain on the Earth plane. They are left with many loose ends and much unfinished business. The process of helping the loved one come to grips with the reality of the situation and complete their crossing can also aid those on the Earth plane in reaching similar acceptance. Establishing a spirit connection can also offer those on both sides the opportunity to say goodbye and bring closure.

Is This All Just Wishful Thinking?

No one likes to think of continuing in this life without the loved ones who bring so much joy and meaning to the journey. Yet inevitably, some loved ones will pass to the Higher side before us, and we will feel the separation as loss and pain. This is natural and normal, part of the experience of being human and of our existence in the physical world. (Many believe this is a core element of the soul's mission on the Earth plane, as loss and pain can be paths to enlightenment and insight.) So, is the desire to make contact with those who have passed from Earthly life just wishful thinking, a means of easing hurt and grief?

To some extent, it certainly is. The sense of loss that comes with a loved one's passing validates the spiritual existence for both the one who has passed and the one who remains on the Earth plane. But beyond the pain, there is still the sense of connection. Regardless of where in the Universe each of you is, you never really lose touch with those who are important to you. (Notice we said "are," in the present tense, and not "were," in the past tense.)

That your spirits are now on different planes changes your relationship, just as a friendship will change when one friend moves from Boston to San Francisco. The move doesn't mean the end of your friendship. It just means the courses of your respective lives have changed and your relationship is changing as a result. Instead of meeting for coffee twice a week, you might send daily text messages, weekly chats, or telephone each other late at night when the chaos of your busy daily lives finally quiets enough for you to enjoy uninterrupted conversation. Maybe you love old-fashioned letter writing and enjoy sending a message in your own hand, as human beings have for centuries. Will you miss each other and the relationship you had when you both lived in near proximity? Surely! But will you still remain dear friends? Most certainly if that is what you both desire and work to maintain.

Spirit contact is, of course, more complex than managing a friendship across the miles (in the human dimensions of space, distance, and time). Your two spirits are now on journeys no longer contiguous. The separation is momentous for each, and it allows each to move toward achieving its unique and personal mission. Communication across this separation is momentous, too, because in addition to keeping you in touch with someone greatly important to you, it affirms (you know this as well as we do by now, so say it with us) *the continuity of life*. Once this happens, there is no wishful thinking about it! Life, like love, endures, beyond the transition from Earth to Spirit.

Spirit Guides

Wouldn't it be nice if you could share in the wisdom and learning the Higher Side has to offer … from this Earthly plane? You can, and probably already do, even though you might not know it! Spirit guides are with each of us all the time. Some people are very aware of their guides and can even tell which guides are present. Some people only sense a Spirit guide's presence in times of need or stress, while others sense the presence of their guides a good deal of the time.

Spirit guides are here to watch out for us, help us understand life lessons, and help us find joy and wonder as we journey through our Earth plane existence. And often, contact serves for the Spirit guide's progression as well. Spirits can learn by helping us through our experiences, too.

You and Your (Spirit) Shadow

Although your Spirit guides are with you all the time you aren't always aware of their presence, any more than you're aware of the presence of your shadow. Just as familiarity blurs the details of your regular commute route or daily activities, the continuous presence of your Spirit guides sometimes makes them just part of the psychic scenery.

Whether or not you know it, your Spirit guides are always with you. They communicate with you on a higher level. Some of the information they have to share is instructional, helping you to discover the learning of your lessons in this life. You might *hear* or *see* or even *feel* this communication and be as consciously aware of it as you would be of a dialogue with an Earth plane friend. Other times, you simply take an action or make a decision that turns out right, and you might marvel at having done so. Do you feel as though Spirit is smiling at you then? Take a deep breath. Do you feel a deep breath deliver the energized warmth of vital life force energy to your body and soul? Thank your Spirit guides!

A key concept with Spirit guides is *guidance*. Guidance is something that is optional. It is additional information, a different perspective that you can use or not use as you choose. You are not required to follow a Spirit guide's advice. What you do with the information your Spirit guides provide is entirely up to you.

Spirit guides aren't with us to live our lives for us or to keep us from making poor choices and mistakes. Ultimately, you are responsible for your own life and the path it takes. Spirit guides are extra resources for you to tap into and to draw from in considering the many elements of information that go into the decisions you make. It's up to you to use or discard that advice, according to how it fits with other advice and information. You, and you alone, are accountable for the course of your life.

Someone to Watch over You

Do you sometimes feel that your Spirit guide is some sort of a heavenly protector who watches over you and keeps you from getting into harm's way or into trouble? You might even refer to this protector as a Guardian Angel (although technically speaking, a Guardian Angel is an entirely different entity). You might have Spirit guides that function in this way. They stay with you, surround you with light and energy, and help you find your way safely through the day and to your destination.

Your safety always remains your responsibility! Don't rely on Spirit guides, however protected they make you feel, to keep you safe when you put yourself in hazardous situations. Remember that Spirit guides are with us to help with the lessons of our lives, not to keep us from the consequences of potentially risky decisions.

A Little Help from Beyond

During your existence on the Earth plane, you develop a certain expertise. (If you're truly talented, you might have several areas of expertise.) You might be a graphic artist, a banker, an accountant, an engineer, a carpenter, a baker, an attorney, a doctor, or a writer. When you pass to the Higher side, this expertise goes with you. As you evolve on the Higher side, your first order of business is to complete whatever personal matters need attention. After that, you can use your expertise to guide people on the Earth plane.

This is the help that comes to you through your Spirit guides. They have expertise in areas that are important in your life, and come to offer guidance in those areas. Often, your Spirit guides help you to move toward achieving your life's mission.

Cast of Thousands

Most Spirit guides were once people who walked the Earth plane and now have an expertise that they can share with you. They can offer help with just about any need you might have, from the mundane to the spiritual. You might have one Spirit guide who offers advice about matters relating to your professional life, and another that gives you a boost when you're involved in physical activities. You might even have shopping guides!

Rita has a particular Spirit guide that has been with her for a long time and is with her when she paints for herself. Yet when Rita makes Spirit drawings during readings, she can feel that other Spirit guides come in to guide the process. She can see the shift in the style of her drawings, and then Rita knows different guides are at work, helping her to make the best presentation. Sometimes the spirit being drawn will help to guide the details and even the composition of a drawing. On the occasion Rita paints her own Spirit guides, she can feel them as well, guiding her hand to help create the images that unfold on her canvases.

A Spirit guide might have a heritage that is very different from yours. Yet if you look closely, you'll find that there is some sort of connection. Perhaps there are elements of the Spirit guide's heritage that allow you to look at things differently than your own heritage and culture permit. Our Spirit guides help us through the processes we need to complete so we can make the changes and experience the growth needed to make our own life paths unfold. Each of us is so unique! Some people don't want to go any further than their neighborhood, while others want to travel around the world. Spirit guides give us inspiration for journeys that we want—or need— to take.

Friend, Family, Stranger?

A Spirit guide has a particular skill or expertise to offer you, which is why you have different Spirit guides at different times of your life, and even during different activities. Occasionally, a Spirit guide might be a friend or a family member who has passed to the Higher side. But most of the time, your Spirit guides are not the characters you'll find in daguerreotypes in your ancestry family album. The only time a Spirit guide might be a relative is when this person has an expertise that you need. If you're a painter and your grandfather was a plumber, your grandfather doesn't have much to offer you about painting—even though you might very much enjoy his Spirit visits. A Spirit guide comes to teach or assist you. A loved one comes to fuss over you and to tell you to eat your oatmeal and button your coat!

If a Spirit guide's apparent message doesn't make sense to you, explore it further. Never make changes in your life solely on the basis of information that comes to you through Spirit communication. As with all advice, explore all the possibilities and consequences before choosing a course of action.

Sometimes you might believe a relative has come through to give you some help. Think this through carefully before accepting it. Did this relative have expertise in the area they are now offering assistance with? If Aunt Martha couldn't balance a checkbook on the Earth plane, she's not going to become a financial whiz when she passes to the Higher side! If you have someone coming through, whether directly or through a medium, who says she's Aunt Martha and she's coming to give you financial planning advice from the Higher side, don't feel that you have to accept the advice. Sometimes the signal isn't quite clear; this either isn't Aunt Martha, or it is Aunt Martha, but she hasn't come to help you plan your financial future. Sometimes a visit is just a visit. Ask the spirit to clarify their identity and purpose, and then question whether that makes sense.

We've come across a good example of a Spirit guide's identity being discovered as a distant family member. *The Washington Post* article, "Near the end of life, my hospice patient had a ghostly visitor who altered his view of the world" (January 2, 2021), tells the story of a man in his 90s who is in hospice as he slowly succumbs to the ravages of colorectal cancer. The man had been a supply officer for a World War II combat hospital and had seen many men suffer gruesome wounds in battle. One night, the man gave in to the pressures and horrors of the war and was crying and shaking in his cot, when a vision appeared to him. Bathed in light sat a World War I veteran in uniform, crying and laughing and looking at the man with great compassion. From the WWI vet, the man received the message that all the pain and cruelty of war was nothing compared to the knowledge that we are all loved and connected by love. It left the man with a sense of peace and calm that allowed him to go on. He would be visited by the vision of the WWI vet several times more during the war. After the war, the visits stopped, and years later, the man found a photograph among his mother's belonging after she passed—a photograph of the same WWI soldier in uniform with the inscription on the reverse, "Uncle Calvin, killed during World War I, 1918." It had been Uncle Calvin who had appeared to the man during his time served in WW II with a message of love and peace. And who was the ghostly hospice visitor mentioned in the title of the *Washington Post* article? Uncle Calvin, of course, still wearing is WWI uniform complete with helmet. He'd arrived to assuage the man's depression in hospice over his terminal cancer diagnosis. This time, Uncle Calvin spoke, telling the man that Calvin was there with him, and that he'd be there to help the man "over the hill" when it was time to go. The man's long-time depression lifted, as he realized he'd been accompanied every step of his way by a Spirit guide who cared very much about his struggles and who surrounded the man with compassion, love, and understanding. Without the visitations of Uncle Calvin, the man would not have received the message of love and peace he needed to embrace his life unafraid and not alone, even in the final moments of living.

Who Are Your Spirit Guides?

It's cathartic and exciting to meet your Spirit guides. Most of them are just as eager to meet you. Even though they've been a part of your life for who knows how long, they've operated, for the most part, in the shadows. Everyone enjoys recognition, and Spirit guides are no exception. Many Spirit guides, as we saw with WWI vet Uncle Calvin, will go out of their way to help you figure out who they are.

Rita was painting a picture of her Spirit guide when a friend came in and asked, "What's his name?" Rita struggled with fragments of words and kept coming up with "Frangelico, Angelico, friar," with words going back and forth, until finally "Fra Angelico" came to her. But this didn't mean anything to Rita or her friend, so Rita just pushed it to the back of her mind.

End of the Day, November 1989, oil on canvas. Rita's painting of her Spirit guide Fra Angelico.

Three weeks later, Rita heard her father's voice say, "Look it up!" This had been her father's constant message during his presence on the Earth plane, so it came as no surprise that it was his message from the Higher side. So Rita went to the encyclopedia and found an entry for Fra Angelico, a painter who lived in the fifteenth century. All the information that she had told her friend about this painting monk was verified in the encyclopedia.

The Italian painter Fra Angelico (ca. 1400–1455), whose given name was Guido di Pietro, lived on the early side of the famous Italian Renaissance period in art that produced Leonardo da Vinci and Michelangelo. One of his famous paintings, a fresco called "The Annunciation," is in a church in Florence, the monastery of S. Marco. According to the "standard of standards" in art history basic texts, *History of Art*, art historian H. W. Janson writes Fra Angelico preserves "dignity, directness, and spatial order … but his figures, much as we may admire their lyrical tenderness, never achieve the physical and psychological self-assurance that characterizes the Early Renaissance image of man." Lyrical tenderness is exactly the quality Fra Angelico, as Rita's Spirit guide, nurtured in Rita's life and artworks.

But being the skeptic that she is, Rita dug deeper for more information about Fra Angelico. Could this Italian Renaissance master *really* be one of her Spirit guides? At the Worcester Art Museum's research room, Rita found an article written in approximately 1850, critiquing Fra Angelico in the same way that Rita's work had been reviewed just a few months earlier! In both cases, the critiques stated, "Master of hands and faces but not enough painterly quality. Too interested in telling the story." For Rita, this verified that Fra Angelico was indeed one of her Spirit guides; the chances of something like this happening at random are pretty incredible.

Hilma af Klint's Symbolic Economy of Spiritualism

Many artists' works are guided by Spirit. Hilma of Klint, until recently a little-known Swedish painter of the early twentieth century, publicly acknowledged that conversations with spirits directed her artwork and informed her aesthetic as an abstract painter. Af Klint's paintings fit in well with the works of painters such as Wassily Kandinsky and Piet Mondrian. Yet she was not taken seriously in her own time because, of course, she was a woman, but also because of her Spiritualist beliefs and practices.

With four other women, she formed a group that met to hold séances to contact Spirit. Hilma af Klint's most ambitious work, a series of ten paintings called "The Ten Largest" (1907) are abstract paintings depicting the arc of human development from childhood to oldest old. Af Klint painted the works in response to instruction from her Spirit guides. Her communication with spirits and close relationship with her guides helped af Klint create a unique female artistic voice. Her artworks, now shown around the world as she takes her rightful place among the early twentieth century masters of painting, demonstrate a radical, new interpretation of an abstract painting style. Her work fuses a deep feminine understanding of humanity with the creative spark of Divine Spirit.

You Have One Dominant Spirit Guide

Most people have a dominant guide who is present nearly all of the time. When Deb (Rita's co-author of this book) and Rita talked on the telephone for the first time, Rita immediately "met" Deb's Spirit guide, even though Deb was unaware of his presence. An energetic and powerful presence, this guide is a Native American in full, colorful dance attire. He dances with great energy, and it is this energy that gives Deb her "Never say die!" approach to life. Now that she is aware of her Spirit guide, Deb feels his energy and his presence—especially when flying downhill on her mountain bike! Deb looks forward to getting to know Feather Dancer and to learning what lessons he is here to help her learn.

Like Deb, you might become aware of your Spirit guides when a medium introduces you to them. Or you might already have a sense that a presence accompanies you through the activities of your daily life; you might even have a clear vision that you can already identify as a Spirit guide, like Uncle Calvin, the WWI vet. Whatever the case, your guides are with you to help you get the most from your life. Your guides are your friends in Spirit, and you can initiate communication with them just as you might pick up the telephone to call your Earth plane friends.

Among your Spirit guides, there is generally one that is a dominant presence. This dominant Spirit guide serves as the guardian who decides what other contact with Spirit to permit. In this gatekeeper role, your primary Spirit guide "screens" your visitors from Spirit to keep you from being overwhelmed by contacts from Spirit guests eager to visit with you. As you get to know your dominant Spirit guide and become aware of their presence and interactions in your life, you'll know when your gatekeeper steps aside to allow other communication to come through. Mediums like Rita often observe this happening when doing readings.

Don't worry that your dominant Spirit guide will keep you from asking for particular kinds of help from other spirits. Your Spirit guide is there to support and nurture you, to challenge and grow your understanding of life and the Divine. You will have many spiritual influences during your lifetime, and your dominant Spirit guide is just another important key mentor for you. Your dominant Spirit guide will bring spirits to you, making all kinds of beneficial introductions, and journey with you on your soul's search for enlightenment.

Meet Your Spirit Guides: Guided Meditation

Who are your Spirit guides? Here is an exercise that can help the guides disclose themselves to you. Guided meditation, or directed communication, is a common method of helping your conscious self to step aside. This opens and frees your mind, body, and spirit to be receptive to contact with Spirit. You might want to read through it several times. In that way, you can go through the steps without interrupting them to see what comes next. It's not important that you follow each step exactly. What matters most are that you are comfortable, relaxed, and open to the experience and whatever information it reveals to you.

1. Make yourself comfortable in a location where you won't have any distractions or interruptions.

2. Take three slow, deep breaths, in through your nose and out through your mouth. Let the first breath clear your body, let the second breath open your mind, and let the third breath free your spirit.

3. Consciously form the thought: *This is my time to be one with God and for God to be one with me.* (God, of course, being the Divine of your belief system or choice.) Set a clear intent to meet your Spirit guide.

4. In your mind's eye, see yourself sitting on a bench in an open, beautiful garden. There are flowers and trees, and the air smells fresh and clean. It is peaceful and calm.

5. Open your mind and your heart to welcome the visitor you know is approaching, with the same delight and excitement you might feel when a close friend or relative comes to visit.

6. Watch your visitor, your Spirit guide, approach you. Notice it, but don't shift your focus to looking at the guide's appearance, attire, and demeanor. Invite your guide to join you.

7. Open your spiritual senses to allow communication with your guide. Listen with your inner hearing, observe with your inner vision. Ask your guide to share with you whatever information they wish to share.

8. When your visitor from Spirit appears ready to leave, thank them for coming to visit. Say goodbye in comfort and in joy, knowing that you can and will meet again.

9. Smell the clean, fresh air, and gaze at the beautiful flowers and trees in the garden of your mind's eye. Gradually feel yourself rise from your bench. Step back, and feel yourself leaving the garden and returning to your physical location.

10. Draw your attention to your breathing. Feel yourself back in your body, become conscious of your breathing, in and out. Wiggle your fingers and your toes; open your eyes.

Identifying Your Spirit Guide

Now it's time to put on your analytical thinking cap. Who is your Spirit guide? What is their link to you, and what lessons is this guide in your life here to teach you? What information did your Spirit guide share with you? Get your old-fashioned, standard-issue pen or pencil, and write down your impressions while they're still fresh in your mind. If you need more space than we've provided here, write your responses on a separate sheet of paper or record your impressions in your computer notebook or tablet.

1. Did you get a clear image of your Spirit guide? Describe the image.

    _____
    _____
    _____

2. Does your Spirit guide seem familiar? Did you get a sense of a name or a place that might help to identify this Spirit guide? Write down any words or images that came to you.

    _____
    _____
    _____

3. Did your Spirit guide appear to be male or female, or without gender? What physical characteristics could you sense? Write the most complete description that you can.

    _____
    _____
    _____

4. What kind of clothing was your Spirit guide wearing? Did their clothes appear to be historical, contemporary, or from somewhere out of this world?

    _____
    _____
    _____

5. What cultural heritage did your Spirit guide appear to embody? Is this a culture similar to, or very different from, your own? Or is the cultural reference of dress or speech unknown to you?

    _____
    _____
    _____

6. Did your Spirit guide seem familiar, as though you've met before? Describe aspects that feel familiar. Do you believe you *know* your Spirit guide? If so, how? Why?

    _____
    _____
    _____

7. Did your Spirit guide speak to you? What did your guide say? Describe the guide's voice and what your guide said. Is the speech from a language you can identify?

_____

_____

8. Did your Spirit guide tell you their name or provide you with clues to identify? Did you have a sense of a name or a word floating in your thoughts? Write down your impressions.

_____

_____

9. What mannerisms did your Spirit guide have? Did they make gestures, sit with legs crossed, or stand during the visit? Write down all that you can remember about what happened.

_____

_____

10. Write down any other relevant details about the visit from Spirit that remain strongly in mind. What feature or characteristic of your guide can you just not forget?

_____

_____

Cosmic Counsel

Rita's Spirit guide Fra Angelico is an ever-present teacher who helps Rita refine and improve her technique and skill as a painter. She can ask Fra Angelico for help, or he can come through with inspiration. Spirit guides are with us to teach and help us learn. Your Spirit guides can help you enhance the abilities and talents that you have, and they can even help you discover those abilities and talents that you didn't realize you had. However, they cannot give you talents, skills, and potentialities that you don't already have nascent within you. It is always your role and responsibility to develop your gifts and aptitudes and make the most of your experience of life.

When Rita did a second exercise to meet her Spirit guide, Fra Angelico appeared again. Rita expected the room that the monk created for their second meeting would look like the cell in a monastery, but instead it looked like a large, elegant dining room. In the center of the dining table was a bowl of fruit. When Fra Angelico walked into the room, Rita waited, extremely excited to talk with him, but the monk stopped to eat a pear. She said to him, "I am a painter." He smiled back and said, "I know." (And of course, he would know.) Rita said, "I paint with much larger brushes than you did." He chuckled and said, "I know that, too." Then in the meditation, they walked over to one of Rita's paintings. She picked up a brush to paint, as Fra Angelico's hand slipped over Rita's hand like a surgical glove. Their two hands painted together.

Life Lessons: A Guided Meditation

You, too, can seek the counsel of your Spirit guides. In the mediumship classes she teaches, Rita uses the following exercise to help her students learn more about their Spirit guides and the lessons they have come to teach. (The first three steps are the same ones you followed to establish contact with your Spirit guides.)

1. Make yourself comfortable in a location where you won't have any distractions or interruptions. If possible, make it a space that holds special meaning for you and surely a place where you are relaxed.

2. Take three deep, full breaths, slowly in through your nose and out through your mouth. Let the first breath clear your body, let the second breath open your mind, and let the third breath free your spirit.

3. Consciously form the thought: *This is my time to be one with God and for God to be one with me.* Set a focus of intent to meet your Spirit guide or teacher.

4. With your eyes closed, see yourself on a magnificent university campus, library, arts center, or other inspiring place of learning. There are beautiful gardens and timeless classic buildings constructed of white marble all around you. (You can close your eyes if this helps you to concentrate, or you can focus your sight on a specific point or object.)

5. As you stand, in your mind's eye, on this campus, you see many footpaths of white, crushed stone. You know that one of these paths is yours, and you start to walk it.

6. Walk your path until it takes you to a beautiful building with a grand staircase leading inside. Climb the staircase and enter the building.

7. Stand quietly in the entrance foyer, waiting for instructions about where to go next. You will be directed to the room where you will meet your Spirit teacher, one who is guiding you from the Higher side.

8. Go to this room, and enter it with an open mind. Have no expectations, no precon-ceived ideas about whom or what you will find in the room. Allow the room to pres-ent itself to you, and wait until someone else enters the room. Notice the shape and configuration of the room, its light, and purpose (Are you in the kitchen, the library, a bedroom, or a green house?)

9. The one who joins you in this room is your Spirit teacher. Ask your teacher what lesson you need to learn. A lesson will be given to you. Be still, stay in the quiet, and let the lesson impart itself to you through your teacher's wisdom.

10. When the transmission of the lesson from teacher to student is complete, thank your Spirit teacher, say goodbye, and know that you can and will meet again. Promise to give your highest and best toward gaining understanding and peace as you work on the lesson intended for you in this life.

11. Walk back to the building's entry foyer, go through the door to the outside, and walk down the grand staircase to the footpath that brought you here. Follow the path back to the edge of the campus. Look around you, see that the sun is high, the sky is blue, and all is well. Breathe deep, full breaths.

12. Bring your attention to your breathing, in and out. Feel yourself solidly in your body, grounded to the Earth, at one with its energy. Become conscious of your life force moving through your body with your breath. Wiggle your fingers and your toes; open your eyes.

Understanding the Lesson

Now, while your lesson from Spirit is fresh in your mind, write down the images that came to you. This is often very much like interpreting your dreams. Images and concepts might be symbolic and representative rather than literal and direct.

1. Were you able to determine right away which footpath was yours to follow? How, and why?

_____

_____

_____

2. What thoughts, emotions, or feelings did you experience when your Spirit teacher arrived and the lesson got underway?

_____

_____

_____

3. Did you get a clear image of who your Spirit teacher was? Describe the image. If you completed the "Meet Your Spirit Guides" exercise earlier in this chapter, was this the same Spirit guide that came to you then?

_____

_____

_____

4. Describe the lesson you were given, as it unfolded during the meditation.

_____

_____

_____

5. Did the lesson make sense to you? Did it relate to something that you do in your life, such as your profession, a talent that you have, or a hobby or special interest? Does the lesson have to do with some aspect of your personality?

_____

_____

_____

6. What images appeared in the lesson? Were there certain colors, sounds, or words? Did you experience anything that you recognized, or that seemed foreign (unknown) to you?

_____

_____

_____

7. How did you participate in the lesson? Were you eager or reluctant? Did the lesson seem easy, or difficult? How and why?

_____

_____

_____

8. Did you have questions during the lesson? Did you ask your questions? Did your Spirit teacher offer answers? Did those answers make sense to you? Whether talkative or mute, how did your Spirit teacher make you feel? As their student? Engaged? Angry? Bored? Fascinated?

_____

_____

_____

9. What meaning does the lesson from Spirit have for you right now? What parts of your life does the lesson inform?

_____

_____

_____

10. What aspects of the lesson from Spirit will you want to explore further to try to understand their meanings or purposes? How has your Spirit teacher offered to help guide you as you attempt to learn your lesson? Will keeping a journal or calendar or some other method help you to follow a study plan for your lesson? How will you continue to explore your lesson and its life-changing potential?

_____

_____

_____

The Path of Spirit Progression

The help that Spirit guides give us is invaluable. It can take us to levels of understanding, skill, and ability that would take much, much longer for us to achieve without their help. Often, this interaction is a two-way street; that is, Spirit guides benefit, too. They are progressing and evolving on the Higher side, moving along the paths of their soul-missions, just as we are doing the same in the paths of our physical lives. Teaching and learning are flip sides of the same coin; it is impossible to separate one from the other. In teaching us, our Spirit guides are also learning for themselves.

Feel the Energy!

Your Spirit guides bring much positive energy into your life. All you have to do is plug into this vital flow of the life force, and its many advantages are yours for the taking. Keep your heart, mind, and spirit open to the energy, and it can be the ground swell that carries you to new heights. Spirit lessons and advice can be enlightening. And they can be fun, bringing you much joy. Let the light of Spirit bring out the highest and best for you in this life. Embrace your life lessons. These lessons are given to engage and stimulate you, challenging you to grow as you create a better self. Do not be afraid or daunted. Spirit is with you!

Every Day in Every Way...

A simple practice can help direct and activate a conscious intent within you to explore your highest and best. Each day, especially at the start and end of the day, repeat this mantra: *Every day, in every way, from every point of view, I'm getting better and better.* Say the mantra in front of a mirror, don't be shy! First postulated in French by psychologist Emile Coue in the early twentieth century as *"Tous les jours à tous points de vue je vais de mieux en mieux,"* the saying demonstrated a method of conscious autosuggestion. Coue believed that imagination, more than willpower, prompts the human mind toward making changes in our unconscious thought. What we can imagine enters the realm of the possible. Coue's formula of autosuggestion is still used today; read more in his book *Self-Mastery Through Conscious Autosuggestion* (1922).

When we call upon our Spirit guides, remember that it is still up to us to improve our lives. Our Spirit guides will not do the work for us. But with the aid of our guides, we are able to see new paths and truths, new possibilities for living our best lives. Coue's mantra is a call to action that reminds us of the great invitation our Spirit guides offer us every day. Who can *you* become? Let your Spirit teachers comfort and guide you as you walk the path of this life, every day, a little better and better.

Chapter
8

Earthbound Spirits

In the decades framing the turn of the twentieth century, the heiress to the Winchester rifle fortune built an elaborately confusing mansion to hide from and fool the ghosts she was convinced were haunting her. But what some consider ghosts, we refer to as Earthbound spirits. Often, they remain on the Earth plane because they have unfinished business that prevents them from transitioning. In a location where people observe phenomena happening, there's always a reason the Earthbound spirit has been unable to make its transition to the Higher side. Releasing an Earthbound spirit is not a matter of "ghost-busting" to rid a house of an unwanted guest; it is a process of encouraging the soul to move on, to make their transition from the Earth plane to the light of the Spirit plane, and join loved ones on the Higher side.

However, most spirits that appear on the Earth plane come to us from the Spirit realm just for a visit. Often, they come to provide comfort and to even share in Earthly joys, such as the birth of a child, a wedding, or other life milestones. If you *feel* someone you love who has passed over is present with you, they probably are—and their appearance is all about love, comfort, and healing.

A Perfect Life That Wasn't to Be

Most ghost stories have an element of tragedy to them. The spirits of people whose deaths were in some way untimely are unable to complete their transitions, and remain sadly and often noisily stuck in the middle. Such tales are told around campfires and at slumber parties. One such story is that of the Winchester mansion.

In 1860, the American Civil War was just getting underway when a small company that was soon to become the Winchester Repeating Arms Company developed the weapon that would forever change the hazards of the battlefield. The Henry rifle had a magazine that could load and fire a bullet every three seconds. The North's Union Army soon equipped its soldiers with this devastating weapon, and the man at the helm of Winchester Arms, Oliver Winchester, became instantly and phenomenally wealthy. Two years after the Henry rifle made its debut, Oliver's son William took a bride: Sarah Pardee.

William and Sarah seemed to have the perfect life ahead of them when Sarah gave birth to a daughter four years later. But even wealth and social status couldn't protect the fledgling family from the dangers of illness, and their baby Annie died not long after birth. The loss was more than Sarah could bear, and she slipped into the dark depths of depression, where she remained for nearly 10 years. Sadly, it wasn't long after Sarah has recovered her mental health and returned to normal family life that tragedy struck again. Tuberculosis claimed William's life in 1881, leaving Sarah a widow and alone at age 42.

Sins of the Family

According to the lore surrounding Sarah Winchester's story, after several years of grieving that took her to the brink of depression again, Sarah consulted a medium. Although Sarah hoped to be reunited with her husband and daughter, the reunion wasn't quite what she anticipated. The medium claimed to make contact with William, but she brought the dire message from him that Sarah must use the vast fortune she inherited to atone for the sins of the Winchester family.

Sarah was to use her wealth to build a house where all the spirits of those who died because of Winchester rifles could come to live for all eternity. Sarah was to go West, the medium told her, until she found the location for this home. Because the Winchester fortune had accrued at the cost of countless lives (with a legacy of tragedy stretching endlessly into the future), the medium said, Sarah was to dedicate the rest of her life to this endeavor of atonement. William's task of atonement for Sarah recalls the task Jacob Marley set for Scrooge in Charles Dickens's *A Christmas Carol*, published only about 20 years earlier. (See Chapter 5.) The notion of performing atonement in this life for Earthly sins in order to gain entrance to Paradise was a strong belief of the time.

Sarah packed her things and moved West in 1892, where she found and purchased a small farmhouse on 160 acres on the outskirts of San Jose, California, about 40 miles south of San

Francisco. The house didn't stay small for long. With a $20 million inheritance and an income of $1,000 a day, Sarah began a building project that continued, day in and day out, until her death in 1922. She even had a private railroad constructed to bring building materials and furnishings to the property. At that time, the Winchester house sprawled over 6 acres and had 160 rooms, some finished and some still under construction. Through the years that Sarah lived in it, the house was reported to have had more than 600 rooms built and then torn apart to make way for other rooms to accommodate spirits deceased of gunshot wounds!

Dead-End Doorways and Stairways to Nowhere

The most important room in Sarah's mansion was the séance room, where she went every day to commune with the Earthbound spirits who told her what to build next. The Winchester mansion's séance room was hidden deep in the center of the sprawling house. It had just one entrance but three ways out. One exit was through the door leading into the room; one through a closet and then a door with a knob only on the side of the séance room; and another that opened to a 10-foot drop into the kitchen below.

At some point, Sarah's focus shifted from constructing a spirit sanctuary to building a safe haven for herself, apparently for protection from the ire of Earthbound spirits angry at her and her husband's family for designing and producing the instruments of their deaths.

The house was filled with stairways—40, by one count—that often went nowhere. One contained 42 steps that only rose 9 feet because each step was just 2 inches tall. Another stairway climbed to the ceiling, with no door at the top. Some doors opened to walls or drop-offs, either to other rooms or to the outside. Chimneys rose to within feet of ceilings and then stopped or extended beyond the roof but connected to nothing within the house. Earthbound spirits, of course, had no need of logical modes of ingress or egress—they could move through walls, doors, ceilings, stairs, and floors—and so the Winchester mansion became a maze devoted to the movements of Earthbound spirits. Sarah reportedly slept in a different bedroom every night, choosing—apparently at random—from among 25 or so human-accessible bedrooms in the mansion.

Thirteen … Everywhere!

Many structures within the Winchester mansion reflected Sarah's fascination with the number 13. There were 13 hooks in the séance room upon which hung the 13 robes of different colors that Sarah wore while communing with the Earthbound spirits. Windows inside and out contained 13 panes of glass, and stairways had 13 steps. Sink drains had 13 holes, and chandeliers held 13 lights. The house had 13 bathrooms. Even Sarah's will continued the pattern, containing 13 pages.

No one really knows why the number 13, traditionally viewed as unlucky, captivated Sarah to such an extent. It remains, along with the many other oddities of the mansion she built, a mystery. Today, the Winchester house is registered as a California historical landmark.

For all of her eccentricities, Sarah Winchester had a generous and giving spirit. In 1909, Sarah donated half a million dollars to the Connecticut General Hospital Society to build a tuberculosis hospital in memory of her husband, who died of the disease. The facility Sarah's ongoing donations built, a tuberculosis sanitarium called the William Wirt Winchester Hospital, outlived the disease it was designed to treat. Today, nearly a century later, the New Winchester Chest Clinic continues as an affiliation with Yale University's School of Medicine to provide medical care for patients with a wide variety of lung and chest ailments.

Pray for Peace

Between 1968 and 2011, nearly 1.4 million people died in the United States alone from the use of firearms. Traumatic gun deaths continue to be a plague on American society and are responsible for senseless violence and the devastation of families. The locations "Columbine" and "Sandy Hook" stand in as examples of the unbearable grief and loss caused by firearms. When traumatic and sudden deaths occur due to gun violence, families often anguish over the transition of the loved one from the Earth plane to the Spirit plane. Loved ones can seek clarity by contacting a professional medium that can help determine whether the spirit has transitioned and is at peace. Regardless, prayer for the souls lost to gun violence and accidents that are directed at Earthbound spirits eases them toward the light, and peace for all.

Paranormal Phenomena: Is It a Haunting?

Paranormal phenomena—the events and sensations people attribute to the presence of ghosts, such as unusual sounds and sights for which there are no obvious explanations—are amazingly common. Among the people you count as your friends and even family, we'd bet that more of them than not have experienced what they believe to be ghosts. "I was walking through the hallway when suddenly there was a young girl standing there, just standing there looking at me!" says Aunt Sue at dinner one evening. Or your friend Jonathan confides, "It was eerie, man, but there was this guy standing in the hallway, and when I said 'hey' to him, he just faded away!"

Hauntings are rife in American lore and literature. Consider the officer in full dress uniform who gives in-depth tours to today's tourists of Baltimore's 1854 sloop-of-war, *The Constellation*, the last sail-only warship built by the United States Navy—only to find no such tour guide exists! Earthbound souls who suffered gruesome deaths at sea upon its decks or in its sickbay are said to manifest at night with the banging of pots and pans and other phenomena. And then there are the ghostly inhabitants of The Overlook Hotel's room 217 (237 in the Kubrick film) of author Stephen King's classic scary novel, *The Shining*. While ghost stories like these can leave goosebumps, Rita reminds us that spirit contact comes in goodness and healing, not for vengeance or violence. We should firmly separate the ghostly chills and thrills of the horror genre from the real-world efforts of confused Earthbound spirits, who need love and encouragement to transition successfully to the Higher side.

It is possible that hauntings, paranormal phenomena, or sightings may be contacts with Earthbound spirits. The phenomena that manifest as a result could be the spirit's attempt to gain attention. It might be because the spirit is angry about something, such as having passed before feeling ready or being angry at a particular person about events that took place before the spirit's physical death. It could also be the spirit's attempt to ask for help in completing its transition. A spirit that feels trapped isn't necessarily going to have the best communication skills! Think about it: When you are confused, angry, or hurt, you also don't think, speak, or act with great clarity.

As a Spiritualist medium, Rita is often called upon to visit houses where people feel there are hauntings by Earthbound spirits. In one house she was asked to visit, Rita and the others with her could feel a heaviness as soon as they entered through the house doorway. It was as though the air itself was heavy, and it felt difficult to breathe. The house's new owner had a similar response and had become afraid to go into certain rooms where the sensation was particularly strong.

Rita and her group sensed the presence of a man, a woman, and two children. They felt that the man was very angry and abusive and that he had locked the woman and the children in the attic—the room in the house where the unpleasant energy was the strongest. Rita and her group prayed and felt that they released the Earthbound spirits in the house to move on to the light. In the days following Rita's visit, the house's owner felt an immediate shift in the energy throughout the house and was vastly relieved.

But six months later, the owner called Rita and her group to come back and experience the house's energy again. The Earthbound spirit had returned, this time as a more threatening presence. To the group's surprise, the negative energy was indeed back—and much stronger. Rita and her colleagues finally realized that this negative energy surged when the homeowner, a woman, was home alone, with her husband away. It became clear that the Earthbound spirit was very strong and defiant and could hide at will. An abuser in his physical life, this spirit had developed a pattern of behavior that made him extraordinarily abusive when he was alone with his wife and children, though he was outwardly ordinary when others were present. It took three visits for Rita's group to finally release the damaged spirit, so he could complete his transition to the Higher side—where presumably, he had a lot of work to do.

Apparitions and Visions

You've probably experienced visual manifestations of Spirit presence—a flash that you see out of the corner of your eye, a shadowy figure that appears and then disappears, or perhaps even a clear image of a loved one who has passed. Apparitions are among the most common experiences people have among paranormal phenomena. Sometimes apparitions just appear and then disappear, while other times, the spirit's image remains to engage in communication of some sort. Often, making a visual appearance is a spirit's way of saying, "See! It's really me!" to validate or authenticate its identity.

Did You Hear That?

From footsteps to moans and cries, the sounds of spirits tend to frighten people more than visual images because there is more of a mystery to them. When you can see something, it takes on a level of tangibility, regardless of whether you can actually reach out to touch it. When you hear something that doesn't seem real, you find yourself questioning it. What is it? Is it harmful?

Sounds and noises are simply other ways in which energy becomes tangible. They activate a physical sense in you—hearing—that gets your attention. Sometimes this is the only means by which a spirit chooses to communicate with you, while other times, the spirit might subsequently appear as a visual image as well.

I Didn't Touch It!

One of Rita's friends was among the early casualties of the AIDS epidemic. A fun-loving prankster in physical life, Richard wasn't about to let his friends mope about his passing—or celebrate the joys in their lives without him. He wanted to make sure they knew he was still with them. At a dinner party, he filled the air with the fragrance and sensation of rich Godiva chocolate—his favorite indulgence. Another time, Rita returned to her painting studio one evening to find a doll sitting on the top of a finished portrait canvas that was hanging nine feet above the floor, posed exactly as the figure in the painting! Spirits often move objects around to let you know they're there and to let you know who they are.

Why a Spirit Stays

Spirits generally remain Earthbound when they have not accepted their passings. Perhaps the spirit's physical life came to a sudden end as the result of an accident or an act of violence, leaving the spirit confused about where it belongs. Sometimes the spirit cannot let go of its Earth plane existence, either afraid to complete passage to the Higher side or unwilling to release its connection to a loved one still on the Earth plane. While we tend to think of Earthbound spirits as "trapped," they're really just in need of help to make the transition from the physical world to the Spirit world.

An example of just such a transition is found in the poignant and eerie film, *A Ghost Story* (2017), directed by David Lowery and starring Rooney Mara and Casey Affleck. *A Ghost Story* is as much a story of place as it is a story about an Earthbound spirit's struggle to reconnect with his wife. Throughout the movie, the spirit remains in his old house, watching his wife and waiting. Even after the wife has left it, the spirit stays with the house through the experience of its new inhabitants. The spirit stays even after the house has been destroyed and a new high-rise built in its place. For a time, the spirit even finds itself time-traveling back to witness the history of the ground upon which the house will be built before he will spend his Earthly time there with his wife. The Earthbound spirit cannot transition until it succeeds in deciphering a message the wife has placed within the walls of the house and is finally able to find peace.

Being Earthbound doesn't do much to advance a spirit's progression and evolution, of course. It's as though the spirit is treading water, so to speak. An Earthbound spirit doesn't necessarily choose to resist passage (although some spirits do); it just doesn't realize it has the choice to continue the passage. There are circumstances and events in your life that leave you feeling confused and unsure of what to do next; imagine the confusion and uncertainty you might feel if you were suddenly uprooted from the existence that's become familiar!

Sometimes a spirit has unfinished business on the Earth plane, especially if physical death came unexpectedly. A spirit might want to guide a surviving spouse or partner through the difficult decisions that accompany physical death, such as making funeral arrangements or wrapping up financial loose ends. We don't usually think of such a spirit as Earthbound in the traditional sense; once the unfinished business is completed, the spirit will feel free to move on in its transition.

Just Visiting

Sometimes spirits who have successfully transitioned to the Higher side just like to visit to let you know they are fine and to stay in touch with you, like your Earth plane friends and family do. At first, this kind of contact can be disconcerting, as it was for one family whose son, Jeff, passed tragically and unexpectedly as a young adult. Although the family was stunned and grieving, they also remembered with great joy the happiness and delight the fun-loving young man had brought into their lives. They often reminisced about his kind and generous nature.

Not long after Jeff's passing, family members started noticing phenomena. The flowers on the dining room table seemed to be in a different place every time someone came into the room. Sometimes, there were voices and noises that sounded like Jeff and his friends had come over for an afternoon of socializing, as had often been the case during his life. The family called Rita and planned a time for her to come to their house to verify whether these phenomena were indeed communications from Jeff.

When Rita entered the home, she anticipated that she would encounter the energy of an Earthbound spirit that would need help in transitioning the young man's spirit. She did her opening prayers and then began walking through the house. Much to her surprise, joyous spirits on the Higher side filled the house. Many, many relatives and friends were there, strong presences that felt like they were gathered to celebrate a momentous occasion.

Rita shared her perceptions with the family, who was overjoyed. They all began talking about Jeff when suddenly, something caught Rita's attention, and she pointed to the dining room table. "Do you see the flowers moving?" she asked. The family members nodded. This was one of the phenomena they saw frequently.

At the family's invitation, Rita opened herself to contact with the spirits who were present. The first to come through was Jeff's grandfather, who gave such a full description of himself that his identity was undeniable. Over the course of the next few hours, no fewer than a dozen of the young man's relatives and friends came through with messages of love and thanks.

Later in the evening, as Rita sat talking with the family, each time she mentioned the grandfather, she would hear the sound of tinkling glass, like wind blowing through a chandelier. After this happened a few times, the mother asked Rita if she could hear the sound, and Rita realized that everyone in the room could hear it. Everyone was very excited; this was yet another validation. The tinkling sounds continued through the evening as if in response to the conversation.

As Rita was getting ready to leave, the young man's mother gently touched her arm. "Can you tell me who held Jeff's hand when he made the crossing?" she asked. Rita put the question out. To everyone's surprise, the spirit who came through was a woman, the mother of a friend. The woman had been very ill in the months before her death, and Jeff had visited her most afternoons. When Jeff passed, it was this woman's spirit who reached out to take his hand to ease and guide his passage to the Higher side.

Spirits sometimes visit to offer comfort in times of sadness and encouragement when times are tough, and they offer healing energy when you are injured or ill (physically or emotionally). You might feel this contact as a gentle touch, a breeze, or even a surge of energy. It is for you; it is to help you. Welcome these contacts, and give thanks to those who bring them to you.

Advice and Warning

"Don't step off the curb!" shouts a voice in your head; startled, you hesitate, one foot floating just above the street. The crosswalk light is green for pedestrians; why shouldn't you cross? Then, from nowhere, a car screams into the intersection, running the red light. Had you started across the street, you'd now be a hood ornament. Give thanks to your Spirit guides and Spirit visitors!

Advice and caution from those on the Higher side can take many forms and often influences your actions without your awareness. You might "just have a bad feeling" about someone who smiles at you in the coffee shop and leave without getting your morning latte, then read the next day in the newspaper that the person had frequented the shop to target young women. Or while walking your dog through your neighborhood, you come across an estate sale, and while browsing through it, you discover the exact antique cookie press your grandmother had used and that you'd been looking for everywhere at online auctions. When you talk to the seller, you discover your grandmothers both had the same first name and grew up in the same state thousands of miles away! Coincidence? We don't think so! Our guides and visitors from Spirit help us along the way, always leading us toward grace and healing.

Helping an Earthbound Spirit Find Release

The real issue with Earthbound spirits isn't "busting" wandering spirits, so they're no longer nuisances in the physical world. It is helping them to complete their transitions so they can move on to the next phase of their evolution and growth as spirits.

When an Earthbound spirit is present, you often feel a sense of heaviness in the air. You might get goosebumps and feel like you need to leave right away—the "uh-oh" feeling. It's important to pay attention to these messages; they are warnings. Earthbound spirits are troubled and confused, and they need help to cross to the Higher side where they should be.

We on the Earth plane can help Earthbound spirits break free from whatever is holding them. Just as with all contact with Spirit, it is important to do this with the highest intent and with Divine protection. Do not embark on this alone; even experienced mediums go in groups when called upon to help Earthbound spirits find release. Instead, seek help from a professional who is consistent with your belief system—clergy, shaman, medium.

And remember, many so-called "hauntings" are nothing more than visits from friends and relatives in Spirit who just want to stay in touch with you! They might have messages of advice or comfort for you, or they might simply want to let you know that they are well and still connected with your life, even though they are no longer in physical forms.

Waking Up the Dead

Is it possible for an Earthbound spirit to return to life? Consider the myth of Orpheus, the ancient Greek poet and musician, and his great love, his wife Eurydice.

While out walking, Eurydice is attacked by a satyr with lascivious intent. To escape, she begins to run and falls into a nest of vipers where she is bitten and descends to the Underworld. In his grief, Orpheus travels there to plead for her life from Hades and Persephone, the Underworld's rulers. In this classic story, Persephone is so moved by Orpheus's grief that she pleads with Hades to allow Eurydice to return to life. Hades grants Orpheus's request with the caveat that Orpheus may not turn to gaze on Eurydice as they climb up out of the Underworld and back to the world of the living.

But Orpheus, overcome with joy and still reeling from the strong emotions of grief and love, turns impulsively to Eurydice as he reaches the light, condemning her to return to the Underworld, separating the lovers while Orpheus lives. Just like Orpheus, our strong desire to gaze upon a loved one who has passed, to be reunited and reclaim a shared life lost is not enough to release an Earthbound spirit back to Earthly life. However, our love can help release our loved ones to Spirit. And this should be our desire—to help our loved one find the light of Spirit. Consult a medium or spiritual adviser to guide you.

Roaming Visitations

May a person who is near death make contact or actual visitations from Spirit *before* the moment of passing over? Many, many times, people have come to Rita saying that funeral attendees bore witness to having contact from Spirit with their loved one in the days before passing. The veil between the living and the dead is especially porous near the time of transition from the Earthly to the Spirit plane, allowing a dying loved one's spirit to travel to visit and/or make amends with the living before departing this life. Perhaps someone comes to you in a dream, or a friend serendipitously offers you the loved one's favorite book to read. One client of Rita's revealed that three generations of women—mother, wife, and daughter—shared the same dream the night before their son/husband/father passed to Spirit. A dying loved one might appear, as in physical form, and even speak. This happened to a friend of Rita's. As the friend's mother lay in a coma, the friend showered and prepared to take her mother to hospital, praying all the while for her mother to stay—to stay alive and not to leave her. In the middle of her shower, the curtain was drawn forcibly back, and the mother stood before her daughter angrily asserting, "I'm here!" This occurrence so shocking that the daughter confessed to Rita that she wondered if the whole thing had been imagined.

These traveling visitations in the veil between planes of existence are to be honored and treasured. In preparing for death, your loved one is preparing for the work to be done in Spirit, making amends or growing and evolving in light and love. The transition to Spirit is always filled with healing, comfort, and peace.

Enjoying the Company of Spirits

Your loved ones who enjoyed sharing the adventures of your life when they were on the Earth plane want to continue enjoying that sharing, even though they can't be with you physically. They come in and out of your life at will, free to move between the Spirit world and the Earth plane. They are not Earthbound spirits, but they simply come to visit you and to remain a part of your daily life—even if you're not aware of their presence. And if you do sense that the spirit of Great-Aunt Julia or Uncle Jimmy is admiring your new baby or your new house, smile!

PART 3

Calling Out
to Spirit

Spirits on the Higher side can be creative when it comes to
making contact with the Earth plane and conveying their messages.
Spirit communication often is highly symbolic, as are dreams.
This can make it challenging to figure out the true nature of the
connection, its source in Spirit, and its meaning. Often, a message from
Spirit isn't what you expect—but it is always a message that you need to
receive and understand. Mediums, like Rita, use their highly developed
psychical skills to help others make contact with loved ones on the Higher
side. Many ordinary people have some mediumistic abilities; you may be
among them! Spirit messages are often emotionally powerful. They can
bring love, resolution, apology, and comfort.

Let's explore the symbolism of Spirit communication and provide
information about the skills it takes to allow a human connection to
Spirit to take place. Exercises give you opportunities to practice
your abilities.

CHAPTER
9

Better Check Your Messages

It's an important day in your life—could be a graduation, a wedding, the birth or adoption of a child, a move, a promotion, the start of retirement, or any event of significance. To gear up for the moment of change, you retreat to a favorite quiet space to meditate and prepare yourself. But suddenly, you feel as if you are surrounded, even though clearly, you are alone. You might even experience the sensation of hearing voices or actually seeing people seated or standing around, though you know no one else is present. No, no one is lurking on Skype or Zoom, eavesdropping on your private thoughts. Siri and Alexa and all the personal digital assistants are silent (and hopefully not listening). In your house, it's quiet as a mouse. So, what's happening?

Don't get stressed out … you're not hearing things or hallucinating. You're in full possession of your faculties. What you are experiencing is just your support team from Spirit, here to give you encouragement and loving advice! Significant life events require great life force energy—physical, emotional, and psychical. Just as your Earth plane friends might rally around to give you strength and support, so, too, might spirit visitors and guides from the Higher side.

Picking Up the Signals

When you perceive a presence from Spirit, it's no accident. It might be just the spirit of a loved one who wants to drop by to say hi, taking joy in your new, heightened awareness of existence beyond the Earth plane. Often, spirits have been around you for much longer than you recognize, just waiting for you to reach a point of openness that permits you to know of and acknowledge their presence.

Sliding into Your DMs!

Just as your friends and family here on the Earth plane drop in by text or by tagging you on social media, the spirits of loved ones on the Higher side like to pop into your life for a visit now and then. You might sense a loved one's presence in Spirit when you are engaged in an activity you and your loved one enjoyed together when you were both on the Earth plane, such as hiking, baking, or working in the garden. You might have the feeling of a loved one standing beside you as you admire your children at play, or giving you a hug of comfort during a difficult time.

How do you know that this is a loved one and not a Spirit guide (which we discussed in Chapter 7)? Sometimes it might be hard for you to tell, but generally, your Spirit guide is present to provide specific expertise, and a loved one's spirit comes to give loving advice. Of course, if a loved one had a particular expertise that you happen to need, you could end up with the loved one's spirit serving as a guide from Spirit! By and large, the spirits of friends and family visit just as friends and family might visit on the Earth plane (no masks or social distancing necessary).

Robin brought her young daughter Lilly to the Angel's Loft to have her Spirit guide drawn. Under Rita's hand, a drawing started to appear on the paper of a youngish woman, about 30. Robin recognized the woman from photographs she'd seen of her mother-in-law, who indeed had passed to Spirit at a young age. When she brought the Spirit drawing home her husband, Richard, he gasped, speechless. He truly felt his mother's presence, guiding their daughter, Lilly.

Many people find their relationships with friends and family in Spirit become deeper and more connected as spirit contact continues. Perhaps you were unable to form the kind of relationship you wanted to have with your father or your sister in the physical world. As a spirit evolves on the Higher side, they learn lessons that, for whatever reasons, couldn't be completed during physical life. On the Higher side, these lessons become apparent, and the spirit progresses in understanding and knowledge.

Part of the healing that can take place through spirit contact is a mending of rifts that existed on the Earth plane, allowing the relationship to heal and evolve. Though one is in Spirit and the other alive on Earth, relationships can still grow. You might gain valuable knowledge and understanding, feeling closer to your father or your sister in this heightened Spirit relationship than you experienced in your relationship in the physical world.

Who's There?

How do you know who is trying to make contact from Spirit? This can be a great challenge. When you are working with a medium, the spirit will convey images and impressions intended to give you indisputable evidence of their identity. Many spirits that come through to Rita begin by sharing the experiences of their passings. These details are generally easy to verify. The spirit might then offer pieces of information only you, the loved one on the Earth plane, could know or would understand.

Rita once held a circle to communicate with spirit loved ones of a group of friends. Because Rita knew each of these people quite well, when she opened the circle with a prayer and established intent, she asked that each spirit give some piece of information she couldn't already know. One by one, spirit visitors came through to greet the friends in the circle. When it came to Rita's husband, David, it was his father who came through and showed himself sitting in a canoe. Rita immediately said to her husband, "But this isn't the canoe we used to use," referring to family canoe trips they used to take.

David asked what the canoe looked like, and Rita said it was green with wood trim. David then asked what color of green, and Rita replied, "Really a God-awful house paint green." David was stunned. When he was 16, he'd brought a canoe home from camp. The first thing his father said to him was, "Where did you get that God-awful house paint green canoe?"

This single detail became the validating comment for David, who until that time, had been quite a skeptic about communication with Spirit. It is this level of detail that you should expect when a spirit claims to be coming through for you. Irrefutable identification is just that: There is no mistaking the message as something else!

Making the correct spirit identification isn't always this easy or straightforward. At first, it's important to accept that the information that comes to you without attempting to pin down an identity or shape the information to meet an assumption or expectation. Sometimes the spirit coming through is a distant relative you might not recognize at first or is a person outside your family. You might need to look through photos, search your memory, and even talk with other people before you are able to figure out the visiting spirit's identity. However, when you do finally make the connection, there will be no question in your mind about the spirit's identity!

Rita's reading with Lee Ann brought through her Sicilian immigrant great-grandmother, Vennera, who came to America at the turn of the twentieth century—and for whom no photograph existed. Through Spirit, Lee Ann was able to see her grandmother Jess's dear mother, about whom Lee Ann had heard Jess tell so many wonderful stories. Vennera came to Lee Ann with a special message from Spirit, instructing Rita to create a blue-sky background to give her great-granddaughter hope and encouragement.

Establishing Intent

Establishing intent is about making it clear why you are seeking contact with Spirit. You are asking for Divine assistance and protection. And you are agreeing to proceed with an open mind, heart, and soul and that you are receptive to the spirits that choose to communicate with you and to the messages of hope and healing they bring.

Establishing intent is not, as people sometimes misunderstand, about asking for contact with specific spirits or for specific information. You can do either of these, of course, but you may or may not get what you ask for. Only when you free yourself from the limitations of expectations will you be able to receive what Spirit wants to show or bring you.

Rita, like most mediums, begins every Spirit contact with a prayer to establish intent, welcome the Divine, and invite the light. This reminds those on the Earth plane who are participating in the Spirit communication of the special and Divine nature of the contact and puts out positive energy signals to the Higher side to attract positive energy in response.

Fear Not ... These Are Friendly Forces

It's natural to be afraid in unfamiliar circumstances. It might scare you to realize you have visitors from the Higher side if you're not accustomed to being aware of their presence. But these visitors *are* familiar to you—just not in the ways you might be expecting. Your Spirit guests show up to give you support, encouragement, and sometimes, just company. There is no reason to be fearful.

If you continue to feel afraid, you need to look for the reason. Are you in a strange location? Is there something about the circumstances that is activating a psychical alarm within you? Is this an intuition alert that something isn't quite right? It's important to pay attention to these signals and to respond appropriately. Always remember: Spirit visitors don't come through to scare you.

Physical Phenomena

Spirits might choose to use physical phenomena to make their presence known to you. You might see shadows, flashes of light, objects moving (or objects having been moved). You might hear voices or other sounds or feel a touch. Spirits love to work with electrical appliances, and they will sometimes turn them on and off with only the use of "spiritual remote" or spirit energy. Spirits choose the means of contact that is most likely to be effective. If you are skeptical by nature, the contact is likely to be bold and unmistakable, so it catches and keeps your attention. A visiting spirit might appear as a full and complete image standing in your hallway or sitting at your kitchen table because the spirit knows that you will immediately recognize their image and identity.

If you are accustomed to Spirit contact and are familiar with the spirits who visit you, the physical phenomena might be subtle. You might wake up in the morning to the smell of coffee brewing when you don't own a coffee pot and instantly think of your uncle who used to drink a dozen cups a day. You might come home from work and automatically throw your jacket over the back of a kitchen chair, only to have it land on the floor because the chair has been neatly pushed against the table—not where you expected it to be.

Some forms of physical phenomena are quite sophisticated or specialized, such as Spirit drawing and automatic writing. Typically, these are phenomena that manifest to mediums (and can manifest to you when your mediumistic abilities are activated) or may come to you because you have an ability that allows you to use them. We discuss these phenomena in Chapter 10.

Mental Phenomena

Mental phenomena make use of your psychical or spiritual senses: clairvoyance (inner vision), clairaudience (inner hearing), and clairsentience (inner sensing or knowing). Sometimes, it is harder to recognize mental phenomena as Spirit contact because your mind is the screen upon which so many of the interactions of your life play out. These phenomena can be extraordinarily lucid. Yet, you know very well they are not "real"—that is, the phenomena are activated by Spirit realm, not the realm of the tangible world. It's more about you *sensing* the phenomena, even as they play out in such vivid detail that it all feels distinctly real.

You might worry that these experiences are nothing more than the products of your (active) imagination, or you might even dismiss them as such. At first, communication with Spirit does feel like imagination! Rita tells her mediumship students to think of it like learning to play the piano. When you first start, you hit a lot of wrong notes, maybe even more wrong notes than right ones! But as you play more, you get better. You sound fewer wrong notes, and those that you do play are more obvious. You correct them immediately, and fluidly play the piece you've been working so hard.

The same process unfolds with Spirit contact. At first, it all seems like imagination or like wishful thinking. Of course, the image of your BFF is in your head; you love her and miss her now that she's passed to the Higher side. And it makes sense to have this little internal dialogue going with her. After all, the two of you could talk and text for hours. You must be just remembering conversations that once took place. But then it occurs to you that the dialogue is actually about something that occurred *after* your friend's passing and is something current. It feels as though you and your BFF are having a real-time, intimate conversation about the things that really matter to your present-day life—your life beyond the experience of your friendship on the Earth plane.

This is the point at which you begin to realize this phenomena goes beyond your imagination. Could it be that you truly are communicating with the spirit of your best friend who's passed? "Yes, of course, Missy!" comes the response in your friend's unmistakable tone and with the nickname for you that only she could get away with using. Yes, you could've imagined the whole thing. But you know you didn't. This is not just your imagination. This is Spirit communication.

It's the minutiae, the detail, that makes contact with Spirit real. It's not, "Your mother used to bake cakes," but instead, it's "Your mother *always* used Duncan Hines box cake mixes ... and her cakes were delicious."

Setting Limits

You don't have to accept Spirit contact just because it's there, anymore than you have to answer your mobile phone because it's ringing. (Likewise, spirits don't have to accept your "calls" when you want to make contact.) But how often will you let your ringtone go unanswered? Most of us jump to take the call or answer the text, no matter what else we're doing, or whom we're with! Learning to just "let it ring" is a key lesson in taking control of your life. And so it is with Spirit contact. Just because your BFF wants to chat from Spirit doesn't mean you have to let her in. You can refuse Spirit contact by gently and kindly asking that she come back when you're finished with whatever is keeping you busy at the time. You might even want to say this out loud. If the message is important, such as a warning of some sort, the spirit will persist, and you'll have little choice but to notice. But for most other communication, spirits will simply call again.

When it is *you* who is initiating contact with spirits, a good opportunity to set your limits is when you establish intent. As you invite Divine light, request the limits that you desire. Rita establishes limits around how much she is willing to physically feel through Spirit. She will allow a tingling sensation in the affected part of the body that took the spirit to the Higher side, but she will not accept any sensations that go deep enough to cause discomfort or pain. This arises from her first experience as a medium, in which she so strongly felt the spirit's passing from a heart attack that she felt like her own heart was about to explode. Her teacher immediately intervened, and from that time on Rita established limits with spirits coming through as to what she was willing to accept.

Your limit range might be "please respect the time I've set aside for family" or "let's communicate after I finish my work." Sometimes, spirits want to come to you at night when you are sleeping because people are more receptive in the dream state or in the altered state of sleep. Setting limits helps define and shape the signals from spirits that come to you. A spirit cannot make or continue contact unless you allow it, although you might need to articulate your desires to make them clear.

Sometimes, messages from spirits come in fast and furious, and you might want to shelter your receptiveness, or there are times when you don't want to be disturbed. You can establish a boundary of protection—what Rita calls "closing the door but not locking it." This lets your guides from Spirit know that they can still reach you if there is an urgent message. Otherwise, you don't want to be disturbed for the defined time. Begin by saying prayers of your understanding and surrounding yourself with white light. Some people see this as a tower, others see it as a globe, and still others see it as a pyramid.

If *ever* you feel uncomfortable during a contact with a spirit, break off the contact immediately. Say out loud, "This contact is over!" Just as you wouldn't continue an interaction with a physical entity if it made you uncomfortable, don't do so with an entity from Spirit. If you are in a mediumship class, ask the teacher for help rather than disrupting the circle.

Many times, Spirit communication is brief and self-limiting. A spirit breezes in for a chat and breezes right back out again. When you've had a more extended visit from a spirit, you can end the contact by saying goodbye, just as you might end a visit with any friend. It's nice to thank the spirit for visiting and sharing with you. Sometimes, the spirit just leaves, and you know they are gone even though neither of you brought the visit to a formal end.

Cosmic Clutter and Spirit Static

When you think about it, there's really a lot of communication taking place between the Earth plane and the Higher side. How do you know how much of it is relevant to you? At first, signals from the Higher side can be confusing. This newly awakened receptiveness in you is eager to accept whatever comes its way. But like a satellite radio that receives a dozen signals on the same frequency, there can be so many signals coming through that they overwhelm your ability to sort and understand them.

Often, your lead guide from Spirit will screen these signals on your behalf. Your guide might block the irrelevant signals and restrict the relevant ones to times and settings in which you can be receptive. A medium can function in a similar way, accepting one spirit at a time to come through with their message.

Psychic Confusion

It is possible to confuse psychic contact with mediumistic contact, particularly if a medium is making contact on your behalf. This is why it is so important for you to establish your intent to be open to whatever will be and try to clear your mind of expectations. A good psychic (and all good mediums are good psychics) will receive the psychical signals of your expectations, which can cloud mediumistic signals. Instead of allowing Auntie K to come through because that's who's there with a message, the medium might get the image of your husband Liam because that's who's on your mind.

Does the message or communication from the spirit seem oddly jumbled or not quite right? When you experience confusion, you need to step back and sort things out. You might end the contact for the time being and think things through in your mind. Try writing down your impressions. Put them away for a day or two, and then look at them again. Consider these questions:

- Are there inconsistencies that jump out at you?
- Can you detect fragments of identifying characteristics that point to different people?
- Who's been on your mind lately?

- Are you truly open to receiving whoever comes through from Spirit, or do you have your heart set on making contact with someone in particular?

- What do you want to have happen, or what do you desire from this contact with Spirit?

When you try again to establish a connection, speak your intent out loud. If you truly want to make contact with a specific spirit, make that part of your intent. It may or may not happen, depending on whether the spirit wants to make contact with you, but at least your desire for the contact is out there, and the focus of your mind is now consistent with your intent.

Resolving Fear and Apprehension

A little apprehension is normal whenever you are doing something important to you or that you are unsure about. But you should also feel excited and happy about establishing communication with spirits on the Higher side. Doing so gives you wonderful opportunities to feel the love and healing that those on the Higher side want to extend to you.

If you are fearful about contact with spirits, try to identify what exactly it is that worries or frightens you. Write it down or speak it out loud, so it is out there in a tangible way. Then you can explore why you feel the way you do. Seek the services of a professional medium; a medium can make contact on your behalf and help you understand the messages that come through for you from Spirit.

The Gift That Keeps Giving

Spirit communication is the ultimate gift of love. It establishes that there is, in fact, life beyond physical death, and that what matters to us in our physical lives has value in the bigger picture of existence. It gives us comfort, healing, and knowledge, enriching our lives on the Earth plane. Spirit communication also shows us that the connections that bring pleasure and joy to our souls continue, unlimited by the borders of physical existence.

Mediums Facilitate Contact

To make contact in Spirit with *your* loved one, why would you need an intermediary—a medium—for communication between the two of you to take place? You don't always; many people enjoy regular and ongoing communication with loved ones who have passed to the Higher side, but contact with Spirit is often subtle. Communication on the Spirit plane is much different than here on the Earth plane, and it often requires the assistance of an interpreter to get messages through—going both directions.

Just as it isn't always easy for us to get a good connection with those on the Higher side, it's sometimes challenging for spirits to communicate with us in ways that make sense in our physical world. Mediums have highly developed abilities in these areas and put their skills to use to help those of us on the Earth plane make contact with loved ones on the Higher side.

Medium, Well Done

From graphic designers to accountants, most professionals complete some sort of specialized education and training that gives them the core qualifications they need to work in their fields. This establishes a certain level of consistency, at least in theory, about the professional's capabilities and proficiency. When you go to a doctor or a lawyer, you can assume that there is a certain baseline of education and expertise in place. Doctors, lawyers, great chef/restaurateurs and many other professionals must pass certain certification or licensing tests before the law allows them to be in practice.

Being a good medium requires a blend of psychical skill, education, mentorship, and practice. There is much more to contact with Spirit than simply putting yourself out there as a conduit for energy from Spirit! A medium must know how to handle situations that might arise from the Spirit world, as well as from the physical world. Spirit communication is often intense for those involved—you, the visitor from Spirit, and the medium. Many mediums have some background in counseling or psychology, which gives them additional skills for helping people deal with the information that comes through from Spirit, as well as their grief, and often their overwhelming emotions.

When considering the services of a medium, ask about the medium's education and experience (more about choosing a medium a little later in this chapter). Both are important because it is through their blending that a medium acquires expertise.

Training and Experience

Good mediums spend considerable time learning and refining their skills and abilities. There are a number of schools and organizations throughout the world that provide teaching for mediums, including the Morris Pratt Institute, the Lily Dale Assembly, and Arthur Findley College. Such programs not only will teach the student mediumistic skills but also knowledge, concepts, and theories about matters of Spirit and existence. Some programs are structured to take a certain amount of time, while others are self-paced and designed to accommodate people who also have other activities in their lives.

Many mediums also teach mediumship classes (as Rita does). Not only does this extend their expertise to those new to mediumship, but it also helps practicing mediums to keep their own skills sharp. In so many ways, the best way to learn is to teach!

In most locations in the United States, there are no laws that regulate the qualifications of mediums (beyond the general laws that apply to anyone in any kind of business, of course). It doesn't hurt to check with your local Better Business Bureau and your state's Office of the Attorney General to see whether there are complaints about the medium you are choosing.

Finding the Right Medium for You

The best way to find a good medium is to work through a source you trust. If you have friends in metaphysical fields, start by asking for their recommendations. Schedule appointments to meet with several mediums, either by phone or online meeting, so you can understand the medium's training, experience, and expertise. Ask questions such as:

- Have you received formal training in mediumship? If so, where?
- Are you affiliated with any organizations or groups, such as the Spiritualist Church, Church of the Divine Man, a metaphysical center or college, or other faith-based structures?
- How long have you been a practicing medium?
- How many readings do you do in a week or a month? Can you do online readings?
- How would you describe your mediumistic approach?
- What other education, experience, and background do you have?
- Have you been interviewed for any publication, periodicals, or published books? Do you maintain a website, write a blog, or have a podcast?
- Are you on social media as a medium?
- How do you protect the privacy of your clients?
- What do you charge for your services, and what payment methods do you accept?

Often, the answers you get will lead you to other questions and discussion. And pay attention to your intuition! Are you feeling that this is someone you want to work with? Keep in mind that this person could connect you with very powerful and personal messages from Spirit. Do you have a sense of trust when you talk to this person?

At the end of your interview with a prospective medium, ask for three professional references that you can contact. Then contact them! Ask very generally about the medium's skills, and then listen—let the person answer without prompting.

You might feel that you just *know* this is the right medium for you, and that is good. But if you are new to communication with spirits, it's to your advantage to at least go through the same conversation with other mediums recommended to you. Pay attention to the testimony of references you are given by each medium to contact. This gives you a broader base of information from which to make your decision.

What a Medium Experiences During Contact

Spirits manifest themselves to mediums in different ways, and each medium has a different way of experiencing contact with Spirit. Most mediums have a dominant mode—clairvoyant (psychic sight), clairsentient (psychic intuition), or clairaudient (psychic hearing)—through which they experience contact with spirits. This is the psychical, or spiritual, sense through which a spirit first makes contact.

For Rita, contact with a spirit often begins as a blend of clairvoyance and clairsentience. The first information to come through is usually an awareness of how the person appeared in their physical life, such as whether they identified as a man or a woman and how the person passed to the Higher side. Rita often can *feel* the person—she feels how tall the person was in physical life, and she feels the person's weight as though her body is growing larger or smaller. Then Rita typically feels the condition of passing, which expresses itself as a twinge in the related part of her body. Finally, all of Rita's inner, or psychic, senses become activated to provide full information about the person.

Other mediums might work differently based on what gifts they have. Spirits will use whatever abilities and talents the medium has and use them in ways that are comparable to the medium in terms of intellectual and emotional development. It's important to remember that the medium's abilities, interests, and biases all influence messages the medium brings through. A good medium will tell you this up front again and again, reminding you to put the information you receive into the proper framework of *your* life experiences and relationships.

The medium should not ask a lot of questions about you before doing a reading. The less the medium knows about you, the more confident you can be that the information coming through is genuine.

Special Forms of Spirit Communication

Spirits can be quite creative when it comes to finding ways to communicate. Activating psychical senses sometimes isn't enough; the spirit desires a more tangible impression. For the medium to become truly skilled, these techniques require practice, practice, and more practice.

Automatic Writing

In automatic writing, the spirit takes control of the medium's hand, guiding it to move a pen or a pencil across paper. (Some modern mediums will even use computers—automatic typing!)

The message might be in a language other than those the medium speaks. The handwriting is often strikingly different from the medium's handwriting and might be difficult to read or even illegible. It takes great patience for a medium to develop adeptness with automatic writing. Compared to psychical abilities such as clairsentience, automatic writing is quite slow and laborious. But some spirits prefer this means of communication.

Sometimes, automatic writing is your first clue that you have mediumistic abilities. You might be sitting there doodling when suddenly the pen takes off on what seems to be its own accord and begins forming symbols or words. Go with the flow! With much practice, automatic writing can become a tool of communication for you. Those who are skilled in automatic writing often blend it with other psychical skills and develop a system of asking questions and receiving answers. More typically, automatic writing conveys messages that the spirit simply wants or needs to deliver.

Spirit Drawing

Spirit drawing is Rita's special expertise. A spirit comes through to her, and her spirit guides use her artistic talent to draw the spirit's image. A spirit drawing presents a visual likeness of the spirit as they are showing at the time, which can be younger or even older than the person was at the time of passing. Spirits tend to show themselves either as they know you will recognize them or as they want you to see them.

The latter was the case when Rita did a spirit drawing of her co-author Deb's father. When Deb first saw the drawing, she felt disappointment. Some of the features looked like her father, but overall, the drawing wasn't what she remembered. So, Deb started going through the pictures she had of her father, from his childhood through the year of his passing. Nothing really matched up.

Disheartened, Deb started putting everything back. She picked up a stack of old pictures and papers, and a newspaper clipping fell out and landed in her lap: A faded photograph of Deb's father, exactly the image in Rita's spirit drawing! Debbie's father directed Rita to produce an image of himself that he preferred and that he wanted to convey to Deb. He wanted Deb to see him not only as her father but also in the larger context of his experience of life beyond family—his life as he knew it, out in the world.

For many people, spirit drawings are the ultimate evidence of the continuity of life. There is nothing quite like the feeling that rushes through you when you see the image of a loved one appear at the hands of a medium who could not possibly know what the spirit looked like in life. As the cliché goes, sometimes, "a picture is worth a thousand words." Often a spirit comes through to show you a view of their physical life that you could not have experienced in your relationship on the Earth plane. Spirits do this so you can deepen your understanding of their humanity in life, as well as deepen the connection between you.

Rita and Deb live on opposite coasts, so Rita did Deb's reading by phone and then mailed the spirit drawing to her. Deb's father chose to present himself in a way that was at first unfamiliar to Deb but as he was familiar to his friends and coworkers. The drawing didn't match any of Deb's family photos, but it turned out to be an amazing likeness of a photo from an old newspaper clipping.

Psychometry

Although we have an entire chapter about psychometry later in this book (see Chapter 16), we want to touch on this important mediumistic form here because it is a psychical skill with widespread applications. Psychometry is the ability to read the energy imprints of objects that can act as springboards for the medium to connect with the spirits to whom the energy belongs. For example, a medium might hold a set of antique skeleton keys and sense the energy of the person(s) who once carried them. This can generate an energy message, so to speak, that travels into the Universe like a beckoning wave. When the spirit responds, the medium can establish connection and communication.

Transfiguration

During transfiguration, the medium's features take on the image of the spirit that is coming through. The spirit uses ectoplasm, a tangible substance created from the energy field that surrounds the spirit, to superimpose its image over the medium's form or face. Transfiguration typically occurs when spirit contact takes place in a circle (see Chapter 11).

Spirit Photography

Photographs that end up including spirits generally happen by accident, although some people do set out to take pictures of locations where they know spirits to be present. Unfortunately, photography is a medium (no pun intended) that is easy to manipulate, and Spirit photography has lost much credibility as a result of fraud.

With the increasing popularity of photography in the 1920s came an increase in attempts to photograph spirits on the Earth plane. Anyone who has a basic knowledge of twentieth-century film developing and printing techniques, has a darkroom, and has a little imagination could create amazing images. This is even truer today in the twenty-first century with digital photography and computer manipulation of images. The resulting lack of credibility causes Spirit photography to fall out of favor as a legitimate means of representing the presence and appearance of spirits among us.

What to Expect in Readings with Mediums

You've found a medium you trust, and you're ready for some contact with spirits. Now what? Well, odds are high that this is more than just a random adventure for you. Most people want to make contact with specific loved ones who have passed to the Higher side. It might be feelings of loss, grief, love, worry, and even curiosity that drive your desire for communication. You might have some unfinished business with the person who passed—it could be that you didn't have a chance to say goodbye or there were some uncertainties about feelings or actions on either side that were left hanging when the person passed. Perhaps you made a pact to communicate across the great divide, and you are now curious to find out what it's really like on the Higher side.

So many families who lost loved ones to the COVID-19 virus were not able to be present at passing, and in many cases, they weren't even able to grieve together at a public, in-person wake or funeral. Saying goodbyes to a live-streaming image on a tablet held by an ICU nurse proved to be heartbreaking consolation for many—or no consolation at all. The direct exchange of life force energy between a person near their moment of passing and the family surrounding them is so powerful and important. Our global society owes much to the nurses, doctors, and healthcare workers who stood in for families day after day, often multiple times a day, to experience this life force energy exchange on families' behalf during the COVID-19 pandemic.

Don't worry about what a medium might think of your reasons for wanting to contact a loved one on the Higher side. Mediums understand their role as a form of compassionate care. The best mediums recognize the connection with Spirit is its own form of therapy and do not intrude upon the purity of that connection to Spirit you feel during a reading. Like good nurses and doctors, experienced mediums have witnessed many, many situations surrounding passing. A professional medium will not make judgments about your interests and needs in contacting Spirit. A good medium simply wants to help you find whatever information and answers you are seeking from Spirit and present them to you for the highest good and in light.

Your reading should take place in an environment in which both you and the medium feel comfortable. If you are meeting with the medium in person, the surroundings should be inviting and make you feel welcome. The same is true of readings done via video conferencing. If you are not comfortable or experienced with video conferencing and cannot meet in-person, doing a reading by phone is perfectly acceptable. When you are doing a reading by phone, you should be somewhere free from distractions, and you should have the sense that the same is the case for the medium.

Before a reading begins (in person or remotely by phone or video conference), ask the medium what they expect from you. Can you talk to the medium during the reading? Can you ask questions of the spirits who come through? Consciously clear your mind of expectations and anticipation and focus on being open and receptive to whatever happens. Sit in an open posture, with your legs and arms uncrossed. You can close your eyes or leave them open, whichever you prefer. Let the medium know when you are ready to start.

For the Highest Good and with Light

The medium should always begin the reading with a prayer or a blessing that asks for Divine light and goodness to guide the communication with Spirit. It is very important to establish your intent in this way; through communication with the Higher side, you are opening a doorway, but you don't want just *anyone* to come through. The medium's intent is focused on bringing through whatever connection to Spirit will be for the highest good for you.

Evidence of the Continuity of Life

Validation is the most crucial aspect of Spirit communication, and it should be the first thing that takes place in a reading. You must know, beyond a shadow of a doubt, that the spirit the medium says is your father is indeed your father. The medium should present you with information that is undeniable—straight up, without having to ask confirming contextual questions along the way.

Often, as we've mentioned in earlier chapters, the first information to come through from a spirit is about their passing. It might be because this is the last Earth plane memory the spirit has or because it is the detail likely to be most vivid in your memory. Rita often experiences sensations in her body that correlate to the cause of death. The sensations are often vivid and mimic the physical ailment. She might feel a headache when someone passed from a stroke, central chest pain in the case of a heart attack, or a wider chest pain in the case lung disease.

The medium should have more to offer than, "I have a woman here who passed of a heart attack." The medium should be able to give a description of the person or of certain physical or personality characteristics that at least hint at the person's identity. When Rita did a reading for Deb, she didn't know anything about Deb's personal circumstances or her family members and friends who had passed. When Rita said, "I have a gentleman here who is showing at about 60 years, with salt-and-pepper hair brushed back and to the side in a soft part, with a full face and a broad nose," Deb immediately suspected this to be her father who had passed several years ago. When Rita said, "On the Earth plane, he was quite set in his ways and didn't like it when people disagreed with him—and neither did they!" Deb was certain (and delighted) that this visiting spirit was indeed her father.

Mediums certified in the Spiritualist Church are trained to identify a spirit totally, so the person knows it can be no one else. Even among talented mediums, this skill requires a high level of consistency that typically takes a number of years to achieve.

The Message

Spirits do come through just to say "Hi!" and to let you know that they are there and still in contact with you. They take as much delight in this contact as you do, but the spirits who make contact for extended communication typically have specific reasons for the contact and specific messages to convey. Messages might be directly from the spirit to you or from a spirit serving as an intermediary.

Rita had a man come to her for a spirit drawing. She described two spirits who came through: The man's mother and uncle, and then did a spirit drawing of the uncle. When Rita showed him the spirit drawing, the man said, "Yes, that's my uncle but I wanted my father!" So, Rita went back to the spirit to see if the father would come through. He would not. Rita shared with the man what the spirits communicated: "Your father was a very shy man, while his brother, your uncle, always took center stage. So, he came through first and wanted to be drawn!" The man confirmed that, in fact, his father had been extremely shy.

Energy Healing

A special form of contact with Spirit is energy healing, which usually takes place in a circle or other group setting (more about circles in Chapter 11 and about healing in Chapter 18). In a healing, the medium calls on spirit physicians and chemists—spirit healers—to send healing energy through the medium, or *healer*, to the person in need. A healer is a person (who may or may not be a medium) who has the ability to receive healing energy from the Higher side and direct it to people on the Earth plane who are ill or injured physically, emotionally, or spiritually. In Spiritualism, a healer is always referred to as a healing medium. Spirit healing can be very powerful. People sometimes feel the effects immediately, or they feel them over a period of hours or even days.

Steering Clear of Fakes and Frauds

Times of struggle and challenge are opportunities for personal growth and insight. Sadly, they are also openings for the unscrupulous to become opportunistic. As with anything else in life, if it seems too good to be true, then it probably isn't either good or true. Put away those rose-tinted glasses … you need to see clearly when you reach out to the Higher side.

Fakes and frauds, we're sorry to say, lurk wherever sorrow and sadness coexist with the inability to "prove" anything and the potential for money to exchange hands. A fake is someone who pretends to make the desired contact to Spirit, sometimes with the best of intentions (to help you feel better). A fraud is an intentional fake motivated by self-interest, which is almost always financial. These folks—sometimes well-intentioned but often simply unscrupulous—are willing to offer you what you want because there's something in it for them.

Misguided Intentions

The well-intentioned fake sincerely feels your pain and wants to make it go away. Such a person might enhance, or outright pretend to make, the contact to the spirit you desire, leading you to experience what you (desperately) want to believe. This might be a person you know who has psychic abilities, a stranger you've gone to for help in making contact with a loved one who has passed on, or even a professional medium. This person doesn't intend to hurt you in any way and sees their actions as kind and good. And what you don't know, after all, won't hurt you if it's in your best interests.

Who knows what's in your best interests? Not this person! And you're bound to find out at some point, either because you make a genuine connection at another time or because you eventually figure it out. In the end, the well-intentioned fake can cause even more pain than the outright fraud because you *trusted* this person.

The only intention the fraud has is to take your money—namely, for their personal good. This individual is nearly always a stranger to you—someone you've selected to help you contact the Higher side. Perhaps you came across this person's business card somewhere, or you found the name in a web posting. The first question that this person asks you is your best clue whether they are legitimate. "How will you be paying for your services today?" is surely a tip-off about this person's interests!

Once More, for the Highest Good

Remember, an ethical, truly compassionate medium will let Spirit do the talking, honor that connection, and trust that you will make the most of the message delivered. The genuine, authentic connection to Spirit is the greatest comfort a medium can offer. It validates the continuity of life through specific details and context that will have meaning—not for the medium but … *for you.* While many mediums do have some amount of psychological training and education, the difference between what is intended as connection to Spirit and what is intended as therapy surrounding the reading should always be clear, well established, and follow professional therapeutic guidelines and norms.

Tricks of the Trade

Frauds are so effective in their trade because it's impossible to prove their actions, but there are some common tricks to put you on the alert. Your fraud warning alarm should go off if the medium …

- Discusses money before asking what you need. Yes, a good medium is worth the price they ask and needs to discuss charges up front. But the medium's first questions should be about your interests, needs, and expectations.

- Requires your credit card information or cash payment before doing a reading. Of course, payment should not depend on whether you like the reading, but you should receive the service before you're expected to pay.

- Is on the other end of an anonymous psychic hotline or web reading. Yes, the webpage is tempting; you can reach them any time, and you don't have to leave the comfort of your own home. But what do you know about that voice on the other end of the line or the person behind the web reading? It's better to steer clear of any service that does not identify the medium or give their credentials and experience.

- Asks a lot of personal questions before beginning your reading. Those who are particularly adept make this questioning appear as though it is casual conversation, while the medium is actually *fishing* for the details that will become part of your "reading." Fishing for information or contextual detail is generally the hallmark of someone who, at best, is inadequately trained and, at worst, is an outright fraud.

- Promises connection with a specific spirit or loved one or promises specific information or results. There is no way to guarantee anything with a reading.

- Makes specific predictions about your future. Your future is the outcome of the choices and decisions you make on your way through life and is ever-changing. Although there are likely signs that point to probable outcomes, we have one important word for you: freewill. Nothing about your future is carved in stone.

- Tells you to take specific actions. No medium has the knowledge to tell you what to do or what events will result from your actions. This is your life, and only you can make the decisions that direct it.

Desperate Illusions

It is possible for you to be the fake, so to speak. Not that you intentionally set out to delude yourself or others, of course. It's just that sometimes you can want to hook up with that special someone on the Higher side so badly that you see signs of connection everywhere that aren't genuine or aren't really there.

This is where it's particularly important to pay attention to authentication messages. What clues are you getting that suggest this *actually* is your brother or your mother or your best friend from college? The evidence of identity should be irrefutable, and it should be evidence that is not especially common. If it's not, then the identity of the spirit contacted remains uncertain. (Sorry.)

If you are desperate to make contact with someone specific, all that you know about that person is highlighted in your conscious thoughts as well as in parts of your memory that are just below the surface of your recall ability. A medium might pick up these psychical signals, misinterpret them as mediumistic signals, and convey them to you as messages from the Higher side when they are really just a reflection of the signals your subconscious mind is sending out. The medium is in essence "reading" your mind. The energy that you are putting out there is so powerful that it creates images the medium can't help but pick up. And it isn't always possible for the medium to be aware of this happening. Only you can know.

Keep your mind as open as possible. You can make it more difficult for the medium to connect with spirit if you are sitting there concentrating on what it is that you want to have happen. That energy can block the communication.

Mediums Are Facilitators

The function of a medium, whether for connection to spirits or for receiving healing energy from Spirit, is to help you access something that is always around you—and that you could see on your own if you studied and trained to sharpen your skills and mediumistic abilities. Mediums allow those on the Earth plane to communicate with the Higher side. A truly gifted medium is one who produces a level of detail and specificity in a reading that leads undeniably to proof of continuity of life.

While mediums can facilitate powerful contact with Spirit, always know that you are *never* alone and that energy from Spirit is always available to you each day of your life on the Earth plane and beyond. Say a daily prayer for the highest and good for yourself and those you love, whether they are here with you on the Earth plane or have passed to Spirit. Give yourself to grace. Know, too, that your loved ones who have passed to Spirit are now doing the work of compassionate healing and growth; they, too, are not alone. We are all, on Earth and in Spirit, united in Divine energy, linked together in eternal light and understanding. Have faith that love endures.

From Séances to
Spirit Circles

Candlelit rooms and special effects worthy of filmmakers—both digital and studio effects—certainly make for grand performances that can at once bedazzle and confound. But this is Hollywood's version of a séance—an antiquated term modern mediums no longer use.

When a group gathers to communicate with spirits, the event is a respectful circle inviting physical phenomena from present spirits. It takes a lot of practice and skill to accomplish this advanced level of mediumship. Circles are not haunted house party-game larks or digital deep fakes; instead, they are profound and powerful vehicles for sacred spirit contact.

Once Upon a Séance

The word *séance* is of French origin and means "to sit." Although certain Taoist sects conducted séances—spiritual retreats at which sect leaders received Divine counsel—as long ago as the third century, i0074 was with the emergence of the Fox sisters and modern Spiritualism in the mid-1800s (see Chapter 3) that the term became synonymous with sitting in communication with spirits.

Through their history, séances have ranged from the subdued to the outrageous, from close-knit gatherings of people intent on making contact with loved ones to groups whose members shared only the desire to meet someone famous (or even notorious) from the "other" side. Some skeptics have made careers from debunking séances, and unfortunately, they've not found a shortage of work. During their heyday in the early decades of the 1900s, séances were favorite events across the United States.

While many were authentic spirit communication experiences for participants, many were simply intended to amuse and amaze those in attendance. The inclination toward sensationalism made it difficult, if not impossible, to separate the valid from the contrived—even in this time before computers and the added confoundment possible using digital and internet effects. Although the phenomena that occur at séances can be authentic spirit communication, the image of the séance is so closely connected with the perception that a séance is all about entertainment that mediums today shy away from the very term.

Legend has it that before his death on October 31, 1926, famed magician Harry Houdini promised he would conduct the ultimate feat: He would escape death itself. Even up to present day, every year on Halloween, in locations around the world, "Houdini societies" conduct old-fashioned séances to attempt to contact the master of escapism. So far, none have succeeded.

Let the Show Begin!

The séances of the late 1880s often took place in a private home, sometimes following a dinner party. Guests seated themselves around a table close enough to hold hands, often in the parlor because this was a room that could be closed off. The medium sat among the participants. As the séance was to begin, the host dimmed the lights in the room. A hush fell over the gathering, and the medium instructed all the attendees to take the hands of those sitting next to them, forming a chain of energy around the table.

"We call upon our guests from Spirit to come forward and to make their presence known," the medium would intone. Those around the table watched each other and the room, eagerly anticipating the first arrivals. They were seldom disappointed. Shadows, flashes of light, bumps and raps, and moving objects (including the table) soon gave evidence of spirits present.

When a trance medium presided, visiting spirits presented themselves through the medium. A trance medium enters a state of altered consciousness that allows spirits to communicate through their body's posture and movements. The medium's demeanor and voice often changed to reflect the spirit's mannerisms and tone. Someone in the group might call out, "Spirit that has joined us, identify yourself!" (In modern circles, participants just offer a greeting: "Good evening!") Under the guidance of a materialist medium, such presence might even take the form of a human image with clothing and features clear to those in attendance. A materialist medium receives spirit messages that manifest themselves in physical appearances, such as images visible to others who are present.

Some spirits cooperated nicely. One might be the departed mother of a person in attendance, another the brother of someone else. Some mediums had specific guides from Spirit that "took over" the séance, giving messages and teaching lessons. At other times, according to reports from the era, the summoned spirits were obstreperous, causing objects to fly about the room, mussing up hair and clothing, and creating a nuisance in general. Other spirits came and went without providing any clues as to their identity and the purpose of their visit, leaving guests to try and figure it out later.

Table tipping is a form of spirit communication in which spirit energy comes through your hands and causes a special three-legged table to tip on its legs or even move across the room with your hands very lightly on it. Usually, two people have their hands together on the table. One asks a question, and the table taps the response—either "yes" or "no" or a sequence of taps that stop at letters of the alphabet. Sometimes the table can really get moving, almost like it's walking up steps. Although table tipping is fun and people enjoy it, it can be a long, tedious way to get answers!

A rare and amazing kind of séance is the cabinet séance in which the medium sits in a small cabinet. One at a time, spirits emerge from the cabinet, seemingly as tangible as the people in the room. These images are formed using ectoplasm, an energy-based substance drawn from the cabinet medium's body. Few mediums have this extraordinary level of ability. Cabinet séances are amazing events to attend!

An entertaining riff on cabinet mediumship appeared in Woody Allen's contribution to the film *New York Stories*, called "Oedipus Wrecks." Here, the cabinet functions as a vehicle for disappearing, a more standard magic trick. Allen's character's mother goes into the cabinet, disappears on cue, but does not come back, at least on the physical plane. Throughout the rest of the movie, mother appears, ostensibly from the Spirit plane, as a floating "talking head," spewing motherly advice from the sky.

This isn't to say that everything about attending turn-of-the-century séances was just entertainment. There were many people who were making authentic contact, such as one-time skeptic Sir Arthur Conan Doyle. But those who used legitimate activities for fraudulent purposes grabbed media attention and public interest, which overwhelmed the genuine work that was going on. Physical mediums became leery of using physical mediumship except in small, private gatherings, causing public interest in Spiritualism to diminish through the middle decades of the twentieth century.

Phenomena or Fiction?

The phenomena manifested at many séances were authentic. Whenever people gather and focus their energy on making a connection between the Earth plane and the Spirit world, they are likely to succeed. Many séances conducted under the guidance of talented and capable mediums certainly made the kind of contact that provided proof of the continuity of life, bringing comfort and closure for those seeking it.

Unfortunately, the temptation to create a memorable experience (and perhaps personal fame and fortune) led a good many séance organizers to contrive the events that took place. Skeptical guests exposed numerous acts of fraud, from strings attached to objects that the medium tugged and moved to elaborately constructed platforms creating the illusion of levitation—the action of a physical object, sometimes a person, lifting into the air.

The séances that were fabrications and fictions made for great entertainment, as was really their intent. At the same time, they discredited the séance as a legitimate venue for genuine contact with spirits. Imagine the distress of believing that you've connected with the spirit of a loved one and then discovering it was all a setup! Such séances are not the efforts of those seeking the highest and the best; they are the manipulations of those driven by selfish motivations.

By the twentieth century, séances were relegated to the popular culture as the realm of haunted houses at Halloween, or a party's entertainment. ("Let's levitate Uncle Joey!") A popular episode of the television show *I Love Lucy* features Lucy and Ethel throwing a séance for Ricky's new boss, Mr. Merriweather. He and Lucy have bonded over a shared interest in numerology and astrology, and Mr. Merriweather expresses his desire to connect with his beloved Tilly. Believing Tilly to be Mr. Merriweather's deceased wife, Lucy arranges to voice Tilly from the beyond, with Ethel acting as the medium. Thrilled to reach Tilly, Mr. Merriweather then asks to contact Adelaide, his wife, causing Lucy and Ethel to panic. If Tilly is not Mr. Merriweather's wife, who is she? Meanwhile, Ethel's husband Fred sneaked into the séance and voices Adelaide while thinking he is voicing Tilly (to play a joke on Lucy and Ethel). Of course, mayhem ensues. Mr. Merriweather, however, is none the wiser and leaves the Ricardo apartment believing he has made contact with both his wife Adelaide and their beloved pet dog Tilly. Confirming their entertainment value, this about sums up a twentieth-century view of séances.

The Real Deal: Modern Circles

Gathering for spirit communication can be a powerful and amazing experience. Modern circles present good opportunities for beginning mediums to use and refine their skills, and they are good opportunities for those who want to experience spirit communication to do so in a sheltered, controlled setting. Often, there are several mediums participating in the circle, giving a range of experience and expertise.

Ideally, a modern circle gathers in a room that is used only for the purpose of holding circles or at least remains unused for a few hours before the circle is held. This reduces interference from extraneous energy. A circle generally begins by clearing the room's energy, which prepares the environment to be as receptive and supportive as possible.

Some circles prefer subdued lighting because it helps set a mood of relaxation and focus, while some sit in total darkness, and others meet in regular daylight. There is no reason to hold a circle in near or complete darkness; a room's lighting is a matter of concern only for those of us on the Earth plane, not for spirits. Like a one-on-one reading with a medium, a circle begins with a prayer to welcome the Divine, to ask for openness and guidance, and to establish intent.

There are many kinds of circles—they can be either *open* or *closed*. In an open circle, anyone can attend and there is a wide range of mediumistic ability. A closed circle is a group that meets regularly with the same members. The circle is closed because the members are working to build a constant group vibration that facilitates easier communication to spirit guides who are also working together from the Higher side.

Open circles welcome participants, from those who just want to experience a circle to those who are developing their skills as mediums. There is one medium who takes the lead, although several mediums might participate in spirit communication. Generally, the spirits who come through have connections to and messages for people in the circle, and a number of spirits make contact during the circle. These messages come through the mediums, and sometimes through participants who don't realize that they have mediumistic abilities.

Those who are part of a closed circle are often mediums, and there is a high level of mediumistic ability in the circle. Mediums sometimes call these medium circles *working* circles. The level of intensity is often higher because the level of mediumistic ability is higher, and spirit communication can take place along a broad continuum of methods—from clairsentience to transfiguration. Closed circles sometimes become teaching environments for guides from Spirit, who come through with generalized information rather than messages for specific participants.

Who Should Be in a Circle

Just about anyone can enjoy the experience of being in an open circle. To find a circle you might join, contact a Spiritualist Church in your area or ask your metaphysical friends about circles they might know of or participate in. Many churches hold services via video conferencing services such as Zoom, so you may be able to experience circles remotely. Many of the guidelines for finding a qualified medium that we recommend in Chapter 10 also apply to finding a legitimate circle.

It's important to set aside any expectations or preconceived ideas about what will happen during a circle and just be open and receptive. Typically, there is a lead medium for the circle who will talk with you before you attend to be sure you understand how the circle functions and what is expected of you.

What happens in a circle is not secret, but it is private. Spirit communication is often intense and deeply personal. While you are free, of course, to share your own experiences with spirit contact, please respect the experiences of others in the circle as confidential.

What if a spirit contact comes through for you? Enjoy! Be open to the experience and welcome the information from the communicator—the spirit that is bringing you the message. As we've said throughout this book, spirit communication is about goodness and healing. The energy of the circle shelters you, and you can feel safe within it. If you feel uncomfortable at any time, ask for help from the mediumistic leader.

Who Should Not Be in a Circle

Participants should come to the circle with positive energy and positive intent. There are people who believe they can use the circle and its psychical energy to control other people or to manipulate aspects of their own lives. For example, they may try to use spiritual energy to control a relationship, to influence personal prosperity, or to boost their profile. If you are not coming into a circle for the highest and best good (for yourself ... and for all present), you can be certain your efforts will backfire. You can call it the law of cause and effect, the law of karma, or you get what you give. No matter what you call it, negative intent ultimately brings negative results.

In an open circle, you can't be sure of everyone's intent despite the care and effort of the circle's lead medium to screen participants. The very nature of an open circle—anyone can attend— makes this virtually impossible. This is yet another reason why it's important to start the circle by asking for Divine protection.

Because mental health affects perception, thought patterns, and behavior, mental illness interferes with a person's ability to establish intent. Conditions such as clinical depression, compulsive anxiety disorder, schizophrenia, and addiction alter perception and make it unwise for a person who has any of these or other serious mental health conditions to participate in a circle.

We Are Gathered Here Today ...

So, the big day is here and you're going to your first circle! What should you wear, what should you expect, and how should you act? The circle's leader should have given you some guidelines about these things already. In general, you'll get the most from your experience when you ...

- Wear comfortable, clean clothing.
- Avoid perfumes and fragrances (which can be disturbing to others in the confines of a closed room, as well as have an effect on a room's energy).
- Leave your expectations or doubts at the door, and enter the circle with an open and receptive mind, heart, and spirit.

In most circles, you can ask questions and request information or a specific spirit contact, although there is no guarantee that you'll get what you ask for.

Setting an Open and Positive Attitude

You have your reasons for wanting to participate in a circle. No doubt there is at least one loved one who has passed whom you would like to contact. This is natural and good. Keep in mind, however, that the Universe has its own intentions! There might be no contact that comes through for you, or what does come through might not be what you hoped for or expected. Nonetheless, it is the communication you are intended to experience. So, get the most from it! If the circle permits you to ask questions, feel free to do so. You should feel comfortable with the others who are present, and you should feel confident they will respect your privacy with regard to what information comes through, as you will respect theirs.

For the Highest Good: Establishing Intent

Establishing intent is not about deciding whom you want to contact and what information you want to receive. Rather, establishing intent is a process of opening yourself to whatever it is that a spirit wishes to communicate and establishing that you desire your communications to take place for the highest good.

Inviting Spirit Presence

The lead medium typically invites, or invokes, spirit presence to join the circle through prayer or a formal greeting. This is called an invocation. Depending on the medium's primary method of contact with Spirit, this might happen within the medium or through external manifestations that are apparent to everyone in the circle. Others in the circle might also receive spirit contact directly, depending upon their mediumistic abilities.

Identify Yourself, Please

The first responsibility of someone who is receiving contact from the Spirit realm is to establish the spirit's identity. An experienced medium does this before sharing the contact with the circle, so they will be able to say, "I have a gentleman here who always wore a New York Mets baseball cap, who wants to tell Marie that she shouldn't be angry with him for not saying goodbye before he passed because he's still here with her, and she should celebrate her birthday next week with a lemon meringue pie from Martha's Bakery."

Now, if that message doesn't convince Marie and everybody else in the circle of the continuity of life and the authenticity of spirit communication, nothing will! Of course, not all contact is that complete or specific. Sometimes, the details are very small or may be difficult to construe as particular to one relationship—and you might not fully recognize the spirit that's come through until sometime after the circle. Just as you are new to this, the spirits who want to contact you might be, too. It can take a little time to settle into a pattern that works for both of you, allowing recognition.

A common and fun exercise mediums sometimes do in spirit circles is bending spoons. You hold a spoon by the bowl and rest one finger on the handle very lightly. You invite the Spirit realm to open, and then let go of the thought. When Rita has done this exercise, the circle starts singing. Suddenly, you can feel the spoon moving, then watch the handle begin to bend. It is the energy of Spirit that causes this to happen, and Rita says the spoon really heats up in your hands! As an exercise, this proves that Spirit can come and work through us rather than just giving us answers. And, we suspect, it's as much fun for spirits as it is for us!

Sometimes it takes a while to figure out who is coming through and why. Rita has taught art for many years. She once had a student who, 10 weeks into a 12-week course, had to leave for medical reasons. The young man had diabetes that was difficult to control, and as a result, lost circulation to parts of his foot. He had to go into the hospital to have a toe amputated, and a few weeks later, ended up having his leg amputated from the knee down. Rita sent cards to him and included him in her healing prayers over the course of a year or so but eventually lost touch with him. A few years later, Rita heard that he had passed.

A number of years later, Rita was in a medium's circle and one of the other mediums said to her, "I have a young man named Greg who is showing as an amputee, and he wants to say 'thank you.'" Rita accepted the message, but she was perplexed; she didn't remember a young man named Greg or anyone with an amputated leg. A few weeks later, she was driving past a restaurant, one that had been a favorite of hers for quite a few years. She felt as though her head was "snapped" to look at the restaurant, and suddenly she remembered who Greg was! He had been the chef at the restaurant and the art student who lost his leg to diabetes. At the next medium's circle, Rita gave thanks in return to Greg and to the medium who had brought his message through.

To Recognize and Interpret Manifestations

Spirit contact can come through in an almost infinite variety of ways. The more people there are in the circle, the more variety there is! A spirit might choose to come through to someone other than the lead medium—even to you!

As we discussed in Chapter 10, at first, these experiences might feel like your imagination has gone into overdrive. This is normal, and others in the circle will give you support and encouragement. Just let the experience unfold; there will be plenty of time afterward to analyze and understand what has manifested.

Common manifestations of spirit contact include the following:

- Hearing words or phrases, often in your head rather than out loud, sometimes in language other than English

- Seeing flashes of a person's face, clothing, or other characteristics
- Images or references to certain colors, numbers, or symbols
- Flashes of scenarios that have the appearance of memories

If you have any of these experiences, share them with the circle even if they seem to have little context. Messages from the Higher side aren't always presented in ways that make logical sense to us. Even if the messages are for you, it might take input from others in the circle for the messages to make sense to you. And if the messages are not for you, you want to get them out there so they reach the right person.

In Goodness and in Healing

When Rita holds spirit circles, she views every circle (and every spirit contact) as a request for healing—emotional, physical, spiritual. Her opening prayers always ask that healing love and light surround the circle. She asks Infinite Spirit, the God of your understanding, to send the spirit guides and loved ones of all who are present to come close and that the people participating in the circle are open to receive.

Those on the receiving end of healing energy have experiences that range from feeling very calm to feeling better, either immediately or after some time has passed. Even though you may feel better, energy from Spirit cannot, and is not meant to, *make* everything better; it is always simply for the highest and the best. Why do we have to suffer? Why *do* we suffer? We don't know! There are spiritual lessons in illness, for example, and many things we don't understand. We are sometimes volunteers for people around us to learn *their* lessons. We don't always know the Divine purpose of a particular situation; it is beyond our capacity to have such knowledge. We do, however, have the capacity to take our feelings of calm and rejuvenation and use them to act, through our freewill, to harness the highest and good for ourselves, our loved ones, and even our communities and the greater world.

Through prayer, meditation, and spirit communication, we can ask for and receive help. Although we don't have to be hurt to learn, it seems that most of the time, we humans don't want to learn, and we get stuck in our egos; it takes a hurt of some kind to kick us into action. Look at how many times people get stuck in dysfunctional relationships but won't leave, or do destructive things to themselves but won't stop. Sometimes, we do things to ourselves (like drinking or smoking too much, for too long, and pushing loved ones away) that amount to a slow rejection of living—a kind of existential suicide. If you can change your life and if you can do what you need to do, your life will change. Spirit energy can help you gain the insights you need to make changes. This is what healing through Spirit is all about—physical, emotional, and spiritual.

Let the Trumpet Blow!

Reality can sometimes be stranger than fiction. There truly are circles called *trumpet circles*. These unique events represent a high level of development in the medium, and they concentrate spirit energy in special ways. It is likely that this "real deal" became the model for the frauds who became so popular for their show-biz séances. A trumpet circle is an amazing experience.

In a trumpet circle, a special, long metal horn is placed in the center of the circle. The room is made totally dark, and those in the circle concentrate on welcoming energy from Spirit. If a spirit accepts the invitation, the trumpet then rises and becomes the mouthpiece for the spirit. In audio recordings of trumpet circles, you can clearly hear different voices coming through the trumpet. Although Rita has been to several trumpet circles, she has not yet experienced the trumpet rising. Several of her teachers have, however, and found the experience remarkable.

Attending spirit circles is a wonderful, rich learning experience if you believe you may have mediumistic abilities, or you simply want to understand more about mediumship in its many forms, so that you may work better with a medium for your own spirit contact. You'll be in the presence of Spirit and a witness to the blessings of Spirit at work in our lives. Seek out the kinds of circles that interest you, while knowing that some circles are more suited to mediums with a lot of training. A great way to start is to attend open circles at Spiritualist church services, either in person or remotely through video conferencing.

The gifts of Spirit may seem miraculous as you witness the spirit communication that can arise for people working with mediums. But the energy of Spirit is around us all, always there, at work for the highest and best. Embrace this Divine energy as a fundamental part of what it means to be human, for our humanity is filled with Divine life force energy. As a talented medium will know and can teach us—we are Spirit, all.

Do *you* have mediumistic talents? Let's explore and find out more.

CHAPTER
12

Your Inner Medium

Most people (and you are surely among them) have had *some* kind of contact with the Spirit world, from just the sense that someone is present to direct messages and advice from loved ones who have passed to the Higher side. Perhaps you want to make contact for yourself, or to use your mediumistic abilities to make contact for others.

Mediumistic skills are like any other skills: You start with a basic or inherent ability (that everyone has to some degree) and a passion to learn more. Through education and experience, you develop and refine that passion and ability into a reliable, *consistent* set of skills. With practice and guidance, you can learn to communicate with the Spirit world. Whether you want to contact someone you feel you know in Spirit or someone who simply knows more than you do, like a guide from Spirit, there are many mediumistic techniques just about anyone can learn.

Could You Be a Medium?!

While everyone has the ability to connect with those in the Spirit world, some people are more open to such connections than others and are more aware consciously of the connections that take place. As an element of the Universe, you are already linked to its energy—you're already plugged in! In accessing that energy to link to Spirit, there comes a great corresponding responsibility as a medium to honor Divine life force and to devote your practice to nurturing the highest and best for both the human beings and the beings of Spirit for whom you foster connection. In addition to mediumistic training, many mediums may also have some training or knowledge of psychology. Both mediumship and psychology take passion for the human spirit and channel it toward applications that help people's lives improve, that nurture peace and understanding.

Developing and refining your mediumistic skills will lead to experiences that are amazing, amusing, entertaining, poignant, and profound. You will certainly experience growth in your personal life, and you will also help others to grow in their lives and understanding. Even if you choose not to develop your own mediumistic abilities, becoming aware of them will let you become more receptive to spirit communication through others.

Your Innate Psychical Talents

You've no doubt noticed that we use both the term "psychic" and "psychical" throughout this book. (And no, the latter is not a misspelling of "physical"!) While they are interchangeable on a certain level, they actually define a somewhat different set of skills. *Psychic skills* are those abilities that you use to communicate in unspoken ways with other people on the Earth plane. A psychic (someone who is using psychic skills) reads from Earth energy, reading the vibrations of what is going on here on Earth.

Psychical skills are those abilities that you use to communicate across the Earth/Spirit divide. The skills are similar to those that a psychic uses. Remember, all mediums are psychics (although not all psychics are mediums; more on this later). A medium (someone who is using psychical skills) communicates with deceased beings through their own sensitivities. Psychical skills include clairaudience (inner hearing), clairvoyance (inner seeing), and clairsentience (inner knowing).

Both psychic and psychical skills differ from psychology, which is the study of human behavior … that is, why we human beings do what we do and how we can become our best selves. Psychology explores and examines the actions of mind, body, and spirit to determine clues that unlock the mysteries of human behavior. Some understanding of psychology can help mediums ground their Divine connections to Spirit in the Earthly context of creating beneficial human relations.

Freeing the Medium Within

Becoming a medium is more often than not a process of being the medium you already are! As a child, you were likely in touch with Divine spirit far more intimately than you are now as an adult. Part of what we view as "growing up" is learning to suppress this spontaneous and unconstrained metaphysical Divine understanding of ourselves. Reconnecting with this truth is just a matter of allowing it back into our lives.

To Be Human Is to Suffer

Buddhists believe that being human is to suffer, and to provide ease from suffering through enlightenment is the task of humanity. This is, of course, a simplistic description of a sophisticated metaphysical practice and belief system. But the very simplicity of the statement opens a path to the depths of human experience and of what it means to feel and experience life, as well as death. As a medium, you will be witness to many intense and intimate details of people's lives and relationships and their manner of passing over to Spirit. Most particularly, you will be witness to the proof of continuity of life that occurs when people connect to loved ones who have passed.

The great pain of loss and grief associated with the COVID-19 pandemic that began in 2020 has actually been given the name *Pandemic Grief* by the mental health community. Research finds this grief is marked in its acute features of extreme anguish, preoccupation, and dysfunction. Experts assert this global grief might not be assuaged for at least a generation, similar to the outpouring of grief associated with the concurrence of losses to the Spanish flu pandemic of 1918 and the Great War (World War I). The witness of history led to a flowering of profound literature of the time—from the work of soldier poet Wilfred Owen to novels such as Rebecca West's *Return of the Soldier*, Ford Madox Ford's *The Good Soldier*, Virginia Woolf's *Mrs. Dalloway*, and Ernest Hemingway's *A Farewell to Arms*.

Today, in our own time, mediums can offer grieving families a way to find peace and closure to their open-ended experiences of profound loss and pain. Humans seek narratives; we are storytellers. When people cannot separate themselves from the traumatic story of the way their loved ones died, such as during the COVID-19 pandemic, mediums can help people, through spirit communication, to carry on their stories by reestablishing the connection to Spirit that has been broken or lost.

Activate Your Mediumistic Abilities

What are your mediumistic abilities? Remember the exercises you did in Chapter 7 to identify your Spirit guide and to discover the lessons your guide has come to teach you? This directed communication exercise can help you identify and activate the psychical skills you used to make that connection. Read through these steps until they are familiar enough that you can follow them without reading through each one.

1. Make yourself comfortable in a location where you won't have any distractions or interruptions.

2. Take three slow, deep breaths, in through your nose and out through your mouth. Let the first breath clear your body; let the second breath open your mind; and let the third breath free your spirit.

3. Consciously form the thought: "This is my time to be one with God and for God to be one with me." (God, of course, being the Divine of your belief system or choice.) Set an intent to explore a spirit contact using all your psychical senses.

4. Envision yourself sitting on a bench in an open, beautiful garden. There are flowers and trees, and the air smells fresh and clean. It is peaceful and calm, and you are open to receive your guide from Spirit, whatever spirit visitor arrives.

5. As your guide or visitor from Spirit approaches, notice, but do not attempt to control, the psychical sense that is first activated. Do you hear a voice or a sound? Do you see an image? Do you "sense" a presence?

6. Welcome your guide or visitor from Spirit and communicate to them using the psychical sense that feels most natural. Make a note in your conscious mind of which sense this is—sight, sound, or intuitive sensing, but don't let your consciousness intervene with its use.

7. Push this psychical sense to use it to the fullest capacity you are capable of at this point. If you begin to feel frustrated, you are pushing too hard, and your conscious mind is becoming involved. Back off until you feel comfortable again.

8. Now choose a different psychical sense. If your initial sense was clairaudience, choose clairvoyance. Concentrate on perceiving visual images using your inner vision. Acknowledge, but don't shift your focus to, these images. If they are just fragments, that's okay. Sometimes images come in bits and pieces (the term mediums use to express the fragmented way in which information sometimes comes to them, especially beginning mediums). They will become clearer. Let the images take shape and form. Focus on what you sense about these images and their meaning.

9. When you begin to feel complete with the messages from Spirit, gently release the concentration you are using to activate the psychical senses. Return to the sense that was first activated, and use this sense to communicate "thank you" and "goodbye" to the guide or spirit who came through.

10. Take three slow, deep breaths, in through your nose and out through your mouth. Feel yourself back in your body, become conscious of your breathing. Wiggle your fingers and your toes, and when you are ready, open your eyes.

When you feel ready to do so after completing the exercise, write down your experiences.

1. Which psychical sense was first activated? What was your initial experience of it?

   _____

   _____

   _____

2. Whom did you meet? Did your Spirit guide return, or did a new spirit come through? What sense of identity did this psychical sense provide about your visitor from Spirit?

   _____

   _____

   _____

3. How did you experience this psychical sense?

   _____

   _____

   _____

4. What was the second psychical sense that you attempted to activate, and what was your initial experience of it? What added information did you get about your visitor from Spirit?

   _____

   _____

   _____

5. What happened with the initial psychical sense as you brought this second psychical sense forward?

   _____

   _____

   _____

6. What interactions did you have with your visitor from Spirit through your psychical senses?

   _____

   _____

   _____

As your mediumistic skills develop, use variations on this exercise to further explore your psychical senses. You might find that your abilities include advanced skills such as automatic writing or, as Rita does, drawing spirit-inspired images.

Learning Focus

The most challenging aspect of using your mediumistic abilities is learning to focus them. Think of this like a time when you entered a room crowded with people who were talking, laughing, eating, drinking, and even dancing to the music that played in the background. A cacophony of "input," to use a term from our digital-driven culture, assaults your senses. Yet within seconds, you locate the friends you are to join and make your way to them. How are you able to do this?

Focus. All your senses align toward identifying and locating your friends. Your eyes scan the room for images of clothing and other physical characteristics. Your ears tune in to frequencies of sound that are closest to what you know signals their voices. Your sense of smell seeks the fragrances your friends typically wear. You search for other details that narrow the scope of your quest to find your friends—foods, drinks, or dance moves. All this transpires without much conscious participation from your mind, of course, and in fractions of time barely measurable. Then click! You're focus aligns with your target, and in moments, you're sharing in the revelry with your friends.

Learning to focus your mediumistic skills is very similar to singling out individuals in a crowded room. You undoubtedly used some of these skills—your psychical abilities—in locating your friends at the party. (One way to further develop these abilities is to consciously concentrate on using them in such ways; but more on that later!) With practice, you become both skilled and comfortable using your core psychical skills—clairvoyance (inner seeing), clairaudience (inner hearing), and clairsentience (inner knowing)—to receive mediumistic messages.

One evening in Rita's circle, a student came to her describing a young man dancing with a top hat and cane. He was tall and handsome with brown hair and was quite the character. Rita could immediately identify him as her friend Tom, a choreographer who danced with a top hat and cane many times and who danced with Rita at parties. He came through with a message that Rita needed to do more dancing and not work so hard, which is definitely something Tom would've said to Rita here on the Earth plane.

Filtering Signals

When you search for someone in a crowd, you simultaneously receive and reject signals. Looking for a friend who identifies as male? Automatically your focus shifts … men in, women out. Short? You glance right past those who stand head and shoulders above the crowd. Always in vogue when it comes to fashion? Your attention migrates to those wearing the latest styles—and overlooks those who are not. Drinks iced green tea … or nothing? Loves avocado toast?? Laugh sounds like a cross between a choking lion and a giggle? You filter all these signals and countless others, consciously and subconsciously.

When receiving signals from Spirit, the filtering process is sometimes more challenging (particularly when you are just beginning to develop your mediumistic skills) because the signals are less tangible to your conscious mind. You might *think* you heard a voice or saw an image.

Did you really? Or was it just your imagination? This kind of conscious questioning is actually a sign of progress in your development. As we said earlier, communication with spirits feels like imagination at the beginning!

Intent and Limits

Mediumistic signals sometime come to you unbidden. Rather than you attempting to invoke connection to Spirit, a spirit comes to you and wishes to make contact. The spirit might desire to convey a message to you or to someone else. As we discussed in Chapter 9, it's important for you to establish intent and set limits. Otherwise, you'll feel like a satellite dish, picking up lots of static but not streaming any clear channels!

Establishing intent makes it clear that you always desire spirit communication for the highest good and with light. Whether you initiate contact or spirits contact you, take time to consciously establish intent. Setting limits reminds visitors from the boundaryless Spirit world that your world has structure and constraints, and that you can't always be available when spirits want you to be.

We Worked So Hard, December 1989, oil on canvas. Rita often worked with troubled inner-city youths, and one young man seemed to attach himself to her. Not an easy person to counsel, Rita decided to ask in meditation, "Who dropped this boy into my lap?" A man showed himself to Rita and told her he had been a migrant tobacco farmer. When Rita showed the boy this painting, he told her that his family had been tobacco farmers and that he thought he recognized the man it portrayed. Rita feels this spirit guided her to work with these youths.

This is a good opportunity to call on your guides from Spirit for assistance. Use the "Meet Your Spirit Guides" guided communication exercise in Chapter 7 to ask for communication with your guide. Then ask your Spirit guide to help you maintain the limits you wish to set. Rita has established with her Spirit guides, for example, that she does not want contact with Spirit to disturb her sleep unless absolutely necessary—the sleep state is a favorite time for spirits to attempt contact because your mind is very receptive. Instead, she makes herself available for spirit communication during her waking hours. She does permit messages from spirits to come to her in the dream state, which is okay because it doesn't wake her up.

Your Circle of Safety

The best place to practice your mediumistic skills is in a circle. (See Chapter 11.) There is strength in numbers, as the cliché goes, and the others in the circle can help and guide you as you are learning. They also learn from you, even though you might feel that as a novice you have little to offer. You might find one circle and stay with it for a long time as participants grow together in their mediumistic skills and maintain a group vibration that those in Spirit will come to recognize, or you might participate in several circles that have different members.

Check with the Spiritualist Churches and metaphysical groups in your area to find out what opportunities there are for learning mediumship.

If you are not able to find an organized mediumistic circle, consider forming one of your own. You might be surprised and delighted with how many people (many of whom are likely already among your circle of friends and acquaintances) are interested in or already have some level of participation with mediumistic abilities and spirit communication. Where there is one, there are usually many; it's just a matter of finding each other. (Chapter 11 offers advice and suggestions for choosing circles and circle participants.)

Beware the scams and the unsophisticated! Some people recognize that they have mediumistic abilities but don't work to develop them before trying to use those nascent abilities for financial gain. This leaves them—and you—open to random spirit contact that may or may not be beneficial. As much as we'd like to believe that everyone offering mediumistic services is doing so for the highest good, the sad reality is that this sometimes is not the case. Always check references and qualifications. If you have any doubts, go somewhere else.

Developing Your Psychical and Mediumistic Skills

Realizing that you have mediumistic abilities is often exhilarating—like recognizing you can sing, paint, or dance when you've always wanted to do those things but thought they were beyond your reach. You are opening yourself to a whole new world—literally and figuratively. But after the novelty of discovery wears off, what's next? You want to learn more, of course, and to explore your unique talents and see where they lead you.

Is this a calling to a career change? You might indeed decide that you want to be a professional medium. But that's really a very personal decision that requires you to consider all aspects of your life. Regardless of how far you think you might want to take your development as a medium, start with the basics.

To some extent, your learning curve as a medium begins with the abilities that seem most prominent. Do you experience voices and sounds? Your predominant psychical ability might be clairaudience, and this is a good place for you to start your development process. As is the case with your physical senses, your psychical senses are intertwined. (Do you *taste* … or *smell* that freshly baked cinnamon roll?) As you develop one psychical skill, you'll discover and develop others.

Medium or Psychic?

You probably already use your psychic abilities in your communications among friends and family here on the Earth plane. You answer your cell right before it rings, and it's always your sister calling when you do it. You impulsively turn left instead of right, and find a parking space. You stop by to see a friend, just in time to see him before he dashes off on an unexpected business trip.

If you take these abilities to the next level to communicate with entities from Spirit on the Higher side, now you're talking medium! (And, a good one, too!)

Finding a Mentor

As with any other skill that you want to develop, finding a mentor who can guide and assist you is a great boost. You can learn from your mentor's experience and expertise as well as from your own experiences and any courses you are taking. You might even think of this relationship as an apprenticeship of sorts. It might be a teacher from your mediumship courses who becomes your mentor, or another medium you meet at Spiritualist services or through a circle.

The difference between teaching and learning is subtle but all important. Teaching is what comes to you via the mastery of another; learning is what you do with that information after you receive it. The greater part of developing any skill is learning. Seek a mentor whose skills are significantly more advanced than yours, someone who is a leader of sorts in the Spiritualist or metaphysical communities. Look for someone whose abilities and integrity you respect and trust, and ask if they are willing to mentor you formally. Because learning and teaching are so intimately integrated, those who want to learn are often also eager to teach.

Honing Your Skills: Cycles of Learning

Practice makes perfect, no matter what skill you're honing. (Well, maybe not perfect, but certainly better!) The more you use your mediumistic abilities, the more competent you will become. Even when you reach the point of producing consistent results, practice leads to continuing improvement. Like playing the piano or riding a bicycle, you meet new challenges, reach new heights of achievement, and rest on plateaus of proficiency until it's time to repeat the cycle of learning—this time with a more complex cadence. In time, your psychical and mediumistic skills will become as second nature, simply part of what defines you and how you function in your life.

Should You Go to School?

The short answer is, of course! If you want to learn more about *anything,* the most logical route is to go to school or take some classes. If there is a Spiritualist Church in your area, that is a good place to start. Spiritualist Churches offer instruction and classes in mediumship. They can also refer you to legitimate, qualified programs in mediumship that offer more extensive study, if this interests you. One such program is the Spiritualist Course of Study for Mediumship, part of the Morris Pratt Institute's (MPI) Course of Study for Spiritualism. MPI is located in Milwaukee, Wisconsin, and their website is www.morrispratt.org. Local universities and colleges, community colleges, and other educational institutions sometimes offer what they might call "extended learning" programs. (Additionally, sometimes these are called "life experience" or "adult continuing education" programs.) These courses are generally not for college credit and are often taught when regular credit classes are not in session and conducted by local or regional experts. Such programs run the gamut from digital skills to tarot reading. You might also find courses in psychic abilities or even mediumship.

As with most learning experiences, the value of such courses depends on the teacher's specific training. Always check the credentials of both the *program* and the *teacher*! Talk with prospective teachers before enrolling in classes, and ask about their training, professional practice, and orientation. Are they Spiritualists? Or do they treat their metaphysical practices more as a game than a spiritual calling? Do they view spirit communication as learning and healing, or do they just see it as entertainment? What if educational opportunities are in short supply in your area? Most programs offer distance learning opportunities. A key benefit with distance learning is that you can progress at your own pace, and within the constraints of other demands placed on your life and your schedule. Not everyone can drop everything to go to school or even squeeze enough time from a busy day to attend night classes!

The disadvantage of distance learning programs, of course, is that much of the time you are on your own. Opportunities for structured practice may be limited because you won't have an in-person instructor working with you to help you receive and give messages. If you're considering a distance learning program, make sure you have adequate access to a medium.

Lessons should be complete with full detailed instruction and should include specific advice for addressing various scenarios that might arise during spirit communication experiences.

There are no universal accreditation procedures for courses and programs that teach mediumship, so choosing one is indeed a process of *buyer beware*. The best way to find a reputable program is to ask sources you trust, such as mediums you might know or organizations you know to be reliable.

~~Great~~ Realistic Expectations

We talk a lot about establishing intent, and we always try to make clear that this means asking for Divine light to guide spirit communication for the highest good and for the greatest healing or learning. A piece of this inevitably becomes, "So what do you want to accomplish with this communication?"

At times, you might desire contact with a specific spirit—your parent, sibling, spouse, child, friend, or colleague who has passed to the Higher side. Often, this spirit is willing to oblige and responds to the energy signals you've sent out. This is always gratifying and comforting; it reestablishes your sense of the continuity of life in very direct and obvious ways.

But spirits aren't always willing or able to respond when we want to call on them. Spirits are active and learning on the Higher side, too! And remember, spirits do have free will. It's important to remain open to the spirits and to messages that *do* come through, even when they don't *appear to be what you want*. There is a grander scheme to the Universe than we, as physical beings, are capable of understanding, and we often simply need to accept that with grace. Otherwise, we find ourselves in a position to ignore or misplace important messages from Spirit.

Expectations for Yourself

If you are using your psychical and mediumistic abilities to communicate with spirits on your own behalf, remain open to whatever the experience turns out to be. The questions you have for Spirit and the contacts you desire may not be the relevant matters in a particular spirit communication, or even in a more general context. Keep your conscious intent focused on spirit communication for the highest good. Be still; let the information from Spirit come through, without interference from you. Avoid trying to direct the interaction with Spirit. You'll have plenty of time afterward to think and analyze the spirit communication to determine meaning. So, keep your mind open and stay out of your own way!

Ask questions of your spirit connections if you are unclear about a received message but realize that the meaning of the message might not become clear to you until quite some time later. A message from Spirit that appears enigmatic might be just a piece of a much larger message that will come to you over multiple spirit connections, or that contains information you aren't ready to receive yet. Be patient; the meaning will come in time!

Expectations When Using Your Abilities for Others

When you use your psychical and mediumistic abilities on behalf of other people, remember *you are just the messenger*. It is not your role to interpret the messages from Spirit that you receive or to judge them (although certainly your consciousness filters them; more on this in Chapter 13). Let the images and concepts from Spirit come through. Always remember that you are in charge; deliver spirit messages faithfully and responsibly.

Sometimes, information from Spirit comes in bits and pieces. If you are patient, the fragments will take shape and make sense to the person who is to receive the message coming through. Sometimes, the meaning of a spirit message will unfold over several spirit communications (not always involving the same spirit each time!)

Lessons and Healing

Your psychical and mediumistic abilities are a great gift, and with them comes the responsibility to use them wisely and always for the greatest good. (We keep emphasizing this point because it is such an essential) Indeed, spirit contact can be, and often is, joyous and fun. Not many of us would be drawn to it if it wasn't! Spirit communication can bring much insight, understanding, comfort, and delight into your life.

Handling Challenges

Messages that come through spirits are sometimes unexpected or intense, and can surface issues you need to confront, address, and resolve. If your intent is pure (meaning you've established that this spirit communication is for the highest good), tremendous healing and learning will come as a potential result.

Many mediums, like Rita, are trained in psychology, ministry, or related fields. This gives them the ability to provide more "Earthly" guidance in response to the effects messages from Spirit have for the people receiving them.

When the messages from Spirit are for you, take time afterward to sort through your emotions and thoughts. Keep a journal about your experience if this helps you. Talk with a friend who understands. Talk with a medium if you know one whom you trust. And if the issues that arise from spirit communications feel overwhelming, seek professional help from a therapist or mental health professional. It doesn't matter what initiates the process of healing; what counts is that you follow through so healing can take place.

Using Your Abilities to Help Others

There is great receiving in the act of giving. It can be tremendously satisfying to use your mediumistic abilities and skills to help others. Bringing messages of comfort and love during spirit communications from loved ones who have passed is a profoundly compassionate action, full of humanity and care. Imagine what our world could be like if we all used our talents, mediumistic and otherwise, to help and nurture each other, whether here on Earth or from Spirit.

What a wonderful world that would be! We can make that world together if we open our minds, hearts, and souls to Divine joy—the peace and understanding of Spirit.

Back in the 1960s, Canadian mass communications expert Marshall McLuhan coined the expression "the medium is the message." He meant that the form of the message informs how the message is perceived. To deepen our context for this expression, the medium is the message is Spirit. Spirit is the message, and the message is love. The message is always love.

Understanding Spirit Messages

Spirit communication brings you messages you need to know—some that you've always wanted to know and some that you didn't realize you wanted to know. Sometimes, the meanings are obvious. "Eureka! I get it!" you exclaim.

Other times, the meanings of messages from Spirit are obscure, even enigmatic. They can be like puzzles for you to solve, slowly revealing the pictures they present. Or, they can be like the children's games in which you move squares around in slots, horizontally and vertically within a frame, until you get them all into just the right position … and then a recognizable scene or image emerges. Meaning can come in a flash, or it can appear only after many months of laborious effort. To make sense of spirit messages, you have to "get" the whole picture, even when it comes to you in fragments.

Despite its often-frustrating nature, spirit communications can be as ultimately satisfying as eating that whole dish of ice cream just to see the picture hand-painted inside the bowl. It's a tough job, but someone has to do it!

Interpreting Information

Spirit communication can be like consulting a therapist ... only more. It can be like an all-night, depths-of-your-souls conversation with a best friend ... only deeper. It can be like waking from a dream and knowing exactly what its symbolism means ... or knowing the dream was important but not being able to piece together its meaning. Spirit communication is an adventure.

Often, your spirit contacts will be with those you knew on the Earth plane who have passed to the Higher side. They are familiar to you, and this familiarity makes you more receptive to communication from them. Just keep in mind that people don't change that much just because they pass to the Higher side! If someone was, shall we say, less than brilliant in their Earth plane existence, don't expect to receive great insights from this spirit on the Higher side to rival the thinking of Eleanor Roosevelt or Albert Einstein. If say, your Uncle Fred could never figure out how to use a smartphone during his life on the Earth plane, he's not going to become Steve Jobs on the Higher side. But Uncle Fred might have other insights and knowledge to share with you—and you may just find the information he does give you quite astonishing and profound.

My Filters or Yours?

Interpretation of spirit communication starts, of course, with the medium who is receiving the messages. It is through their filters—belief system, level of development as a medium, other talents and knowledge—that spirit messages must pass first. On the one hand, this is a clear limitation: You can only receive information within the scope of the medium's background and knowledge to deliver. On the other hand, however, this is a benefit because it focuses the information in ways that make sense to the medium and to you. Modern Spiritualism holds that the psychosocial aspects of the medium attract spirits who are at the same level, to convey messages that are within the medium's scope to understand and communicate.

At a church service, Rita was doing message work, and a rather stiff-standing older gentleman had come through from Spirit who, in his physical existence, had been quite critical and conservative. He always stood in a military stance and didn't have a supportive word to say to anyone. Everything had to be proven to him; he redefined the word "skeptic." The man had come through to connect with his nephew, a young man in the congregation who was developing his skills as a healer. The uncle described a location in the young man's backyard where the young man was establishing his healing work, and then said to his nephew, "Well done!"

The image the uncle described to Rita was of a healing light coming into the place where the young man, a dowser, did much of his healing work. A dowser is someone who uses divining rods or a pendulum to search for water or to check energy fields. In healing, dowsing is also used to balance the chakras (bodily energy centers). The experience was particularly moving because such healing would have been totally foreign to the uncle in his physical life, as would giving any praise or recognition.

Like a Dream

In many respects, making sense of messages from Spirit is like interpreting dreams. Spirit messages are often very symbolic; symbolism is one of the most primal and at the same time most powerful means of communication. Symbolism transcends boundaries (such as language, culture, and belief systems) that divide people on the Earth plane as well as the barriers between the Earth plane and the Spirit plane.

Each medium builds a structure of symbols that spirits use when in communication through that medium. Gold might represent riches and wealth in a universal dream symbolism dictionary, while for a particular medium "gold" represents golden opportunities as yet to be discovered. A good medium knows their personal mediumistic dictionary of symbols and can present to you their meaning rather than the symbol itself. Always evaluate and assess the information you receive from a medium within the context of your life and its realities. Sometimes you need to recast the message from the medium so that it fits the context of *your* life.

If you are receiving spirit communication directly, just let the information come to you rather than trying to interpret it simultaneously as it's coming through. Remember that spirits sometimes struggle, too, to make sense when they communicate! The limitations of the Earth plane can cause a spirit to fumble for just the right images and presentations. Once spirits find the best bridge of communication that links to you, their spirit messages can achieve astounding clarity.

As you explore and develop your own mediumistic abilities and psychical skills, it's a good idea to keep a journal of the symbols that appear to you consistently. They might include certain sounds, smells, or sights. Or they might include numbers, words, colors, or objects. Write down the symbol, and then a brief description of its context. Over time, this will become your personal dictionary of metaphysical symbols.

In the words of the nineteenth-century American metaphysical poet and author Edgar Allan Poe, who knew quite a bit about the limits and possibilities of the symbolic nature of language, wrote, "The boundaries which divide Life from Death are at best shadowy and vague. Who shall say where the one ends, and where the other begins?"

It's in the Details

As Rita reminds us throughout this book, it's the details that make the difference in spirit communication. It's easy enough for a medium (on behalf of a spirit contact) to say, "Your father liked to watch football on Sunday afternoons." Not much of a stretch to make that fit many people's lives! But it's another thing entirely to say, "Your PopPop loved those Green Bay Packers! He never missed a home game at Lambeau Field, and God help anybody who moved his 'cheesehead' from the rabbit-ears antenna when the away game was on television!"

Jim is a member of the Greater Boston Church of Spiritualism where Rita participated in circle on a recent Medium's Day. Jim wanted a spirit drawing done for his mother, Cleo, but he did not reveal this to Rita at the time, so as not to influence the spirit connection. Cleo's father appeared on the paper, and Jim recognized him instantly. As Rita drew, her guides from Spirit showed Rita her own Uncle Tom's hairstyle so Rita would know exactly how to render Jim's grandfather's hair in the picture. Spirit guides sometimes trigger information accessible to mediums, to stimulate what needs to be given out. Rita always felt this drawing couldn't have been more exact if Jim's grandfather had been posing for a portrait while here on the Earth plane.

As a Spirit artist, Rita knows that rich detail—from the broad brush strokes of life-size portrait posture and setting to the intimate, meticulous look of a beloved's mien in a miniature's oval, reveal the essence of a person's character and circumstances. In the film, *Portrait of a Lady on Fire*, two young women of the seventeenth-century—a portrait painter and her subject, grapple with the artistic language of symbols that will reveal the subject's beauty and true essence (both to herself, to the painter, and for her intended). The challenge: to portray both the exterior and the interior life through paint, brush, and canvas—whether on the grand scale of the three-quarter formal pose of the gallery portrait, the nuances of expression and feature in a miniature, and even the intimate truth of the body slipped into the pages of a book. We may not all be Spirit artists like Rita, or even receive information from Spirit in this way, but all spirit communication aims to produce the same level of poignant and true specificity through details and gesture.

Details give our lives meaning, and it is the details that provide evidence of the continuity of life beyond physical existence. It is the details that prove, beyond a doubt, that you are communicating with your loved one. Rita once brought through an older woman from Spirit. At first, all that Rita could see clearly was what looked like a small, fluffy, white stuffed animal the older woman held out toward her.

"I think I'm seeing a stuffed animal," Rita said questioningly and described it. "She wants you to know it is with her and not to worry, that she has it," Rita told the young woman receiving the message from Spirit. "Do you understand this?" a puzzled Rita asked.

It turns out the young woman recognized the stuffed animal as her beloved Maltese dog, Buff, a gift from her parents on her fourteenth birthday. As the young woman had grown up, Buff had become most surely her mother's dog. "Of course, this is what my mom would want me to know," the young woman laughed again. "She loved that dog."

The older woman then gave details of her passing some time ago from the complications of Parkinson's Disease. It all made sense to the young woman, this older woman's daughter, who had been her sole caregiver for many years, up to the time of the older woman's passing. The details are what let you know these are valid experiences, these are authentic messages, and these are feelings you can trust as true.

Digging Deeper

Sometimes the message comes through loud and clear, but you can't recognize the spirit communicator. It might be someone in your distant family, or it might not be whom you expected. Dig a little to find out how this message from Spirit is relevant to you!

Early in her spirit communication experiences, Rita was sitting in a circle with a British medium who did not know Rita or anything about her. He said to Rita, "I have an uncle here for you, his name is Yekah."

The medium gave a lot of detailed information about this uncle, but it wasn't anyone Rita recognized. Because many members of her mother's family had not come to this country, Rita called her mother to see who this visitor from Spirit might have been. She started by asking her mother to name her brothers.

"There's Morris and Mosha," her mother said, and then asked Rita, "What are you trying to find out?"

Rita told her mother of the experience with the British medium and gave the information that the medium had provided. "Yes, Uncle Yekah. He was *my* uncle!" Rita's mother exclaimed.

Even though it took some research to understand the message from Spirit, it was a message that had great meaning for Rita on multiple levels. It gave her information about her ancestry, gave her a shared experience with her mother from Spirit, and it absolutely affirmed the continuity of life. The only way this medium could've received this information was through Spirit, as Rita hadn't even known this great uncle existed.

When the Message Is for You to Deliver

Sometimes during your reading with a medium, a message will come through for you to deliver to someone else. This is usually because you are willing to listen and are open to the communication, while the intended recipient is not. Many times, it is to say "I'm sorry, it's not your fault," to make amends, and sometimes just to say, "I love you."

A woman in Rita's congregation was sitting with a medium when a message came through from Spirit that was for the woman's childhood friend, Martin. The message was from a mutual friend, Carl, who had committed suicide after being arrested for drinking in public. Carl went to jail, while Martin ran away and escaped arrest. Carl hung himself in jail, and Martin had carried the burden of guilt ever since, over not being there to prevent it.

The message was from Carl to Martin, telling Martin it wasn't his fault. Carl had been depressed for a long time, and had committed suicide because of his depression, not because he'd been arrested or because of any sense that Martin had abandoned him. "It's not your fault," Carl wanted to say to Martin. He chose their mutual friend for expressing this because she was open to the communication and Martin would accept the message coming from her.

Prolonged, intractable depression and/or thoughts of suicide are serious and must always be addressed seriously. If you, or someone you love, is having dark thoughts, help them to get assistance from a mental health professional who has relevant training. If you are grieving someone who has passed by suicide, please seek out a counselor who can help you come to terms with what has happened. Remember, you and your loved one, and your family and friends, are not alone. Pray for the grace of Divine love, for the highest and best from Spirit, in the light.

Transforming Difficult Energy

Sometimes messages that come through from the Spirit world seem confused, unhappy, or maybe even dark. Remember, though, we want all spirit communication to come to us for the highest good. Messages might be painful because they stir old resentments and hurts. But this is the path to healing such wounds, for you and probably for the spirit bringing the messages to you.

Spirits sometimes come through to make amends for difficult energy they spread during their physical lives. During message work in a church, Rita had a gentleman come through who was heavyset, scant of hair, and who made it clear that in his physical life he had been an angry and argumentative personality. He never had a kind word for anybody, and often left people in tears. He was coming through at this church service to say to those people in the congregation that day, "I'm sorry, I'm sorry, I didn't mean to be so hurtful."

Another time, Rita had a man come to her for a reading, hoping to find guidance from the Higher side. His mother was getting ready to pass, and he and his brother were having heated arguments about how to handle all the arrangements. It was his grandmother who came through, a kind and gentle woman. She wanted to communicate directly to her grandson, and she said, "You have many good and right things to say, but you need to learn how to present yourself differently, so people will listen and take you seriously."

Emotionally Powerful Messages

Many messages that come through spirit communication are deeply felt. They are messages that convey apology, forgiveness, comfort, and most importantly, love. They touch us in the deepest core of our being, sometimes uncovering both pain and joy we didn't know were there. This is one way we know these messages from Spirit are authentic. They're so intimately *personal* there's no way anyone could deepfake their emotional power!

Deepfakes use artificial intelligence to create digital portrayals that seem so accurate they must be authentic—but they are not. In the future, it will become harder and harder in our everyday lives to discern the real from the copy and the fake. This makes spirit messages all the more important and powerful because they are the emotional intelligence of deeply *felt*, intimately *understood* knowledge and understanding that is given to humanity directly from the Divine.

Once stirred, emotions from contact with spirits are powerful and intense, and can make you feel quite unsettled until you are able come to grips with them (especially if you are someone who keeps your emotions to yourself). Deeply emotional experiences on the Earth plane tend to be clearly defined by time: a wedding, a funeral, the birth of a child. Deeply emotional experiences activated from the Spirit plane often extend across conventional borders of time and place, touching many dimensions of your life simultaneously. It can be overwhelming to feel such intensity.

If you are planning a reading with a medium, schedule it for a time when you will be able to deal with the emotions that might arise. Try not to rush through the reading on your lunch break, if possible! Although the intensity of your feelings might startle you, it's perfectly normal. And it's what allows healing to begin.

After a reading (or any spirit contact), take some time for yourself, to think about the messages you received and begin to examine the bits and pieces to understand their whole meaning. You might want to:

- Take a long walk or go for a bicycle ride. Physical activity occupies your body, and being in nature connects you with a reality larger than yourself. This frees your mind to explore the new information it has received.

- Write in your journal. This activity takes you intentionally within yourself, giving focus to contemplation and understanding (see the journaling exercise in the next section).

- Talk with a trusted friend. Someone who knows you well can help you connect seemingly disparate messages to situations and experiences in your life (or your family). Within the context of love and kindness, this friend can gently show you things about yourself that you can't (or won't) see.

- Pursue clues. Look through family photos or heirlooms to help reveal more detail about your connection through Spirit to your ancestors, or to other loved ones who have passed but who have messages for you.

- Explore and resolve intense emotions, such as anger and hurt, through counseling or psychotherapy. A mental health professional can help you accept past hurts and use them to strengthen and shape your life as you move forward.

Don't fall into the trap of going to a medium to have someone else make your hard decisions *for* you. A good medium (an experienced and ethical medium) will not tell you what to do or what spirit messages mean; instead, an experienced and ethical medium will present you with information to help you choose appropriately. *Never* make changes in your life just because a medium tells you to or gives you information that tells you to do so. Spirit communication is for you *to learn*, not for you to avoid responsibility for your life and your decisions along its path! Spiritualists stress personal responsibility.

A Journaling Exercise to Explore Feelings

Keeping an on-paper journal is a good way to explore your experiences and feelings about spirit communications. It's just for you, so you don't have to worry about spelling or grammar or any of that—or even having what you write make sense to anyone but you. Writing with a pen or a pencil on paper causes you to use different parts of your brain than other forms of communication do, which helps you see things from a different perspective. For this reason, avoid typing or using one of the popular digital notebook applications, unless the app allows you to write longhand with a digital pen. The following exercise lets you explore a message you might have received from a spirit contact:

1. Find a comfortable, quiet place where you can write in your journal without interruption. Put on music and light candles if you like.

2. Write with a pen or pencil on paper, preferably. Or, if you must, use a digital pen to write longhand in a notebook application.

3. Begin by writing down the message from Spirit that you received. Write it in as much detail as you can recall.

4. Who delivered the message from Spirit? How did it feel to connect with this spirit?

5. Now, write about how it felt to receive the message. How did you respond or react? What feelings did you experience? How old did the message make you feel?

6. Write some memories of times in your life when the information of this message would have been helpful or that changed your understanding of events and/or relationships.

7. Write about what changes you might make in your life to make good use of this information from Spirit. What can you do differently? How can you do it?

White Cake with White Frosting

Judy came to Rita a week before her birthday for a reading. This was Judy's first birthday since her mother's passing the summer before. Her mother, a baker, had always created elaborate birthday cakes to celebrate family birthdays. Because this was just a part of who her mother was, Judy had never appreciated these cakes, which were truly works of art. So now Judy wanted to contact her mother to say, "I miss you so much, and I want to thank you, for the care you took in creating your cakes for my birthdays."

Rita started the reading, and quite quickly established a connection with Judy's mother. After presenting Judy with the identifying information that confirmed this was indeed her mother, Rita said to Judy, "Your mother is presenting you with a white cake and white frosting for your birthday."

Judy smiled and said, "That's very sweet, but you must be mistaken. My mother would never have made me a plain white cake with plain white frosting while she was alive, and I can't imagine that would be the message she would choose to send now."

Rita continued on with the reading, presenting Judy with a variety of messages from her mother that ranged from "I'm glad you married Jed, he's a good man," to "I like your new hairstyle; it really accentuates your eyes." Judy was delighted with this communication from her mother and told Rita it was just like sitting down together for a lovely chat.

But Rita kept getting the message about the white cake with the white frosting. Finally, Rita said to Judy, "Your mother is very insistent about this white cake with the white frosting! She wants to present this to you in honor of your birthday celebration." Rita didn't know that Judy's birthday indeed was coming up soon.

At first, Judy just sat there. Then her face turned pale, and she burst into tears. Judy's mother had really liked to bake, and always insisted on making gourmet cakes for family celebrations, but Judy had always begged for just a white cake with white frosting! Now she would have it from her mother, through Spirit. The experience was very affirming and comforting to Judy because she knew her mother was really there and finally hearing her.

Seeking Clarification

Communication, whether in Spirit or on Earth, is not always clear or consistent. When in doubt, ask! Spirits aren't intentionally mysterious or enigmatic; they want you to understand the messages they are bringing. Sometimes, however, they just aren't able to communicate in ways that make sense to you. Of course, communication on the Earth plane has its challenges, too—so much so that we might think of each other sometimes as being from different planets!

From the Spirit World

Is the confusion coming from the spirit? A spirit who was not especially articulate while on the Earth plane, or who has been on the Higher side for a long time (measured in Earth plane time, of course), might struggle to find the right images and symbols. Sometimes, the symbolic language is different between the communicator and the medium. It's fine to say, "I don't understand. Can you put it another way?"

Is it the case that the medium seems to understand the message, but is having trouble conveying it to you? The message might be clear to the medium on a clairsentient level, but difficult to translate into language that communicates the message successfully to you. It's like trying to squeeze a baseball-size orange through a one-inch tube. You might succeed, but although what comes out the other end might smell and taste like an orange, it isn't going to *look* anything like the orange it started as! Again, ask for clarification. Rita always tells people to let her know if there is anything they can't relate to and explains that she will ask her guides from Spirit for clarification.

When receiving a spirit's message directly (without using a medium) that seems unclear, write down exactly what the message is as it's coming through, to the best of your ability to capture it. Put this aside for a few days, and then come back to it. Sometimes things will make more sense when you give them a little distance.

From You

Sometimes it's we, ourselves, who don't get the message, or we interpret it in ways that are different than the spirit bringing the message seemed to intend. This is especially likely to be the case when the message delivered from Spirit is counter to a long-held belief or resistance. If all of your life you viewed your father as distant and uninterested, you're naturally going to resist messages from the Higher side attempting to communicate his love for you.

It could be that the message isn't authentic; perhaps this *isn't* really your father, but another loved one who might have looked or sounded like your father—a grandfather, brother, or uncle. Or it could be that your father's spirit has evolved enough on the Higher side to want to reach out to you to make amends. You should be able to get enough identifying information to determine which is the case. (See also "Desperate Illusions" in Chapter 10.)

Life-Changing Experiences

Sometimes messages from Spirit are so revelatory that they become turning points in your life. When you gain new understanding and insights, great. Let these insights guide the changes you make to restructure your life, and you will truly have learned to evolve through spirit communication.

Just remember, however, that spirits don't usually come through to say, "Invest in Google and move to Denver." Before you make a major life change, consider all of the ramifications, all of the pros and cons. Then make your considered decision based on all the circumstances of your life. If you hate your job, have no one depending on you for support and sustenance, don't like the weather in Phoenix—and you just inherited a cool million dollars from Great Aunt Delia— then you might want to buy some stock, quit your job, pack your things, and move. Don't make a major change in your lifestyle, though, just because a medium or a spirit *tells you to*. This is *your* life, and only you should make the freewill decisions that shape its direction.

The Peace of Understanding

Welcome the messages that come to you through communicating with spirits for the understanding and comfort they can bring to you. Accept the learning and the healing that comes to you from the Higher side. Through communication from Spirit, you often can find answers that have otherwise eluded you.

Drawing You Closer

As a Spirit artist and medium, Rita understands the grace and power of receiving messages for people from Spirit. As the shape, form, and manner of the spirit coming through manifests under Rita's hand, her spirit drawing becomes a document not just of the presenting spirit but also of the spirit connection that's being established during the reading as well. *Spirit draws us closer*—to ourselves, to our ancestors and loved ones who have passed, as well as our loved ones still sharing the Earth plane with us. We are the human family, linked together on Earth by Spirit. Let the emotional power of messages from Spirit draw you ever closer toward Divine understanding, to love and light.

PART 4

Activating Your Spirit Senses

Do you follow your intuition even when it appears to be leading you in directions contrary to logic or common sense? Do you experience spirit contact? Many people have strong psychic and mediumistic abilities but don't recognize them. Clairvoyance, clairaudience, and clairsentience are the psychical senses through which mediums experience contacts with spirits in the Spirit world. Your spirit can use your thoughts and your psychic senses to communicate without using any of your physical senses. Objects and places hold energy in the present from those who came in contact with them in the past. A medium can read their energy to facilitate connection with those spirits. When you are in the dream state, you are very receptive to contact with Spirits. When loved ones who have passed appear in your dreams, they may have special messages for you.

Let's explore some of the advanced abilities mediums use to communicate with spirits. More exercises let you test your own skills.

CHAPTER
14

Medium's Sight, Hearing, and Knowing

From early on in its quest, *Star Trek's* starship *Enterprise* encountered many alien beings and cultures on its science fiction mission to explore the Universe—to *boldly go where no one has gone before*. Season three, episode eight, "The Empath," first aired in December 1968, and features a rare and seemingly delicate creature marooned on a research station on planet Minara II, a planet threatened by destruction from the supernova of its sun. Christened "Gem" by ship's doctor McCoy and admired as a "pearl of great price" by chief engineer Scott, Gem and the Enterprise officers are the subject of an experiment where Gem's gift for healing is tested as she witnesses the *Enterprise* crew grapple with their escape to rescue survivors. Will Gem, born with no vocal cords, find her voice through healing self-sacrifice and save her race—and the *Enterprise* and its crew—from destruction?

Empaths figure as important races in the *Star Trek* Universe, beginning with Gem and going all the way to ship's counselor Deanna Troi, from *Star Trek: The Next Generation*, who is half-human, half-Betazoid. Advanced brain development and heightened nervous system function gave empathic characters a unique ability: They could communicate without speaking, by sensing another's thoughts and emotions. This intrinsically-felt "knowing" allows empaths to take on the pain and suffering of others, to understand it, make it their own, and heal it. If we can see it, feel it, and know it, we have the understanding to heal it. This is true even if we humans need to develop those empathic skills, unlike the Betazoids who needed only to practice their empathic gifts.

Science fiction, then, really isn't *so* far removed from reality! Although we've yet to send crews on spaceships to explore distant galaxies, humankind is ready to perform unmanned flights on the surface of Mars. And NASA's *Webb* telescope, the successor to the *Hubble* telescope, is three times larger and seven times more powerful than *Hubble,* and will unfold its mirrors a million miles out in space to discern faint stars and galaxies at the edges of time itself. Human footprints trail across the lunar dust of the moon's surface. Private companies race to create the first commercial space flights. And many ordinary human beings right here in the real world of everyday life—your friends, your colleagues, your relatives, and maybe even you!—have the psychical abilities that would make them feel right at home on Betazed, the fictional home planet of *Star Trek's* Betazoids.

Exploring Your Physical Senses

Yes, we do mean *physical* senses. These are the five senses you first learned about in grade school science class and through which you experience the tangible world—sight, hearing, smell, taste, and touch. These senses connect you to your physical world, allowing you to gather information—the data that becomes your perceptions.

Learning to use your physical senses to their fullest extent increases your awareness of your surroundings. Look up from your reading right now. What is the first thing that you see? Describe everything about it that you can perceive through vision—colors, shapes, shapes, and textures (as dimensional perceptions). When you've exhausted your visual perceptions, find one more visual detail. Repeat this exercise, calling on each of your physical senses. Make this a daily activity and you'll be amazed at how quickly your sensory capabilities expand.

It's a Tangible World

The energy that gives our physical world its form and context presents itself in many tangibilities. The frequency of an energy's vibration determines our sensory experience of it. We see colors and shapes, smell fragrances, touch textures, taste flavors, and hear sounds. The energies of these experiences are distinct and discreet most of the time. Most of us don't taste colors, for example, or see sounds. (Although many mediums do.)

Nonetheless, our physical senses work in a sort of synchronous way. This is most obvious with the senses of taste and smell. Ever notice how the flavor goes flat in favorite foods when you have a cold that plugs your nose? That's because much of what you perceive as flavor is actually smell rather than taste. The receptor cells for these two senses—technically known as olfaction and gustation—(Eat with *gusto!*)——reside fairly close to each other. Their signals travel to the same section in your brain for interpretation.

Other physical senses complement each other, too, although their interrelationships are often not as obvious. Typically, you hear more clearly and in greater detail when you can also see the source of the sound. This allows you to combine visual signals with audio signals, expanding the range of information that reaches your brain. Similarly, sight enhances touch. Seeing an object's size, consistency, color, and texture gives a framework for the perceptions of that object that come through touch. It also happens that one sense (or more) may compensate for another that is lost. When sight is lost, hearing is heightened, touch is more tactile, and so on.

Expanding Your Physical Senses: An Exercise

One way to expand your physical senses is to focus on one sense, gathering as much information as possible. Here is an exercise to help you do this:

1. Get a notepad and pen or pencil so you can write down your experiences. Then go to a location where there is a lot of activity, such as a walk in nature, a city sidewalk, a tour of a child's playground, or walking through an open-air marketplace.

2. First, look around you. What do you see? Write down at least 10 sights.

3. Next, what do you hear? Write down at least 10 sounds.

4. Now, what can you touch with your hands, feet, and other parts of your body? (Consider the floor you walk on, the bench you sit on, even the pen and paper in your hands.) What do you feel, and with what part of your body do you feel it? Write down at least 10 sensations.

5. What do you smell? Describe at least 10 fragrances and odors.

6. Taste is sometimes a difficult sense to integrate into an exercise such as this unless you stop at a restaurant or other location where you can get a drink and a snack. If you are in such a location, write down your descriptions of the tastes you experience.

How often do you find yourself using more than one sense to form a perception? Think first about the primary sense that you're using and then any other senses that come into focus. You might receive visual perceptions about a person, then add to the information you are gathering when you hear the person's voice and smell any perfumes or fragrances (or other odors). Although the point of this exercise is to focus on what each sense can contribute to your perceptions, your sensory experiences combine in practical use to form impressions that are more densely layered and complete.

Exploring Your Psychic Senses

Your psychic senses are your senses, sometimes called *extrasensory perception* (*ESP*). Extrasensory perception (ESP) uses your nonphysical senses to gather impressions and perceptions about physical and nonphysical experiences. They allow you to take your physical senses to the next level, and they also allow you to gather information that your physical senses alone cannot detect.

Intuition: More Than Just a Feeling

Just about everyone has had "gut feelings"—about people, events, places, and circumstances. You meet someone at a business conference and instantly know, without tangible information, that this person is someone to be cautious around. Maybe it's that every hair on your body is standing on edge or that you can't suppress the shudder that goes through you when you shake hands with this person. But you *know*. Your "gut feeling" is telling you something isn't right.

Take this to the next level, and now you're talking intuition. What images does the handshake evoke? What is your sense of this person? What other psychic senses does this person activate in you? What, precisely, is the message your intuition is giving you about this person? Some people experience vague intuitive messages, while others experience intuition that provides considerable detail.

You might have intuitive feelings about friends and family or about such mundane events in daily life as what song will play next on the radio (a fairly common manifestation of intuition). You can cultivate this psychic sense by practicing it. For example, we know someone who's oldest childhood friend is intuitive. All their lives—up to the present moment—the intuitive friend gave her messages she'd received both large and small. Sometimes this intuitive knowing proved to be an intrusive distraction in their friendship, but over time, it became a part of the friends' bond of affection. It might be something small, such as handing her friend a new package of Sharpie pens and telling her she was tired of receiving the message that her friend was thinking she needed some fresh ones. Or, it might be something larger, like driving to the airport to be sure her friend took a later plane than she was booked for—*No way you are getting on that plane, any plane but that one.* (Later, an astrologer did a chart and confirmed she was wise to have listened to her intuitive friend—some small event, seemingly innocuous, occurring on that plane would have mushroomed to create lasting pain for her life had she boarded it.)

Telepathy: Reach Out and Connect

Telepathy is the communication that takes place between people without using your physical senses. It's not really mind reading, although that's a common perception. Rather, telepathy is a process of sending and receiving messages. You might, however, "pick up" on messages that others don't realize they're sending to you.

Telepathy, like initial mediumistic experiences, can feel more like imagination than ability when you are new to your awareness of it. After all, how can you really know what's in someone else's head? You can, of course, but proof can be elusive. But with practice, you will soon learn to distinguish between what you think or imagine and what you receive and send. Chapter 15 discusses telepathy in detail.

No one, not even the most talented psychic or medium, can "read" your mind and receive information you don't wish to share. Your private thoughts and feelings are always yours; your guides from Spirit help assure this. Sometimes you do send messages about your thoughts and feelings without consciously realizing that you are doing so. This happens because you are willing, on a Spirit level, to share them, which is how it might seem that a psychic has tapped into your innermost thoughts.

Precognition: Sensing the Future

Do you ever sense something, an event or occurrence then find that later it happened? This is precognition, a psychic ability to perceive experiences beyond the boundaries of time. This psychic sense taps into the universal energy field, the energy of all existence that encompasses the physical and nonphysical worlds. A common form of precognition is crisis precognition in which we sense impending difficulties or disaster involving loved ones here on the Earth plane (like our intuitive friends and boarding, or not boarding, the plane).

You might think of precognition as predicting the future. Certainly, when events unfold as you sensed them (especially when there was no way you could have known of their details), this appears to be the case. But remember that precognition transcends the borders of time that define the events and reality of our physical world. This definition construes time as a linear continuum. Time really isn't linear; it's coexistent. That is, all time exists simultaneously. There is no past, present, or future—there are only our perceptions of these conceptual dividing points.

Most people aren't aware of precognitive experiences until after the events they perceived unfold. This gives the appearance that the events were destined to occur. You read a newspaper report about an assassination attempt on a world leader and suddenly realize, "I knew this was going to happen!" But there are myriad circumstances that also unfold. These countless events are the result of choices and decisions we all make each moment—the all-important function of freewill.

Psychometry: Reading the Energy

Many psychics have trouble going into antique stores. The residual energy stored in their furnishings and objects can rush out at the psychically sensitive just as the smell of baking cinnamon rolls floods through a restaurant during brunch service. Touching an object connects you with the energy it has stored from others who have touched or owned it. You might experience this energy through any of your psychic senses. Chapter 16 discusses psychometry in detail.

Exercises to Expand Your Psychic Senses

You can expand the capabilities of your psychic senses by practicing them. Let's use intuition as an example. (We'll give you exercises to build your telepathic and psychometric abilities in later chapters.) Spontaneous intuition often comes to people during everyday activities. Here are some ways to "tune in" to your intuition, making it a more conscious function.

- **Streaming music.** Do you stream music in the car and at work? Try to intuit what song will play next on shuffle. When you get good at this (or tired of it), create a playlist of five or ten songs. Put the playlist on random shuffle and before playing it, write down what you think the order of the songs will be. How close do you come to intuiting the song order correctly?

- **Answering a text.** If you've got specific tones assigned to texters, turn off that feature so that the same tone is used to indicate all incoming texts. Now, when you hear the tone, can you tell who is texting you without looking? If you are right, how much of your knowing was based on context and circumstance rather than pure intuition? Learn to separate intuitive knowing from the ability simply to deduce the texter.

- **Listening to your inner voice.** What inner messages do you receive when meeting people for the first time? When you have the opportunity, write down these perceptions. (Most people will be quite unnerved if you whip out a smartphone or tablet and say, "Just a minute! Let me get this down!") Make sure you keep these notes secured where others aren't likely to view them. Later, go back to your notes and see how accurate your perceptions were.

- **Rolling the dice.** Take a set of dice in your hand. Predict the number, and then roll the dice. How often does your number come up?

- **Cutting a deck of cards.** Get a new, unused deck of cards that you dedicate only for this exercise (so you don't pick up any other energies). Decide that you want to turn up two cards, such as a Jack and a Queen. Cut the deck; see if you cut it on the cards you chose or whether that card is the next card above or below. How close are you?

These simple exercises are only starting points. There are endless ways to induce intuition into your life, and the more you use your psychic senses the better at accessing them you will become.

Exploring Your Psychical Senses

Your psychical senses are closely related to your psychic senses. But rather than using them to explore Earth plane experiences, you use them to connect with the Spirit world. The three key psychical senses—clairaudience, clairvoyance, and clairsentience—correspond to key physical senses (hearing and seeing) and psychic senses (intuition). You were first introduced to the psychical senses in Chapter 12.

Clairaudience: Hearing the Unspoken

Clairaudience is the inner sense of psychical hearing, the ability to hear voices and sounds from beyond the Earth plane. A contact with Spirit might begin with the sense that someone is talking to you. You don't actually hear these words in the same way you hear the words of someone who is talking right in front of you. Instead, you hear them within your head. You might even feel that you're imagining them!

Because contact with Spirit usually comes for a purpose, a spirit attempting to deliver a message might persist with the message until you finally "get" it. You may or may not know the spirit communicator, and the message could be for you or for someone else. You might hear the words over and over or perceive the message as a directive: "Tell Robert not to worry. Change will be for the better and he'll do fine."

It's important to first just receive the message without attempting to filter or interpret it. This is especially important if the message is for you to deliver to someone else; let that person decide what the message actually means.

Early in her mediumistic experiences, Rita was doing a Spiritualist church service and had had few clear clairaudient experiences. She was receiving a lot of information for a woman in the congregation, and the woman was nodding and agreeing. Then Rita kept hearing "Frenchie" without much context, so after a few moments, she just put the word out there for the woman. She was very excited; this was the nickname of a woman who had been her close friend and mentor!

Another time, Rita had a set of parents coming through for two sisters. The father was an accomplished musician, and the music was coming through. Rita was talking about how magnificent the music was and then said: "Now your mother is here." Then Rita heard someone just banging out a tune like a marching band. She shared this with the daughters, who started laughing. "Yes, Mother sure could bang out a tune!" one of them said.

When you receive clairaudience, use the opportunity to refine and develop this sense. Determine the following:

- What does the voice sound like?
- Is the voice male or female, old or young, soft or harsh?
- Do you know whose voice it is?
- What is the message?
- Is the message for you or for you to deliver to someone else?
- If the message from Spirit takes the form of sounds only—no language—are these sounds you can recognize (or that someone else present can recognize)?

- Are the sounds you are hearing relevant to the context or circumstances/location you find yourself in, or are the sounds evocative of some remote location?

- Do the sounds recur? Can more than one person hear them, or is this the first time the sounds are heard?

Messages that are for you might also come through the clairaudience of a medium. When this is the case, remember that the medium's consciousness filters this message; it's unavoidable. If the message is clear and makes perfect sense to you, great! If it seems vague or perhaps even unrelated to you, ask the medium for clarification. There might be symbolism in the descriptive words the spirit communicator chooses to use, or the spirit just might not be expressing the message clearly. Verbal communication on the Earth plane can be challenging enough!

Here's something that happened during the COVID-19 lockdown of 2020: The Daffodil Bowl in Puyallup, Washington, began to make itself heard to the owners after the lines were closed temporarily (for safety from the virus) to bowlers. In the unusual stillness, the owners heard the repeated sound of a bowling ball rolled down a lane. Once word got out, employees joined in with stories of bowling shoes flying out of their cubbies or pans and utensils falling off their hooks in the café kitchen. Sometimes the pin setters turned themselves on. Some believe all this is caused by the spirit of a league bowler who passed on from a heart attack on lane 1. Some say it is the spirit of a former mechanic who worked for decades on the lanes. The owners enjoy this friendly spirit and say, "[We] think he doesn't want to stop bowling!" Without the unexpected silence of a stilled bowling alley, devoid of its Earth plane bowlers, could the presence of the bowler on lane 1 from Spirit be heard and affirmed?

All it took for the spirit bowler's presence to be affirmed was for the Daffodil Bowl to experience a period of prolonged stillness. But what if the clairaudient messages from Spirit are not strong enough to pierce through to the Earth plane—but are still very much energetically present? There are some new computer apps that use Electronic Voice Phenomenon (EVP) to investigate presences from Spirit by using psychoacoustics, which is the science of how humans perceive and understand sound. The apps look for the persistence of sound after a sound is produced, a kind of real-time recording and reverb. The perception of sound stops being a physical mechanism of the body and starts being perception. EVP apps are often used on battlefields from the American Civil War or the Great War in Europe. Recordings often reveal sounds and voices that suggest the presence of entities on the Spirit plane.

Clairvoyance: Seeing Visions

Clairvoyance is the inner sense of psychical vision—the ability to see images from beyond the Earth plane. For example, such visions might be explicit, showing you facial details and clothing (such as Uncle Calvin, the Great War soldier from Chapter 7). More often, clairvoyant images are less specific and might be shadowy or incomplete. In your mind's eye, you might see the image of a person's head and upper body but not the arms and legs. Or you might see a steering wheel but not the car. Even when incomplete, clairvoyant images can be quite vivid—they seem real and tangible even as you know they are not.

At other times, clairvoyant images are more dreamlike. The images might be symbolic or representative rather than literal. You might repeatedly see the color blue, the shape of a triangle, or a marigold in full bloom. Every medium has a "dictionary" of symbols; certain objects and images that have specific meanings whenever they appear. This symbolism may or may not make sense in terms of Earth plane experiences.

During a reading, a grandfather came through. He started out talking about his personality, which was sometimes very sweet but sometimes very strong. Rita kept seeing a newspaper being held in front of his face. Rita told the woman she was doing the reading for, "He sits there with the newspaper in front of his face, almost as though he's hiding because he doesn't want to talk to people." Rita mentioned this three or four times, and the woman finally said, "You never said he was *reading* the paper. Yes, this *is* my grandfather. I didn't find out until after he died that he actually couldn't read!"

When you receive clairvoyant messages, try to experience as much of the images as possible. If you are alone or in a circle, describe out loud what you're seeing. If this is not practical (the images come to you when others are there or you just can't speak out loud), explore the images as much as your mind's eye will permit, and when the clairvoyant experience is over, write down as much as you can recall.

- What exactly do you see? Describe shapes, colors, features.
- Is the image clear and complete (like a portrait painting) or foggy and incomplete (like a dream fragment)?
- Do you recognize the image? If so, what is it? If not, what does it remind you of or make you think of?
- Does the image relate to your life?
- What seems to be the message of the image?

If a medium brings through clairvoyant images, ask for clarification about anything that doesn't quite make sense. If the medium describes someone that sounds very much like your father who has passed, but this spirit is showing with a full beard and wearing a hat, two things never associated with your father, this might seem inconsistent and therefore incorrect. Don't be so quick to jump to such a conclusion!

Rita begins every sitting with, "I am seeing ..." because she is predominantly clairvoyant and sees images all the time. In one sitting, she was clearly tasting all of the father's favorite foods and talking about it. Then Rita received an image of the father with a huge bowl of salad in front of him and then pushing it away as if he didn't want it. The woman laughed; her father had always refused to eat salad!

Spirits present themselves as they want to be seen. Maybe there's a joke in this image for you—did your dad try to grow a beard but was unsuccessful, or did people gently tease him for his beard-growing efforts? Did he have a favorite hat that you hated or found embarrassing? Spirits love humor! Even if your father never wanted a beard or wore a hat on the Earth plane, he might want to present himself in this way to you now as a message that he's perhaps loosened up or is enjoying a carefree existence. And of course, there is always the possibility that the medium has misinterpreted the image, which is why you should ask for clarification when the descriptions seem off.

Clairsentience: Experiential Knowledge

Clairsentience is like intuition to the tenth degree. It is the psychical sense of just knowing, and the psychical sense mediums experience all the time. Mediums feel the presence of spirits, feel the size and bulk of their bodies, and feel the stance of the person, just as though they are standing inside of them. They feel the condition that caused the person's passing and can smell or taste as if they were actually within the person.

Some mediums view clairsentience as a discreet psychical sense, while others perceive it as the combination of multiple psychical senses. In some regards, this is like trying to separate the physical senses of smell and taste. Yes, each is a discreet and individual sense that responds to particular sensations. Yet one sense does not function completely without the other one.

Clairsentience is an experience of the whole. You might get the sensation of hearing a voice, seeing an image, and even smelling a fragrance or odor—all at the same time, just as your physical senses experience a person who walks into the room. Or you might not have any tangible perceptions; instead, you might have just an overall sense of knowing that surrounds a place or an event.

To get the most from clairsentient experiences, open yourself fully to the experience. Let all the information come through. After the experience concludes, try to answer these questions:

- Do you recognize the person, place, or event?
- How are you experiencing these perceptions? Can you identify specific psychical senses?
- What seems to be the nature or purpose of this clairsentient experience? Is the message for you or for you to deliver to someone else?
- How do you feel as this experience is unfolding? Are you aware of external activities and sensations, or has the clairsentient experience completely enveloped you?

Clairsentient perceptions might feel intangible, unreal, and even more mysterious than dreams or imagination, especially when you are new to exploring your psychical senses. With practice and focus, clairsentient experiences can be quite amazing and profound.

But, remember that messages from Spirit come to us for good and for healing, not to do harm. If you are hearing voices or seeing images that are instructing you to hurt yourself or others, this is not spirit communication. Please seek help from a licensed psychologist, therapist, or counselor.

Two very different clairsentient experiences happened recently during a friend's trip to the wonderful City of Light, Paris, France. The first experience came during an organ concert given at The Church of St. Sulpice at sunset. During the concert, a profound presence of angels moved from nave to pew, somehow creating a merging of celestial light and Earthly music in the cathedral. The air as the light changed from afternoon to evening seemed charged with life force energy. Many of the attendees were moved to tears, knowing the lovely notes of the organ music called forth the attendance of angels in this sacred moment of Divine adoration. Celestial music raised its voice to Earthly music that evening in Paris.

On another occasion, Rita visited the tomb of Napoleon Bonaparte—a huge, formal marble sarcophagus that seemed more the size of the general's ego rather than his diminutive Earthly stature. The air in the tomb chamber was heavy and gray, contributing to a sense of claustrophobia and the inability to breathe. Even though the space was grand and definitely not filled to capacity, there seemed a sense of energetic crowding, as if you stood soldier to soldier with the air. Heightened emotion, adrenaline, a fierce battle of wills, and cries of battle and anguish could almost be heard. It felt like imagination, but was it? Exiting the tomb to the fresh air and broad blue sky of a Parisian day seemed the best retreat imaginable. Later, when photos of the trip were returned from the developer, all the pictures of Napoleon's tomb were riddled with blurry splotches. The spirits of Napoleon's army? We believed so.

Setting Aside Consciousness

Sometimes your conscious mind gets in the way of, or limits, your psychical senses. There are a number of ways that you can set aside your consciousness to enhance the perceptions of your psychical senses.

Meditation

Meditation is the process of preparing your mind for openness. It is not, as those unfamiliar with it sometimes assume, a process of emptying your mind. That would be impossible! Meditation is rather a means of refining your focus so that you gradually exclude disruptions and interruptions. There are many ways to meditate and many purposes for meditating; here, we'll just look at meditation as a means of connecting with spirits.

Remember the "Meet Your Spirit Guides" exercise from Chapter 7? That is a form of meditation. In that exercise, you used your mind to place yourself in a receptive mode. You did this by focusing on specific details: sitting on a bench, looking at and smelling flowers, watching your Spirit guide approach. The more you focused on these details, the more specific they became and the less aware you were of the endless other activities of your thoughts, memories, brain, and body functions. You were able to go within yourself to use your inner senses (your psychical senses) to experience energy perceptions from beyond the Earth plane.

Trance

A trance is a state of suspended consciousness into which a medium enters to allow spirits to communicate through them. When this happens, the medium's spirit steps aside to let the visiting spirit "borrow" some of the medium's physical abilities, such as speech. A medium in trance state might also take on the physical mannerisms and gestures of the visiting spirit, seeming to become the spirit's personification.

This is a shared experience between the medium's spirit and the visiting spirit. The visiting spirit cannot make the medium do or say anything they do not want to do or say, nor has the spirit any interest in trying to do so. Visiting spirits come through with messages that they want to convey to us here on the Earth plane—scaring the daylights out of us isn't going to do much for their credibility!

An experienced medium can control both entering and emerging from the trance state. An inexperienced medium might find that a visiting spirit wants to stay a little longer, like a child who doesn't want to leave an amusement park even though it's closing time. After all, visiting spirits enjoy their contacts with us, and some are reluctant to give up center stage! This, again, is why it's so essential to establish your intent for communication from Spirit to come through in light and for the highest good. Experienced mediums have made their limits clear, which sets the boundaries for the visiting spirit's stay.

Dreams

"In Xanadu did Kubla Khan, a stately pleasure dome decree." And so begins William Taylor Coleridge's haunting poem, "Kubla Khan: Or, A Vision in a Dream." The story goes that the poet had fallen asleep and experienced his marvelous poetic vision whole and complete. But, being disturbed from his sleep for a visitor (an Earthly one!), he could only rouse to fragments of his exquisite vision. These remain as Coleridge's famous work. In the dream state, your conscious mind retreats and releases its control and censorship of the activities of your brain. This frees the mind to experience perceptions that would otherwise be blocked. Hopefully, upon waking, you, unlike Coleridge, will preserve your dream vision intact.

The brain, as the physical organ that interprets the vast range of perceptions you experience, is particularly receptive to mediumistic messages during the dream state. Rita often finds that messages from Spirit come to her in the dream state. Although she has established a restriction around spirits waking her from sleep unless absolutely necessary, she frequently awakens with the realization that she's received spirit messages.

Sometimes spirit messages have the appearance of dreams. For example, you might wake up with images of visiting with your mother who has passed and feel as though you "lived" the scenario in your dream. The dreamscape might be a presentation of an actual setting or event from when your mother was alive on the Earth plane and the two of you went somewhere or did something together. This might feel to you like a dream-memory—reliving in your dreams a favorite memory from your life. Or your dreamscape might be someplace fantastical, magical, mystical—clearly not a setting you've ever experienced in your tangible life.

Keeping a journal is an effective way to explore your dreams and messages from Spirit that come to you through dreams or in the dream state. Keep a pad and pencil next to your bed, and write down the images and feelings that are present when you wake up. Later, when you have the time and the opportunity to explore these impressions, write about what you think they mean.

One helpful technique is *free association*. From the notes you wrote about your dream experiences, make a list of what appear to be key words or concepts. Beside each word, write the first thoughts that come to you. Don't let your conscious mind censor this process! Just let the thoughts and images flow. Give yourself 30 seconds to a minute for each, and then move to the next. You don't want to be thinking and analyzing, just reacting.

See Chapter 17 for more about dreams, including special dream states such as lucid dreaming and astral travel.

Transcending Boundaries

One of the most exciting aspects of developing your physical, psychic, and psychical senses is that it expands your awareness of the experiences that are your life. This brings a fullness and richness to your life, like seeing a black-and-white photograph become full color. It can put you in touch with your mission in this life, make you laugh (and make you cry), help you understand why certain things happen, and connect you with loved ones who are important to you in a continuing affirmation of the continuity of life.

CHAPTER
15

Telepathic Bridges

Your mind is a powerful tool. As a bridge between your thoughts and your spirit, it converts energy into images, memories, and articulations. You can't see your mind, although certainly, you can show it! Scientists have explored the workings of the mind for decades. Researchers have identified brain structures called *polypeptides* that conduct the energy impulses we identify as the mind's functions, activating the brain cells that translate the impulses into perceptions. Polypeptides help make proteins by bonding various amino acids together, forming chains of amino acids folded into the shape of specific proteins.

Telepathy comes from Greek words meaning "far feeling." Sometimes called thought transference, it is a process of exchanging energy to communicate, rather than using physical senses. When telepathy takes place between mortal human beings, it's a psychic skill.

Children are known to have high sensory processing sensitivity (SPS), as do 5 to 20 percent of adults. SPS is a personality trait that indicates a highly sensitive person. Just as children are sensitive people, they have strong telepathic capabilities and innate awareness of the presence of Spirit. The unspoken Divine communication between mother and newborn child can be remarkable to observe. Even more amazing is a mother's sudden recognition, without physical evidence and often when her child is nowhere in sight, that something is wrong. (This ability is confirmed, no matter the age of the child.) Every family album has its collection of in-the-nick-of-time, mom-appears-out-of-the-blue rescue stories.

A step beyond empathy and compassion, telepathy is the power to communicate directly (both sending and receiving messages) with another through thought. You could say that empathy and compassion (postulated to reside in the body's vagus nerve) empower telepathy.

Read My Mind!

Scientists tell us that, at most, we use about 10 percent of our mental capacity. That leaves quite a lot of ability untapped! Surely, all those gray cells aren't just hanging around waiting for electrical impulses to stimulate them. Those brain cells might already be hard at work, and you just don't know it.

How often does something like this happen to you:

- You're taking a walk with a friend from the chorus, and you both start spontaneously to sing the same song lyric—and it's not from a piece you're learning for the seasonal concert.

- You're talking on the phone with your brother, and you say what he is thinking, often with the jarring effect of non sequitur mixed with *how did you know that?*

- You stop by your sister's house to drop off the jacket you borrowed just as she's texting to tell you she needs it back.

- Your spouse stops at the bakery on the way home from work and spontaneously picks up a blueberry pie thinking it might be a "nice sweet treat," while you took a break from at-home schooling that same afternoon to bake a blueberry pie spontaneously with the girls as a "nice sweet treat" for dad.

- You pick up the phone to call your mother just as she was about to call you.

- You're walking past Rockefeller Plaza on Fifth Avenue in New York City, in a sea of city dwellers, flaneurs, and tourists all making their way up and down the sidewalk. In a prescient dance, the city dwellers and flaneurs move to anticipate each other's every step, making steady graceful progress without impeding one another or even touching. The tourists, however, are no NYC walking dancers as they awkwardly sidestep or even stop, creating traffic jams in the middle of the sidewalk (and irritating even the most patient of New Yorkers).

All these situations could be examples of telepathy. Telepathy often occurs between two people who are emotionally connected to each other. The deeper the emotional bond, the more likely and frequent telepathic communication is. You think about an event or object, which intensifies its energy in your mind. Someone who is emotionally close to you picks up the signal because it's a change in the normal balance of energy between the two of you. And if you can make eye contact during a telepathic event, your mirror neurons kick in and stimulate empathetic feeling between you, strengthening the sense of understanding that's just *knowing*.

What about the last example in the list? This truly is a random event because the walkers don't know each other. But they're surely sending messages to each other that arise from the small but nonetheless present expectation about who should step aside. Each participant in the sidewalk dance picks up the energy signal the others send—and the signals happen to carry the same message intent. The tourists who miss the signal can't intuit the dance and present obstacles to the smooth flow on the sidewalk.

Was It a Dream?

The dream state is an environment in which you are particularly receptive to telepathic communication from other mortals as well as entities from Spirit. The filters of your conscious mind are asleep, so to speak. The dream state serves as a telepathic bridge, a communication connection that bypasses the physical senses.

You might awaken from a dream in which you've experienced telepathic communication confused about whether you dreamed the whole thing or whether it was real. It can be hard for you to tell but is often easy to confirm if the telepathic communication was with someone you know. Ask the other person who was in your dream if they had a similar dream. Sometimes it takes several days, weeks, or even months before you recognize the telepathic nature of a particular dream.

For example, a man with cancer—intending to pass at home in his own bed—was attended by his mother, his wife, and his daughter, all staying together in the family home. Sometime after his passing, the women discovered they had all shared some version of the same dream on the night of the man's passing. Each dreamed of the family's yearly vacation spot and events surrounding it. The three generations of women decided that the son, husband, and father they loved had also dreamt of this beloved location in the hours before his death.

Telepathic dreams can involve either incarnate (physical) or discarnate (Spirit) beings. If your dream involves communication with a being from Spirit, you can ask the spirit to visit you again. Spirits like to visit during your dream state for much the same reason: You're open to it. It's common to dream of a visit with a loved one who has passed and for you to share favorite experiences. If your mother loved flowers, she might come to you in your dreams and stroll with you through elaborate gardens.

Keeping a dream journal is an excellent way to learn how to understand your personal dream symbolism. The symbolic elements that show up in your dreams are likely the same ones that emerge when there is contact from Spirit for you. Dreams can provide insights and information that wouldn't come to you in any other way. You might even discover that your dreams are also the venues for spirits' visits. (See Chapter 17 for more about dreams.)

Psychic Prying: Stay Out!

So is your mind an open book? Are your thoughts available to anyone who chooses to peek at them? Certain thoughts are openly available if you are not taking any measures to protect them. These are the things moving across the surface of your consciousness. If someone said, "What are you thinking right now?" these are the thoughts you would mention.

It is unethical to attempt to perceive another person's thoughts without that person's knowledge and permission. It's like walking into someone's house without knocking or announcing yourself. This kind of "mind-reading" is intrusive and is seldom done with truly good intent.

You can protect yourself from being on the receiving end of psychic prying. Just establish a protection of light around your being. Envision this as a dome that covers you. Establish the intent that only those with whom you wish to communicate on a telepathic level can have access. This creates a shield around your thoughts.

It's Your Mind, and Only You Can Control It

Some people believe they can use their thoughts to control others. No one can control your thoughts or "will" you to do something you don't want to do. What a dangerous weapon this could be, were it possible! But even extensive government experiments during the Cold War era proved that it's not possible.

Various agencies of the United States and the former Soviet Union conducted telepathic communication and control tests in the 1960s and 1970s. Although psychically gifted test subjects scored high in extrasensory perception (ESP) tests such as perceiving the symbols on cards, they did no better than the odds of chance in using telepathy to "will" other subjects to some sort of action. Mind control over others is a tantalizing concept of science fiction, and so far, it remains in the realm of fiction rather than exposed in the arena of science. However, the ability to use digital technology to aid the human mind in performing actions of its own body, such as lifting a finger, through thought alone do exist and will one day emerge from the laboratory as treatment for those suffering spinal damage and other neurological conditions.

Crisis Contact

Many people experience telepathic communication in times of crisis. One friend suddenly perceives that another friend has been in a car accident. A sister living on the West Coast gets a sense of panic about her brother living in the Southeast, then hears on the news that a tornado swept through the town where he lives.

Energy intensifies in times of crisis. When bonds already exist between people, rapid spikes in energy intensity send a psychic alert. Sometimes more than two people are involved in the telepathic communication. For example, this could happen when a crisis involves a parent and their children, and each of them experiences some form of connection as a result. Every person's individual experience can be different.

Sometimes crisis telepathy presents itself as a warning, a connection of intuition that is sent directly from one person to another without conscious intervention of the mind. You might not even realize that you've sent a telepathic warning to someone until that person texts, calls, or otherwise contacts you.

Validating Telepathy

The first formal efforts to analyze telepathic experiences and understand the processes of telepathy took place in the 1880s when the Society for Psychical Research in London began publishing reports about the phenomenon in its journals. As the circulation for those journals grew, so did interest around the world. In these early explorations, researchers used the term extrasensory perception (ESP) to describe the ability to communicate without using the physical senses.

Sir Arthur Explores Thought Transference

Sir Arthur Conan Doyle, author of the Sherlock Holmes detective novels and an early member of the Spiritualist movement (see Chapter 3), was fascinated with what was at the time called *thought transference*. He and an architect friend in another location decided to see how well and how much faster they could communicate architectural ideas and drawings by thought than they could through the process of writing and mailing their ideas to each other. They agreed that at a specified time every week, each would sit down and sketch his ideas, then concentrate on sending the images to the other. They would then switch and focus on receiving the images the other was sending and sketch those.

They were on target with each other far more frequently than the odds of chance, and Doyle became convinced of the scientific validity of telepathic communication. He later continued some of his studies through the Society for Psychical Research and published many of his writings on the topic.

J. B. Rhine and Zener Cards

In 1930, an American parapsychologist, J. B. (Joseph Banks) Rhine (1895–1980) of Duke University, began conducting experiments following scientific research conventions. A parapsychologist is a scientist who studies psychic phenomena. The word parapsychology means "study of what is around the mind." At first, Rhine used common items to test the ability of subjects to send and receive messages telepathically. Among them was an ordinary deck of playing cards.

Then a colleague and fellow parapsychologist, Karl Zener, developed the set of special cards, known today as Zener cards, with five symbols: red cross, blue waves, black square, orange circle, and green star. The deck contains 25 cards, 5 of each symbol. The odds of randomly guessing the correct symbol are one in five.

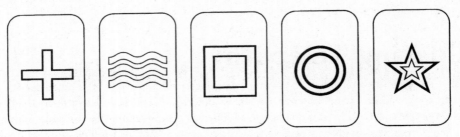

In color, the Zener cards show a red cross, blue waves, black square, orange circle, and green star.
You can use marker and cardboard stock to make your own Zener cards.

In early tests, subjects sat across a table from each other. One subject turned up a card, holding it so the other subject couldn't see it, and concentrated on sending a mental image of the card's symbol to the other subject. The other subject then said what they thought the symbol was.

A score of 20 percent right is the baseline because this is the number of correct answers likely just on the basis of the odds. Scores higher than 20 percent suggest telepathic ability on the part of one or both subjects. More important, high scores validate that telepathy is a real and observable phenomenon. Because of their simplicity and consistency, Zener cards have become a standard for telepathic training and testing.

Later experiments put the two subjects in separate rooms so they couldn't see or hear each other or in any other way use their physical senses to communicate. This came in response to criticism that subjects could give each other subtle signals that tipped off which cards were being turned over. Separation didn't change the results.

Parapsychologist J. B. Rhine was inspired to study psychic phenomena by Sir Arthur Conan Doyle's studies in thought transference. Ironically, Rhine earned Doyle's ire later in his life for exposing as a fraud a medium that Doyle respected. You can use Zener cards to improve your personal telepathic abilities. They are available at many metaphysical shops and bookstores. Practice working with a friend to send as well as receive card images. Telepathy is like any other skill. The more you use it, the more proficient you become.

Early in Rita's psychic development, her friend Judy became convinced of Rita's telepathic abilities, but Rita still felt unsure. So Judy and Rita agreed that, as a test, they would both meditate at 10 P.M. on a Friday to see if they could communicate telepathically. Rita would then call Judy at 10:20 P.M.

At 10 P.M., Rita began to meditate and set her intent on visiting her friend Judy. When she went into meditation, she could clearly see Judy's apartment. She saw Judy sitting on the left corner of the couch, wearing a geometric print caftan. Rita saw an incredible white glow around Judy.

When Rita called Judy at 10:20 P.M. and described to Judy what she had seen, Judy was delighted. In fact, she was sitting in the corner of the couch wearing that geometric caftan. "I'm glad you could see the glow around me as I was meditating," Judy told Rita. Rita "visited" Judy telepathically, just as vividly as if they'd been physically sitting in the room together.

Sharpen Your Telepathic Skills

Do you have a friend who is as interested in telepathy as you are? Here's an exercise that the two of you can do together to practice and sharpen your telepathic skills.

1. Determine a time at which you will sit down to meditate, each in your separate locations. Determine how long your meditation will last (10 minutes is good). Use one half of this time to send and one half to receive a message. (Make sure your times are opposite so that one of you receives when the other sends!) Use a timer to signal the end of each time period.

2. At the agreed-upon time, begin your meditation. Ask for the meditation to proceed in goodness and light. Start with three deep, cleansing breaths.

3. Concentrate on sending a message to your friend. Perceive the message in whatever way feels comfortable to you, but stick with a single representation.

4. When the sending time is up, take three cleansing breaths and shift to receive mode. Concentrate on opening your mind to the message your friend is sending.

5. When the meditation time is up, bring yourself back to the context of your physical environment.

6. Write down everything you can remember about the experience. On one side of a piece of paper, write the messages you were trying to send to your friend. On the other side, write the messages you think you received from your friend.

7. Phone or visit each other to compare experiences. How often were you right? When you were wrong, were you off in consistent ways, such as perceiving yellow when your friend sent you the color orange?

Generally speaking, if you are on target more often than not, you've exceeded the odds of chance. The greater the gap between on and off, the more intense the telepathic experience. Don't be discouraged if at first, you barely hit the odds of chance (or even are below them). You will improve with practice! As you become more proficient, make your messages more complex.

Telekinesis: Use Telepathy to Move Objects

Telekinesis (also called psychokinesis) is the phenomenon of using the mind's energy to move objects without physical intervention. Perhaps the most famous demonstrations of telekinesis came in the 1970s when a young psychic from Russia named Uri Geller came to prominence for his ability to bend spoons and other metal objects without any physical contact.

How does this work? One theory is that the concentration of energy from your mind alters the energy structure of the object you're focusing on. At the point when you release your mind's stream of energy, the object re-forms itself according to the energy pattern you've been sending. If you've sent bending, the spoon bends. If you've sent twisting, it twists.

You can practice telekinesis in a kinder, gentler way. All you need is a twenty-five-cent piece. If you toss a quarter ten times, your odds of calling whether it lands heads or tails are about 50-50. There are only two choices, which keep the experiment simple. Calling heads or tails correctly more times than not demonstrates telepathic ability—you are "reading" the energy of the coin to identify which side is up.

Directing the coin to land either heads or tails demonstrates telekinetic ability. You are using the energy of your mind to guide the coin's fall in a determined way. Go ahead, practice! When you get good with the coin, move on to a pair of dice, or you can use just one die to keep it a little less complicated. Just be sure that you focus on sending energy to direct the number at which the roll will stop rather than trying to determine the number. A fine point, but it's the point of distinction between telepathy and telekinesis in this context.

Astral Projection

Astral projection is the phenomenon of your spirit leaving your body to travel beyond it. You might call this psychic visiting. Sometimes it happens spontaneously. You might have a flash image of a friend working at her desk, and then call and tell her what she's wearing or what she's doing. You also can cultivate this psychic skill through practice. Astral projection is a conscious form of telepathic visitation. You are deciding to "visit" another person or place. Telepathic communication can happen without a conscious effort, such as crisis telepathy.

Here are two exercises that you can use to practice astral projection. As always, when working with Spirit phenomena, start each exercise by asking for goodness and light. Even though you're not asking for contact with Spirit with astral projection, you are connecting your spirit with cosmic life force energy when your spirit leaves your physical body.

How is it that your soul can travel about and then know to return to your physical body? Doesn't it seem that the freedom of *not* having a body would be quite enticing? You have an energy umbilical cord, so to speak, that links your spirit with your body for as long as your body lives. It's called the silver cord.

This is not a tangible or physical connection; instead, it is a link of energy. Your silver cord keeps your body and your spirit connected, no matter what your state of consciousness. It is said that your silver cord appears at physical birth and disappears at physical death.

Astral Projection Exercise for Two

This exercise requires two people. Choose someone you trust who shares your interest in astral projection. As in the telepathy exercise, both of you should be in different, undisclosed physical locations.

1. Determine a time at which you will each meditate and for how long (five minutes is good). Use a timer, so you know when your time is up.

2. At the agreed-upon time, begin your meditation. Ask for the meditation to proceed in goodness and light. Start with three deep, cleansing breaths.

3. Concentrate on your friend. Release your mind to travel to your friend's undisclosed location.

4. What can you hear? What can you see? What can you feel? What is your friend doing? What is your friend wearing?

5. When the meditation time is up, bring yourself back to the context of your physical environment.

6. Write down everything you can remember about what you experienced—sights, sounds, smells, even tastes.

7. Call or visit your friend to share experiences.

Astral Projection Exercise: Solo

This is an exercise you can do by yourself.

1. Sit where you are comfortable, and there are no distractions. Determine the length of time you want to meditate (or let the meditation run its own course, which you can do because you are alone in this exercise).

2. Begin your meditation. Ask for the meditation to proceed in goodness and light. Start with three deep, cleansing breaths.

3. Focus on letting your spirit go to sit across from you so that you can see it.

4. Through your spirit, see your physical self.

5. What do you see? Is the experience similar to looking in a mirror? If not, how is it different?

6. When your meditation is over, bring yourself gently back to your physical environment.

How completely were you able to leave your body? How did you feel during the experience? How do you feel about it now?

The first time Rita tried the solo astral projection exercise, she chose to sit outside on her deck. Because the day felt a bit chilly, she wore a vest. She projected out okay, but then all she could see was the color yellow. So she went back into her body and asked, "What am I doing wrong?" The response came back: "Sitting too close!" Rita had projected her spirit from her body, but only slightly—all she could see was the yellow of her vest! She did the exercise again, and this time sat across the deck from herself.

What's Spirit Got to Do with It?

When telepathic communication takes place between a physical being (like you) and an entity from Spirit, it becomes spirit communication. Most mediums don't use the term telepathy in reference to communication with spirits because usually spirit communication takes place using more specific and sophisticated methods, such as clairaudience and clairvoyance. These psychical methods give more extensive information.

Telepathy between human beings can forge an intensely beautiful connection linking souls directly through universal life force energy. A successful telepathic relationship builds upon already nurturing levels of empathy and compassion shared between you. Even as mirror neurons twin behaviors, a couple feels the bond of two becoming as one. The closer we are to each other, the closer we come to Spirit.

We're thinking of a telepathic bond as strong as the one between Charlotte Bronte's Jane Eyre and her Byronic hero, Mr. Rochester. Mr. Rochester's anguished calls for Jane across the moors reached her ears telepathically and drew her inexorably to him. And yes, reader, she married him.

Psychometry: Objects and Places Hold Energy

Places and objects hold residual energy from the souls that come in contact with them as energy imprints. Sometimes the sense of this is strong, as when you touch an oil lamp in an antique store and the image of a pioneer woman reading beneath its light flashes through your awareness. Sometimes the sense is weak, as when you feel a slight tingle at holding your grandmother's favorite button tin in your hands. Psychometric ability can turn places and objects into links between this world and the Higher side.

When you take a photograph with an analog camera, fragments of light interact with the molecules that form the film's surface to take shape as visual images. The film—or the negatives processed from it—contain those fragments, those bits and pieces of energy, virtually indefinitely (well, at least as long as the film remains intact and undamaged). As many times as you want, you can develop pictures from that film. You can look at these pictures, again and again, the representations of energy that you've captured on paper.

Spirit energy is like light energy in that it alters surfaces that it contacts. It interacts with the molecules that form those surfaces, leaving virtually indelible fragments. When "developed" through psychic expression, these fragments present images. Rather than taking visual shapes, like pictures, these energy imprints can take many forms. But unlike pictures, these energy imprints are dynamic. That is to say, every new energy contact with them (such as you picking up the object that holds them) can evoke something different. You get something like a metaphysical slide show (although the images are not always visual).

Energy Imprints

Whatever you touch, you leave a little of yourself behind. From a physical perspective, you leave molecules of scent and skin oils. These are the substances that tracking dogs can detect. (A dog's nose is so sensitive to smell, it can "read" just a few molecules.) You might also leave fingerprints, skin cells, and DNA (microscopic fragments of your genetic coding). These are the substances that high-tech detective methods can retrieve and use to identify you. Solid surfaces such as desktops, doorknobs, and windows are likely to collect more of these physical tracings from your touch.

You also leave energy molecules. These are intangible and undetectable by physical means. Energy imprints are often micro-vignettes that capture and store representations based in emotion. In touching the object, you might feel a flash of joy or sadness. You might see, fleetingly in your mind's eye, the image of a baby's birth or the gathering at a funeral. The stronger the emotional connection, the more intense the energy imprint … and the more vivid the energy "replay" that occurs.

The more often you touch an object, the more of your energy it retains. Items worn often and close to the body, such as wedding rings and favorite clothing, retain high levels of energy. Items you infrequently touch, such as silverware or jewelry you wear just once a year, typically retain low levels of energy.

An object you touch infrequently can hold a lot of residual energy if the only times you touch it are emotionally intense. Suppose the jewelry you wear once a year is the necklace and earrings you wore at your wedding and now wear when you celebrate your anniversary. In that case, it's going to hold much more energy than if it's a bracelet you bought on a whim and only occasionally wear because you feel guilty about leaving it sit in your jewelry box. Because people pray with them, holding prayer through touch, rosary beads often contain strong personal energy.

Capturing Energy Imprints on Film

In 1939, Seymon Kirlian, a Russian electrician by trade and inventor by avocation, discovered that when he took pictures of his hand, the developed photographs often showed a glow around his fingers—his hand's energy field. One of the most famous examples of *Kirlian photography* came from the University of California Center for Health Science, showing the glowing photographic image of a full leaf, although the leaf in the picture had a piece ripped off. The leaf's energy field completed its image, even though the leaf was no longer intact. Kirlian photography is a process of taking pictures in which the photo shows the object and its energy field.

Since its inception, Kirlian photography has evolved in various technological directions, some of which use electrical equipment rather than cameras to capture images of energy. Currently, researchers are exploring ways to apply Kirlian photography to medical diagnosis and treatment. Doctors have long known that the body's energy composition changes in illness. Whether you look at these changes as physiological—the outcome of biochemical changes within the body— or spiritual, they are verifiable. Researchers hope that someday Kirlian technology will present energy images that can monitor the progress of treatment for serious diseases like cancer and heart disease.

The Things They Carried

Book critic Michiko Kakutani in *The New York Times* wrote this about National Book Award-winning author Tim O'Brien's classic book of stories about the Vietnam War, The Things They Carried: "In prose that combines the sharp, unsentimental rhythms of Hemingway with gentler, more lyrical descriptions, Mr. O'Brien gives the reader a shockingly visceral sense of what it felt like to tramp through a booby-trapped jungle, carrying 20 pounds of supplies, 14 pounds of ammunition, along with radios, machine guns, assault rifles, and grenades...." Psychometry, the study of energy imprints on objects, becomes the metaphorical lens O'Brien, an American war veteran, uses to deconstruct the imprint of the war on the men who fought it through telling stories about, literally, the things they wore and carried.

Intuitively, we know that our possessions become imbued and endowed with the force of the events surrounding their use and the life force of the human being(s) who possessed and used them. Of course, this would be so and is only natural. After all, all matter is energy. It was eighteenth-century scientist Antoine Lavoisier who discovered the Law of Conservation of Mass (1789), stating that mass can neither be created nor destroyed … but only change its form, and so the manner in which it behaves. Just as matter continually changes its form energetically, so is the constant nature of change the hallmark of life itself, of our *human* experience. Our energy imprints upon the things we use and carry, creating a kind of real-time life force energy stamp upon them, which is intuitively accessible to anyone who touches them. That energy imprint is preserved in the very particles that make up the Universe, such that the Universe itself carries the energy imprint of all things. Our bodies, as we know them, are stardust. That ancient power lies within us, and around us, every moment of life.

The Artifacts of Remembrance

On April 6, 2021, the editors of *The New York Times* published in its special series "Those They've Lost" a virtual memorial including photographs of objects reminding those in grief of their beloved ones who passed in 2020 of the coronavirus, or of other causes. Because of the unique nature of grieving during the COVID-19 Pandemic, and that loved ones have not been able to celebrate a lost one's memory in traditional ways, the virtual memorial is meant to serve as a way to honor and acknowledge the collective scope of society's losses. The virtual memorial tells the stories of grief by telling the stories of a person's most beloved possessions. Readers can click on a library of images and uncover an interview about that object and the life associated with it.

Without saying so, the virtual memorial is a psychometric catalog of energy imprints, an acknowledgment that the life force energy of those who've passed to Spirit leaves its mark upon not just upon treasured objects but upon the loved ones who carry out the sacred rituals of remembering in their hearts. Everything from a thimble to a prayer shawl, a figurine, a book, an old sandwich box, eyeglasses, an incense burner, a music box, a vanity set, even a simple sweater, build a sense of endearment and expresses a tangible need to hold onto *the things they carried*.

Our life force energy continues in the objects we love and use long after we have passed to Spirit. This fact can provide great comfort as we grieve. As we feel them, we access psychometric snapshots of memory and character. And this is true whether or not we are consciously aware of the energy the objects carry or whether we have developed our psychical skills to be able to discover objects' psychometric memories.

Take a moment to choose and hold a beloved possession from your own life—a wedding ring, perhaps, a book, a pair of shoes maybe. Hold that object and call to mind the memories it evokes. Is the object associated with memories of a special place or person(s)? Spend some time in meditation with the object and register the emotions it arouses within you. Before you restore the object to its pride of place and continue on with your day, hold the object next to your heart (if its size permits … we know you can't lift that old Chevy Vega hatchback). Consciously endow the beloved object with the energetic real-time stamp of your essence. Pray for the highest and best for loved ones who, even now, look for you when they also look at or handle this beloved object.

Repeat this process with an object that you hold onto from a dear one who has passed to Spirit. When you hold your loved one's treasured object, what emotions are aroused within you? What images are called to mind? And are these images corresponding to your own remembrances of your loved one, or do they seem to correspond to your loved one's memories and experiences using the object? What memories might you attribute to the imagination, and what might be a calling forth of psychometric energy held by the object?

The more skill you acquire in acknowledging psychometric energy, the more compassion and empathy you will develop for our shared humanity and the real-time force of that energy that makes up every particle of the Divine Universe. Remember the words of twentieth-century American poet Stanley Kunitz who mused that the Universe is a web—touch it at any point, and it quivers.

How Do Objects Retain Energy?

Any object that you touch, however casually, will hold at least a little of your energy. Some objects hold energy longer than others. Generally, the more solid or dense the object, the longer it retains energy imprints. Metals, jewelry, and even items such as pottery or crystal can hold a person's energy over generations of time. But even fabric, books, papers, and other more fragile objects can retain energy for surprisingly long periods of time—perhaps however long is necessary for the object to convey its energy messages to the person who needs to receive them.

Metals

The physical structure of any metal is very dense. As a result, it holds energy for a long, long time. Rita remembers Ann, whose grandfather, a firefighter, died in the line of duty fighting a fire when Ann was just four years old. Ann had been the last person in the family, other than her grandmother, of course, to speak to him that fateful day. Many years later, as Ann prepared to sell the house where her grandparents had lived, she came across an envelope pushed to the back of a bureau drawer. Inside the envelope, she found the belongings her grandfather had carried on his person the day he died.

When Ann picked up her grandfather's keys, she felt a tingling, almost like an electrical charge, and remembered herself as a four-year-old, sitting on her grandfather's lap. Image after image of her grandfather and his life flashed through Ann's inner vision, including his last moments in the fire. All these years, these keys retained his energy, and now, 40 years after his death, that energy surged as a gift connecting Ann with her grandfather.

Objects like keys and jewelry retain great amounts of energy, not only because they're metal but also because they're usually in daily contact with whoever uses or wears them. Every morning after putting on his firefighter's uniform, Ann's grandfather took his ring of keys from the top of the bureau and put them in his pants pocket. He carried the keys there, close against his body, reaching for them occasionally, his thumb and forefinger rubbing the medal of the Virgin Mary he hung on the ring for protection until he came home again after his shift and replaced them on the bureau.

Those keys collected energy from every experience Ann's grandfather had all through each day, compiling a virtual energy record of his life. They recorded the energy trail of his life and of his passing. At his death, Ann's father sealed the keys in an envelope and the envelope was stored away by Ann's grandmother, where they stayed until Ann found them. The envelope helped to contain the energy imprints the keys held. And each time Ann touched the keys, she experienced a different perception of her grandfather. Ann carries the keys with her now, and her grandfather's energy walks with her.

Jewelry of emotional significance, particularly wedding rings, also stores significant energy. Part of this comes from the intensity of emotion of the jewelry's first use, and part of it comes from the everyday contact the jewelry experiences. All the joy and sadness, success and disappointment, calm and outburst … these emotions that are the expressions of life become attached to possessions such as jewelry in the same way that electromagnetic energy becomes embedded in a digital recording.

To replay a digital recording, you need a compatible machine. But to "replay" energy imprints, all you need is to tune into your psychical sensitivities! Holding your dad's watch or your great-grandmother's ring could bring forth a flood of energy experiences.

When Rita was in her first psychical development class, another student, a young man, brought a bottle cap. It was a simple, plain, Coors beer bottle cap. He asked for someone to psychometrize this. Two students tried and couldn't get anything, and then the teacher handed the bottle cap to Rita. As she held the bottle cap in her hands, Rita saw a vision of being in the woods and then saw a very, very dark place with a pool of water in it. Although it embarrassed her to say the words out loud, she said to the young man and the class, "I see funny-looking men in yellow suits!"

The young man laughed. He had been up in the New Hampshire woods and had gone caving with his friends. They had gone into a cave that had a big pool of water inside. In the pool, left behind by other cavers, was a bottle of Coors chilling in the frigid water. The four young men shared the bottle and brought back the bottle cap. They were all wearing yellow neoprene suits!

Furnishings

Where do you spend the most time when you are in your home? You might say the living room or the kitchen or even the bedroom (as we spend a third of our lives sleeping). And none of these answers is wrong. But in truth, the most extensive interaction you have with your home is actually with your furnishings.

A good number of furnishings are nothing more than functional, of course. You use them and then put them at the curb for recycling or disposal after they wear out. Some furnishings, however, become family heirlooms. Through the years, they take on emotional and historical significance. The delicate china tea set a distant cousin carried home from a trip to the Far East … by sailing ship. The marble-top dressers that Great-Great-Grandfather Pete carved as a 14-year-old apprentice the year the American Civil War ended. And even the handprint of your daughter, from when she was three years old, now frozen in plaster of Paris and hanging in a frame on the wall.

The objects of our daily lives pick up considerable energy. How long and to what extent how strongly they hold onto that energy depends on the object's use and the number of people who use it. Deb was in an antique store when she rested her hand lightly on top of a small table. Like a flash, she saw the image of a Victorian-era woman, dressed in a long, dark skirt and a white blouse with a high, buttoned collar and long sleeves. The woman's dark hair was pulled back and wrapped around her head.

At first, Deb thought the vision was a spirit, but it remained still, like a photograph. When Deb lifted her hand from the table, the image disappeared. When she touched the table again, this time in a slightly different place, the woman's image reappeared. But this time, the woman sat in a chair beside the table, holding some sewing or embroidery in her hands. Each time Deb touched a different place on the table, a different image of the same woman appeared.

The shop's proprietor noticed Deb's apparent interest in the table and told Deb that it had just come into the store earlier that week. The woman who had owned it had recently died. The family held an estate sale, and the table had been among the items that didn't sell. It was a lovely piece that had been in the family for several generations, the proprietor said. The woman would sit for hours at the table, which stood in front of her living room window, sewing or reading.

Many people with highly refined psychic or mediumistic abilities might find it difficult to be around antiques. Antiques are often treasured family heirlooms, passed down through generations of family members. They can retain many energy imprints, which can present a flood of images and information to someone who is receptive.

Fabric and Clothing

When a tracking dog is about to set out in pursuit, its handlers try to have the dog smell an item belonging to the missing person. An item of clothing that has not been washed since the person last wore it is ideal because it captures and holds the person's individual scent. The more contact with the cloth, the stronger the scent signals the dog can read. The dog then searches for matching signals, following them until the trail runs out or the dog finds further evidence of the person or finds the person.

Fabric can hold energy imprints for long periods of time, too, and for much longer than it holds a scent. Dresses, scarves, hats, and similar items that end up stored in trunks in attics for years and even decades hold tight to the energy imprints they've collected. Pull such an item from its sanctuary, and those imprints might seem to float out, just like dust particles.

The rise of consignment sites and apps selling and sometimes even renting upcycled or vintage clothing, shoes, and accessories speaks to the appeal that quality, affordable clothing has. But it also speaks to the psychometric energy held by the things we wear and the shared humanity of a piece of clothing that's had more than one owner. Collections of antique textiles and clothing from previous eras are increasingly valued by museums and college archive collections, many of which have been digitized to view online. As curators know, styles may change, but fashion is timeless. Wearing vintage acknowledges the Divine life force energy held by the clothing we wear. And honors the life force energy that we pass on to the next owner, who will treasure and delight that vintage 1980s cocktail dress we wore to the Palladium in Manhattan. When you hold the dress's fabric between your fingers, can't you feel the music? Sweet echoes resonating through time.

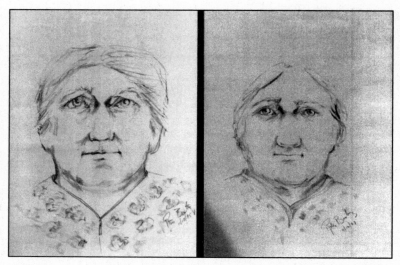

Bonnie came to see Rita at the First Spiritualist Church of Quincy in September 1995. During the sitting, a drawing came through of her grandmother, Margaret. Bonnie recognized the face immediately, with delight. Two years later, in April 1997, Bonnie's daughter, Aileen, came to Rita for a spirit drawing, and the same woman wearing the same housedress appeared on the paper.

In one of Rita's classes she teaches at the Spiritualist church, she asked her students to bring items to practice psychometry readings. One student brought his most treasured possession, a woolen New York Yankees baseball cap. He handed it to Rita and said, "Here, see what you get from this."

Rita held the cap in her hands and felt the most incredible adrenaline rush of her life! She had the impression of being on the baseball diamond, looking out at the pitcher. Her heart was pounding, and her hands were sweating. She described these responses to the student, who was tickled. The cap, he said, had belonged to a former New York Yankees catcher! What Rita "read" from the cap was the experience of the catcher crouched behind the batter during the high excitement of a baseball game.

Paper and Vinyl

Paper and vinyl—do you understand the code? "Paper and vinyl" translates to "books and music." In an age of e-books and digital playlists, many people, especially younger generations, are still enthralled to the bound book and the vinyl album as their preferred way to read and to listen. Hand bookbinding and letterpress are still thriving artisanal methods for quality bookmaking. But even if you are reading a manufactured book, the act of reading a book is a distinctly *physical* experience. How you sit, your comfort and concentration, the weight of the book in your hands, and the turning of pages all impact the way you receive the story.

The same goes for "listening to records." The physicality of the turntable, sitting (or dancing) in proximity to the turntable, and the variable sound quality all impact your experience of listening to the music. With vinyl, the bespoke quality of performance is enhanced by the capture of real musicians playing in a unique studio setting. A record like The Beach Boys' "Pet Sounds" is a great example of a bespoke studio sound. Digitally enhanced recordings lose much of the immediacy and the humanity of live studio recordings to vinyl.

Whether you're reading a library book or a used book that's passed from hand to hand, from eye to eye, or you're browsing through a used record store, flipping through the stacks of recordings, you're picking up on the psychometric energy of these objects. You're contributing a bit of your own life force energy as well. (And we love the things people leave in books inadvertently. Receipts, tickets, cards, and paper are all ephemera of a life experienced while carrying that book.)

Picking Up the Trail

Psychics who work with police to find missing people read the energy imprints of objects connected to the missing person. These energy vibrations become a trail the psychic can follow, providing details about the person's fate that police have been unable to determine based on physical evidence. Often, a psychic working in this capacity can hold an object from a crime scene and describe information about the person who committed the crime.

Psychics have been involved in many famous crime investigations, including a 1940 case involving the murders of three civil rights workers in Mississippi, the disappearance of Patty Hearst, and the search for victims of mass murderer John Wayne Gacy in the late 1970s.

Rita has been involved in a number of missing persons situations. In one, a 14-year-old girl had disappeared. A friend of the girl's mother knew of Rita's work and called Rita to see if she could help. The girl had been missing since Friday evening, and it was Sunday afternoon when Rita got the call.

The family feared the girl had been abducted. Her hairbrush was still on her dresser, and the girl never went anywhere without it. So Rita asked if she could hold the brush. As soon as she took the brush into her hands, Rita knew the girl was safe and fine. "She's at a house just south of route 37, the house of somebody she knows," Rita said. "I'm seeing three brick steps going up to the front door and a storm door with the initial 'K' or 'R' on it."

Later that evening, Rita got a phone call. The girl had been found, safe and a little embarrassed, at the house of a friend—you guessed it—just south of route 37, with three brick steps going up to the front door and a "K" on the storm door! The girl had gone to spend the weekend with her friend, thinking her mother knew of the plans.

Develop Your Psychometry Skills

You have countless opportunities to practice and develop your psychometry skills. Here are two exercises to get you started. The first is a structured meditation; the second is an exercise of opportunity.

Exercise: Reading Familiar Energy

For this exercise, you need the help of a friend. Ask the friend to bring a small object they wear frequently, such as a watch, a piece of jewelry, or a scarf. Also, ask your friend for permission to do an energy reading from this object. Don't look at the object. Make yourself comfortable where you aren't going to have interruptions, and ask your friend to join you.

1. Take three cleansing breaths, and ask that your energy meditation proceed in goodness and light, for the best intent.

2. Close your eyes and ask your friend to place the object in your palm. Feel its weight, its pressure against your skin. Feel whether the object is light or heavy, cool or warm, and dense or soft. Is it metal? Is it wood? Is it fabric?

3. Without trying to create a mental picture of the object, let its image form in your mind. Be open to any perceptions that occur, including visual images, sounds, smells, or tastes.

4. If you know what the object is, set that knowledge aside. Focus on receiving the object's energy. It might come to you in vignettes or flashes.

5. Describe to your friend what you're receiving. Don't attempt to filter or interpret the information in any way; just convey it.

6. If something about the energy imprint is unclear, form a question about it in your mind and wait for an answer. (It will come!)

7. When you feel the energy exchange is over, gently return to your normal state of consciousness. Become aware of your toes, your legs, your fingers, and your arms. Return the object to its owner.

It's most helpful to you in developing your psychometry skills if your friend is willing to discuss the possible meanings of the energy messages you received through the object. But understand they might not want to do this if these messages have evoked unexpected emotions. Psychometry, like other energy reading, can reveal deep meanings. As you become more comfortable with reading energy in this way, you can try reading objects from people you don't know quite as well.

Exercise: Reading Random Energy

As you go about the many activities of your daily life, look for opportunities to experience the energy imprints of objects around you. Although you won't get much feedback to confirm the accuracy of your perceptions, this exercise helps you make psychometric skills part of your everyday life. Here are some examples:

- Hold an apple in your hand. What does it taste like?

- Go into an antique store. Touch the first object that catches your attention. What do you feel?

- In a music store, touch or hold an old instrument (if the proprietor allows you to). Can you hear music or see the musician who once played it?

- Try on a vintage suit jacket, dress, or hat. What impressions come to mind? Are you comfortable wearing vintage?

- Go to a used bookstore. Walk until you reach a shelf that compels you to stop. Pass your hand slowly in front of the books on the shelf. Take down the book that seems to draw your hand to it. What is the title? Who is the author? What is the topic? Do these have any significance for you? Open the book. What is the copyright? Is there anything about the book that has special meaning?

- Walk slowly through the exhibits at a history museum. Stop at the first display that compels you to look closer. What is the exhibit? What do you feel, hear, see, sense?

As you can begin to understand, the potential for opportunities to use this exercise to develop your psychometric senses truly are unlimited!

Linking to Spirit Contact

Psychometry certainly has many applications in psychic contexts. But what about in contact with Spirit? Many mediums use psychometry to establish a link to a loved one on the Higher side. Handling an object imbued with the loved one's energy instantly signals other holders of the same energy—the loved one—to connect. It's like a cosmic search engine!

The contact established using psychometry as its bridge can be especially powerful and is very helpful when you want to contact a particular spirit entity. Often, this approach quickly establishes evidence of the continuity of life because it transitions from the tangible world to the Spirit world in a way that appears logical to us.

Sometimes the energy readings the medium gets from the object help direct questions the medium can ask of the spirit entity. This might provide direct information you are seeking or the information you need to have (even if you don't yet know that you need it).

When Jeanette came to Rita for a session, she brought a wedding ring with her. Rita took the ring and held it in her hands, and within moments a man came through from Spirit. Rita described the man in full detail, including physical characteristics and personality. "That's my father!" Jeanette said. Then Rita very clearly tasted chocolate-covered coconut and heard the father singing the commercial jingle, "Sometimes I feel like a nut, sometimes I don't!" Rita asked the woman, "Did your father ever bring you Mounds candy bars?" The woman laughed. "Absolutely!" she said. Spirit will always trigger information that's stored in your memory.

Spirit Presence, or Residual Energy?

Places retain energy, too. Locations are just collections of objects; a house has walls, floors, stairs, and other surfaces people contact all the time. Much of what people perceive as "haunting" is really not the presence of Spirit at all, but rather an energy imprint called residual energy, which captures and replays a significant event. Because such events typically have intense emotional connections, they are generally connected to a person (or people) and might have to do with some sort of trauma or tragedy.

It isn't always easy to determine whether presence of Spirit is genuine or residual because the same kinds of events can connect either to the physical world. Generally, an energy imprint doesn't involve any kind of interaction. Its presentation might change so that you have a different perception of the energy experiences that are retained. An experienced medium can tell whether the energy is active or residual.

Rita was asked to visit a home its owners, two adult sisters, believed was haunted. The sisters had not had pleasant childhoods in the house, and for many years as adults had been estranged from their parents. The women inherited the house after their mother and then father passed away, and they wanted to sell it. But every time they went into the house they were overcome with fear and left without venturing much further than the vestibule.

As Rita walked into the house, all seemed calm enough with no evidence the father's spirit was present. Rita did detect distinctive energies. Among them was the energy of a mentally disabled great-aunt who had lived with the family for a time. Hers was a confused but benevolent presence. Rita and the sisters prayed to help the great-aunt find her way to the Higher side, and her presence was gone.

As Rita continued walking through the house, she could feel the energy, sometimes intense, of childhood traumas the sisters had experienced at the hands of their abusive father. These traumas lingered as energy imprints that activated memories in the sisters. As soon as Rita explained this to the women, they immediately felt better. Knowing there were no spirits remaining in the house, only memories and residual energy, they were able to clean out the house and sell it and move on with their lives.

Trauma, of course, leaves intense energy behind. But not all intense energy is traumatic. Many homes are filled with energy imprints of the moments of joy and laughter that marked the lives of the families who lived there. You might step onto the lawn of an old home and suddenly hear shouts and giggles of children playing hide and seek or see in your mind's eye a yardful of tents made from bedsheets. You might see stacks of books and a most comfortable reading chair. Happiness leaves its imprints, too.

Remember, all matter is Spirit.

A Dream, or a Visit
from Spirit?

"I had the weirdest dream last night …." This must be one of the most common morning greetings in the English language! It sets the stage for what you know is going to be a presentation of events defying logical understanding. And yet, it's a phrase that intrigues us all because we all have "weird" dreams. By listening to the dreams of others, we hope to learn more about what our dreams might mean—or at least to feel secure in knowing that everybody has dreams that don't seem to make sense.

Despite many scientific discoveries about the nature of sleep and its function for our mental and physical health, much is still to be known. Whether we believe the dream state is purely a biological function of the body or a spiritual window upon the subconscious mind, the dream state presents a mysterious existence. Some say it allows the soul to roam freely, unconfined by the parameters of reality as they define consciousness.

When you dream about a loved one who has crossed over, could this be a spirit visitation? The dream state offers a natural doorway for communication with Spirit. The filters of your conscious mind are at rest, unable to block signals they otherwise would restrict or reinterpret. This leaves you receptive to the messages from Spirit these signals might bring.

The Dream State

We talk about the dream state as if it's a place we can go to, like we might think of going to California or New York. The journey holds the promise of exciting adventures that will take us beyond the realm of our everyday lives. It's a little scary, sometimes, but we can calm our fears by reminding ourselves, "It's just a dream …."

What happens during the dream state? The earliest written records speak of dreams and their mysteries. In many cultures, ancient and modern, dreams sometimes represent visitations from the Divine of your belief system. According to this belief, some cultures believe that the soul leaves the body during dreaming to visit a special world in which it actually lives in dreams; to wake someone during a dream is to risk severing the soul's connection to the body. Modern psychology looks to dreams as providing insights into your waking concerns, worries, and fears.

From your body's perspective, the dream state is as essential as sleep itself. There are two clear stages of sleep, *REM* and *NREM,* which cycle throughout the time you are asleep. REM (rapid eye movement) sleep is the stage of sleep during which the eyes move rapidly and dreams take place. NREM (no rapid eye movement) is the stage of sleep during which there is little dreaming and no rapid eye movements. Your body starts a sleep cycle by drifting off into NREM sleep, during which all physical functions become quiet and still. Not even your eyes move, which is why this is called the "no rapid eye movement" stage of sleep. About 90 minutes into NREM sleep, your brain suddenly wakes up—you are dreaming!

During REM (rapid eye movement) sleep, your eyes move rapidly behind your closed eyelids, as though watching a movie. Although your body generally is still, your brain is as busy as when you are awake. Over the course of an eight-hour sleep, most people cycle through four or five REM stages. Each tends to be longer than the one preceding it. The first REM stage might last five to 10 minutes, while the last one can last an hour or longer. This is partly why you are more likely to remember the last dream of your sleep—it's usually the longest, most detailed, and most vivid.

Sleep studies show that the REM stage of sleep is essential for your body to feel rested. This suggests that dreaming has a physiological importance; that is, your body needs not only to sleep but also to dream so that it can restore itself.

Clearing Your Brain: Data Dump

One theory about the importance of dreaming views dreams as "data dumps" for your brain. During your waking hours, your brain collects and processes a seemingly endless volume of information—stimuli from your physical senses, your thoughts, your emotions, the functions of your body. Your brain somehow processes everything you encounter while you are awake, even if you are unaware of this act of processing as it happens.

Because the vast majority of collected content has no context, it doesn't really qualify even as information. Your brain has no idea what to do with it, quite literally, and so it stores it away. When you begin to dream, the conscious parts of your brain that keep this data "behind the scenes" ease their control, and these fragments begin to float, as it were, into the parts of your brain that process thought. As you sleep, your brain then shapes these floating fragments into images you perceive as dreams.

Within this framework, there is nothing more to dreams than a discharge of electrical energy that is part of the filtering and cleansing process sleep provides to the brain. Dreaming is a "clearing" of your brain's circuitry, preparing it for the next day's data collection. Rather like a computer's hard drive, your brain collects and then filters and discards data in a cycle tied to waking and sleeping.

Studies in which researchers deprive volunteers of sleep or interrupt sleep when EEG signals show the brain has entered the dream state show the clear importance of dreaming to sleep. When sleep interruptions, disturbances, and deprivation that prevent dreaming continue over a period of days or weeks, the chemical balances of the brain change. This affects just about every function in your body, from heart rate to mood. When study volunteers are permitted to return to normal sleep and dream patterns, the chemical levels return to normal.

Researchers have also demonstrated there is no such thing as "making up for lost sleep." Sleep, once lost, is lost forever—your brain does not "make up" for the loss. So, maintaining regular and healthful sleep habits is essential to good health and one of the most important things you can do for yourself. In doing so, you also avoid bursts of micro-sleep, barely detectable to you but dangerous to your functioning, especially when driving. Caffeine also cannot restore your brain after sleep loss, substituting chemical stimulation for a sleep-deprived lack of energy and alertness. Only sleep itself can restore our brains for a new day of waking activity.

Working Out Your "Stuff"

From the framework of psychology, the brain's filtering process of dreaming allows you to experience and understand emotions and feelings that you don't address during your waking hours. Within this context, the content of dreams takes on symbolism that is personal to you. By writing down your dreams or talking about them, you can begin to see the patterns of your personal dream symbols and relate them to events and emotions taking place throughout your life. In this framework of interpretation, dreams seldom mean only what their images suggest.

What a Nightmare!

We've all had bad dreams, nightmares from which we wake up scared and shaking, sometimes not certain if we're still dreaming. The content and images of nightmares also become symbolic to us, generally representing major fears or worries. Some cultures believe dreams are an altered state of reality, and if you can work out your lessons in the dream state, you don't need to work them out in the waking state. If you are afraid of an issue or person and can face your fears in the dream state, you don't have to work them out when you are awake.

You might think of nightmares as the ultimate "working through." We can interact with our dreams, making contact with the visions that appear there. Whenever something disturbing happens in a dream, you can immediately surround yourself with a "safety zone" and remind your dreaming self that you are safe. Then you can question your "dream" actors as to their purpose in your nightmare and confront them if necessary. "I don't want this to happen anymore. Stop! Tell me why you're here!" You might be surprised at how effectively this ends the nightmare (and what answer you receive to your question!). If you can do this, you are working through your concerns.

Rita's husband has strict instructions not to wake her if she appears to be having a nightmare! If you aren't used to interacting with your dreams, think about the nightmare's issues upon waking, and the fearfulness of the dream will dissipate as you begin to analyze what happened in the dream. See more on interacting with your dreams later in this chapter.

Freud's "Royal Road to the Unconscious"

Still considered the father of psychoanalysis, Sigmund Freud (1856–1939) held that dreams revealed repressed desires (often sexual) and that dreams were the "royal road" to the inner sanctum of the unconscious mind. His book, *The Interpretation of Dreams*, published in 1899, was a groundbreaking work that attempted to explain dreams in the context of waking experiences and unexpressed thoughts and wishes. Analyzing and interpreting one's dreams, Freud believed, was the route to understanding one's needs. Though many of Freud's theories about the psychology of the mind have undergone reconsideration and much has evolved in the field of psychology, Freud's emphasis on the importance of dreams to nurturing mental health remains undisputed.

Carl Jung and the Archetype

Psychotherapist Carl Jung (1875–1961), initially a student of Sigmund Freud, viewed dreams as the unconscious mind's efforts to convey messages to the conscious mind, often by tapping into what Jung termed the *collective unconscious*. The collective unconscious, Jung said, is a vast repository of shared human experiences—*all* shared human experiences. Because of its vastness, we connect to it through universal symbols Jung called *archetypes*. Archetypes represent a range of interpretations, such as "hero" or "lover;" the key is identifying those archetypes that are relevant to you within the context of your life experiences.

Dreams, according to Jung, are a direct link to the collective unconscious. What we remember from the connection, upon waking, we perceive in the form of archetypes. As author James R. Lewis succinctly defines in his book *The Dream Encyclopedia, Second Edition* (Visible Ink Press, 2009), "archetypes ... predispose us to organize our personal experiences in certain ways unconsciously. Archetypes are not concrete images in the collective unconscious. They are more like invisible magnetic fields that cause iron filings to arrange themselves according to certain patterns."

Archetypes are icons of human experience you must then apply to the specifics of your life experiences. They might appear in dreams to explain past or current events or to provide glimpses of the broader context of your life mission and your soul's journey. Common archetypes and their representations include the following:

- Actor or acting a role, representing the parts of yourself you consciously present to others
- Anima/animus, representing the elements of the "opposite" sex that are present within you (feminine qualities in men, masculine qualities in women) and also how you view human sexuality through the lens of a feminine yin and masculine yang interpretation of the supposed poles of gender identity
- Four of anything, including the number itself, representing stability, completion (such as in the cycle of the four seasons), wholeness
- Father, representing power, authority, responsibility, tradition, procreation
- Mother, representing life, love, caring, nurturing, creativity
- Old man, representing wisdom and forgiveness
- Old woman, representing the energy of life (through birth) and death
- Rebirth, representing repressed issues that are resurfacing or another chance to do or receive something you thought was lost
- Shadow, representing the dark side of your personality or the parts of yourself that you keep hidden (sometimes even from yourself)

Jung further connected dreams to mythology, observing that despite the many and varied mythologies of world cultures from ancient to modern times, common themes—in the form of archetypes—emerge that link them. He speculated that mythology represents the efforts of the conscious mind to organize the information received through dreams into structures (stories and belief systems). As universal symbols, archetypes permeate nearly all aspects of our modern culture, from character representations in movies, books, and even the comics to the symbolisms of astrology and Tarot.

Esmirelda, December 1989, oil on canvas. Rita asked to see the Spirit guide who works with her when she reads Tarot cards. An old Gypsy woman revealed herself as Rita's inspiration.

Understanding Your Spirit Archetypes

As symbolic representations, archetypes appear in communication with Spirit. Remember from earlier chapters that we've talked about developing your personal dictionary of mediumistic symbols. Archetypes can help you understand the deeper meanings of some of these symbols by giving them a universal context.

Archetypes are useful only to the extent that you can connect the universal knowledge and understanding they represent with the events and circumstances of your own life. This representation can be physical, emotional, and spiritual. A technique called *free association* is a good method for understanding the archetypes and symbols that appear in your dreams and in spirit messages that you receive (directly or through a medium). Free association is a process of saying or writing the first things that enter your mind when you think of a particular word or symbol.

Free association is easy to do. Get some paper and a pen or pencil. Find a comfortable place to sit, where it is easy for you to write longhand and where you won't be distracted.

1. Choose one image from a dream. Write it at the top of a piece of paper.

2. Set a timer to give yourself a time limit—one to three minutes. This encourages you to work quickly without giving your intellect an opportunity to interfere.

3. Write down every word the image you selected evokes. Do this without thinking about what you're writing. The faster you do this, the more intuitive your responses. It doesn't matter whether the words seem to be related to the image; just write them.

4. When the timer goes off, stop writing.

5. Look at the words that have found their way onto the page. Do any of the words instantly relate to your chosen dream image? Do any of them seem so unrelated as to be far-fetched?

6. On another slip of paper, write some of the archetypes these words on your first page seem to represent. Under each archetype, list the words that relate.

7. What pattern do you see emerging? Sometimes this isn't immediately obvious to you. You might need to journal, meditate, or otherwise ponder the archetypes, words, and dream images to make the archetypal connection.

8. If a pattern doesn't appear, set the exercise—the word list and the archetype organization—aside for two weeks. Then come back to it, and see if you can now recognize a pattern.

Do this exercise regularly to build a foundation of understanding about what archetypes mean to you. Not every dream element has extended archetypal symbolic meaning, of course. Over time and with practice, you'll come to easily identify those that do.

A Doorway to the Higher Side

The dream state is particularly conducive to spirit contact and spirit visitation. When you dream, your conscious mind eases its control over what you think and perceive, allowing you to be more open. This happens because the dream state is the closest to an altered state from waking consciousness that most of us achieve on a regular (daily!) basis. So it's the easiest way for a loved one to contact you from Spirit. You might not know whether you're dreaming; the dream may feel more real, more vivid than usual—as if it has actually happened. It's common to see deceased loved ones and to receive messages from them in the dream state.

There are many times that a spirit will visit you in the dream state. There is a very different feeling when this happens than when you just dream about the person. It feels real, and it makes sense. Six months after Rita's father passed, her daughter came running into her bedroom one night and said, "I was dreaming, but I know I wasn't dreaming, and Poppa was in my room."

Rita held her daughter and asked her how Poppa was. Her daughter said he was fine. Rita asked, "Were you worried about Poppa?" Her daughter replied that she was. Rita told her daughter, "You know, he probably just came to visit you to let you know he was okay because you were so worried." Her daughter smiled, gave Rita a big hug, and went back to bed.

Some people believe the dream state is actually the soul's opportunity to leave the physical body and travel as a spirit. It reconnects with cosmic energy and exists in a discarnate state for the duration of its travels. Where does your spirit go? It's hard to say, although meditation might reveal this to you.

Inviting Spirit Visitation to Your Dreams

You can intentionally invite spirit entities to visit you in your dreams. If you have situations you didn't resolve with someone who has now passed to Spirit, you can resolve them through visiting in Spirit in the dream state. Or you can just reconnect with a loved one for the joy of experiencing that connection again! The following exercise can help you initiate a dream visit with Spirit:

1. As you are beginning to fall asleep, set the intent that you are going to meet in the dream state with a specific person who has passed to Spirit, in which a dream will play out any unresolved situation.

2. Permit yourself to go to sleep.

3. When you wake up, don't worry about whether you remember the dream. Instead, focus on how you feel. Do you feel you've achieved resolution or at least established a reconnection?

4. Ask a question about the conditions surrounding the situation and see how you feel. Your dream journal can help with this. If you still feel the situation is unresolved, try again the next night—with your question in mind as you set your intent.

Joseph had problems with his father throughout his life. When his father passed to Spirit, Joseph was afraid these problems would never be resolved, and he was left with a feeling of need because there was unfinished business between them. So Joseph did this exercise. The first night he felt nothing. The next night he tried again, and this time was a little more forceful in setting his intent.

Joseph said, "Dad, I've waited 39 years to speak to you. I want to speak to you tonight in the dream state." The next morning, to Joseph's surprise, when he tuned into the situation with his father, he felt total peace. He didn't remember the dream, but he feels a new peacefulness every time he thinks of his father.

When you wake up in the morning (or if you wake up during the night after a dream), write as much as you can remember about your dreams in your dream journal. Did you dream of the person you were thinking about when you fell asleep? Did it feel like you and this person were enjoying each other's company?

Don't be discouraged if you wake up and remember dreams that have nothing to do with the spirit loved one you hoped to contact, or if you remember nothing at all. Spirits, you recall, are not always willing or able to respond when we want them to. Just be patient, and keep trying. Eventually, your dreams will connect you with Spirit.

A brilliant songwriter and musician in his own right, the former Beatle Paul McCartney, recounts in the media that he often dreams of his bandmate and songwriting partner John Lennon. McCartney believes his dreams of Lennon are visits from John in Spirit. The dreams are often humorous and sometimes prank-filled, such as picking up a favorite guitar and discovering the frets are covered for a moment in a sticky substance. ("What's this?") Paul welcomes John's spirit and enjoys simply spending time with his friend, working on songs, and making music together in his dreams.

Past Life Dreams

Your past lives are always part of you, and sometimes your dreams give you the opportunity to connect with them. Famed American psychic Edgar Cayce (1877–1945) taught that when you have a past life dream, the way you recognize it is that everything in the dream presents in the relevant context. If you dream that you're walking down the street in 1840 in Kansas, you are not likely to see a red convertible Mini Cooper drive by! The roads are dirt, not pavement. Clothes and surroundings are appropriate for the period; nothing appears out of historical context.

You can set the intent for experiencing past life dreams. Do you have strong feelings that you've lived other lifetimes, and do you carry fragments and impressions—sense memories—of those lifetimes with you now? Do you have the sense of setting the rigging of a sailing tall ship at sea? Or can you feel the heaviness of your heavily jewel-encrusted, hand-embroidered gown as you lift it to climb a set of cold stone circular stairs (such as might be found in the present-day ruins of a castle)?

Just as you can set your intent for a dream visitation from Spirit, try setting your intent to recall a past life. Even if you don't remember the dream upon waking, write down in your dream journal any feelings, colors, sounds, or other impressions that come to mind when you think of the dream.

Keeping a Dream Journal

Do you wake up from an intense dream and know, just *know*, its message is vitally important … then fall back asleep and remember very little in the morning? How frustrating! If you're interested in exploring the meanings and messages of your dreams, you can't rely on memory. You need to keep a dream journal.

A dream journal doesn't have to be anything fancy, although many bookstores sell very nice dream journals and blank journals that you can use to record your dreams and your thoughts about them. A plain old composition book will do. You might want to keep a notepad and pen at your bedside to jot down dreams when you first awaken from them and later transfer the information to your official dream journal. Use your dream journal to record …

- The details of your dreams as you remember them, without interpretation or filtering. Just describe the dream as it occurred, as best you can remember it
- Your free-association exercises for each dream. You can do these on separate paper and then transfer the information to your dream journal or do the exercises right in the journal
- What is going on in your waking life—what's happening at work or school, with your family, with your significant other
- Your thoughts and ideas about what the archetypes and symbols of your dreams might mean in a common or universal context, as well as in the context of your personal life
- Any learnings or "ahas!" that you get as you work through a dream's interpretation
- Any connections of your dreams to Spirit and whether any of your mediumistic symbols occur in your dreams—and what that might mean

Keeping a dream journal gives you documentation of your dreams so that you can go back to look for common patterns, themes, and symbols. What wakes you up? Can you see a connection between your dreaming and possible sleep interruptions. For example, persistent waking from reflux might be accompanied by dreams of feeling like your mouth is stuffed with a cud-like substance your dreaming self finds worrisome. The dream symbol becomes a clue toward understanding what you need to do in your waking life to restore your restful sleep.

What Dreams Mean

Can a dream be, well, just a dream? Do all dreams have hidden meanings and messages? What about dreams that seem so literal they are like replays of the events of your day? Dreams often have multiple layers of meaning that extend from the literal to the symbolic. Sometimes a dream is just the events of your day, bubbling through your subconscious mind so they can break free and disperse. Other times, a dream brings you a specific message or insight.

Where do premonitory dreams come from? Some believe your soul can read your Akashic record (see Chapter 5) during dreams, which gives access to all past and future information of your soul's travels and experiences. When you return to a waking state, remnants of this access remain. When these fragments involve events that have not yet occurred in your physical existence, you interpret them as precognitive or premonitionary (see Chapter 14). This access is also how some people explain past life memories. Learn more in Part 6, "Soul Lessons and Karmic Cycles."

Interpreting Symbolism

Symbolism is the language of dreams. Dreams, like thoughts, move in fluid images. And a dreamspace often does not follow the rules of perspective that dictate our physical waking environments. Like a Cubist painting by Picasso, a dreamspace might show simultaneous perspectives or points of view impossible when awake. There is no sense of time or the structure that time imposes in dreamscapes. There are many books available on the subject of dreaming, dreamscapes, dream interpretations, and dream symbols. But no understanding is more relevant than the one you will build yourself when you begin to follow your dreams, to keep a dream journal and an accompanying personal dream dictionary of symbols.

Some symbols have common meanings (that may or may not be archetypes). Water, for example, often represents the emotions (Tarot's Major Arcana Moon card). It can also suggest significant change and transition ("sea change"). Dreams of death, dying, and being killed are common and frightening, but they generally represent transformation and "letting go" of something that has been part of you or your life for a long time (Tarot's Major Arcana Death card). Other times, dream symbols have particular meaning for you. You might always dream about driving on a highway that never turns, goes up, or goes down whenever you find yourself in a rut in your work or your life.

The best way to identify your personal dream symbols is to keep a dream journal in which you record elements of your dreams and your thoughts about what they could represent or mean. Over time, patterns will emerge that will help you identify your unique dream symbols. Personal dream symbols often fit within archetypes or common dream symbols. But sometimes, they do not.

Here are some common dream symbols:

- Anchor—staying in one place, weighed down
- Automobile—the means by which you move through life
- Baby—something new in your life

- Bed—intimacy, rest and/or comfort, recovery
- Blanket—cover, hiding
- Bridge—connection, link, transition
- Climbing—struggle to overcome an obstacle, to reach a pinnacle
- Clothing—your persona (the self you project to others), the physical body, past lives
- Death—renewal, end of one thing and beginning of another, metamorphosis
- Elevator—change, ups and downs
- Flying—freedom and joy, rising above, an omniscient viewpoint
- Garden—growth, nature, flowering, the cycles of life from seed to bloom to lying fallow
- Gate—exit from one place or circumstance and entrance to another
- House—your spirit, your mind, your inner self
- Key—solution, answer, unlocking, instrument of change
- Losing teeth—loss of control
- Naked—uncovered or exposed, feeling natural, unfettered
- Public Transportation (trains, ferries, planes)—literally, being transported or carried from one place or dimension to another
- Trash—disorder and confusion
- Wall—obstacle
- Dream symbols may change context according to religious or cultural beliefs or even your physical, geographical location in the world. What is *your* most persistent dream symbol? What is your most persistent mediumistic symbology? Do your dream and mediumistic symbols correspond? If so, how?

Premonitions and Warnings

It's unnerving to wake from a dream that a friend was in a car accident or that a fire swept through the apartment complex where your sister lives. Such events are within the realm of possibility, and indeed often appear as news stories. How do you know if these kinds of dreams reflect your fears and worries or are foretelling actual disaster?

The first step is to write about the dream and any surrounding circumstances you can recall. Did you fall asleep with a television or a video podcast streaming? Perhaps you dropped off listening to video of a live news reporting—a protest march or a raging forest fire? Did you read about one in a magazine or newspaper article earlier in the day, or even a few days ago? If so, it could be your worries during waking hours that manipulate your dreams. Writing about why these events worry your dreams can help you reach insight about them.

So many people dream of a disaster in the family and then it happens. It's common to be afraid that the dream caused the disaster in some way or to just be frightened when you recognize that you've had a precognitive dream. Don't be afraid! Spirit is trying to give you information so you can be strong for other family members, to make sure there is someone who will not be in shock and can take on the position of strength and leadership coping with life's disasters requires.

If there don't seem to be external influences, pull out your dream journal and look for other dreams like this, either in subject matter or symbolism. What were they? How are they similar, and how are they different? Have you had premonitionary dreams before? If so, what does this dream have in common with those dreams?

In the end, it doesn't hurt to call your friend and ask him to be especially careful when driving today or to phone your sister to remind her to check the batteries in her smoke detectors. You might never know whether you helped avert a disaster, but you will feel better that you acted on a potential warning.

Interacting with Spirits in Your Dreams

Whether in spirit communication or situations you are trying to work through, you can consciously interact with your dreams to get more information from the dreams or to work out events, trauma, or situations with other people. Did you ever wake yourself up from a dream? Most people have. Earlier, we talked about working through issues in nightmares by surrounding yourself with a "safety zone" and then confronting the situation or person creating anxiety for you in the dream. You can do this with any dream that you're curious about.

Waking Up

If you can wake yourself from dreams, then you can learn to consciously interact with the dream. Work up to this level of participation in your dreams by first writing your dreams down in your dream journal. Then, when you have a dream you are curious about, invite a "clarification" the next night when you go to sleep and see what dreams come to you. Eventually, you'll be able to interact with the dream while it is occurring.

In a dream that is a spirit communication, allow yourself to interact with the visitor from Spirit as though you were in the same room—which, really, (through the dreamscape) you are. If you have questions or seek information, ask. This is an ideal opportunity to try to work through lingering concerns or issues that you still might have with the person. You don't always remember these interactions, although you will usually feel calmer about the issues after the dream takes place.

Passing Over, Love's Shared Dreamscape

In Chapter 8, we made mention of a mother, wife, and daughter—three generations of women present at the bedside of the man at the time of his passing. He was a man who was son to the mother, husband to the wife, and father to the daughter. The night before the man's release to Spirit, all three women dreamed a shared dream about a beloved yearly family vacation spot at the ocean in Maryland.

The man's mother, an Italian immigrant, dreamt of slicing potatoes for hand-cut french fries and wiping her brow with the hem of her apron before deep-frying crabcakes and fried hard crabs for supper. As she lifts her gaze to the breeze from the open beachfront cottage window, eyes open for her family returning from the water's edge, she awoke. With that morning's light, her son had passed to Spirit.

The man's wife of thirty-two years, a "housewife" by the lingo of her generation, dreamt of walking the cottage path toward the beach dunes and ocean wave's edge while calling the name of her young son. From her skyborne viewpoint, she looked down upon herself and the small black-headed figure of the boy walking toward her. The boy, loaded down with bucket and raft, kicks a multi-colored beach ball. Her eye caught the ball that seems to float as if by magic up into the bright cobalt blue of a cloudless sky, and she awoke. In the crisp, clear November morning's light, her husband had passed to Spirit.

The man's daughter, grown now and working as an editor in New York City, dreamt of her teenage self, wedged into the backseat of the family station wagon loaded up for the beach holiday. While sitting between her grandmother and her brother with her mom's jewelry case on her lap and her feet resting on the backseat hump, the teenager looked out the rain-streaked car window to see a beautiful coal-black stallion running alongside Eastern Shore Route 50. The stallion was running full-out in the grey of a hard-driving rain, like one of the wild horses she'd seen roaming Assateague Island with her father. Somehow, the girl watched the horse run right ahead of their car, and as he disappears, she awoke. In the startling dawn light, she answers her mother's call and closes her father's eyes. Her father had passed to Spirit.

Rita believes there can be little doubt that the three generations of women shared a dreamscape with their dying loved one. Before passing, perhaps the man spent one more spirit vacation at the beach, taking his beloved family of attending women with him. Our dreams are powerful. Shared, they become the collective unconscious of humanity and a conduit to Spirit's Divine light.

What do *you* dream about? Where do *your* dreams take you? Who will you meet on the dreamscapes of Spirit?

PART 5

The Essence of Spirit Is Being

Even as you exist on the Earth plane in a physical life, inhabiting a physical body, you remain connected to the energy of the Spirit plane. This energy sustains you, is full of love, and is available to you whenever you need it. You can receive healing energy through contact with Spirit, and you can also be the one who directs healing energy to others. Spirit lives everywhere around us. Spirit energy is an integral part of our physical environment that is present in all the Earth's elements— Fire, Earth, Air, and Water, and is revered by many indigenous cultures around the world. But while we are anchored on Earth, we reach to Spirit. People who return from the brink of death have similar experiences of seeing a bright light, as well as loved ones who have passed to the Higher side. Spirit energy is Divine energy. As such, it links us all—on the Earth plane and on the Higher side—with the God of our understanding. Making connections across the border of physical existence or temporal space gives you insights into your thoughts, feelings, behaviors, and actions.

CHAPTER
18

The Healing Power of
Spirit Energy

Life is a constant energy exchange. You acquire energy from and give energy to others in your life—both on the Earth plane and on the Higher side. Sometimes this is intentional, as when you focus on sending healing energy to a loved one who is ill or aiding someone you love in crossing over to the Higher side, or when you call on a friend to lend you a hand in a time of need.

But sometimes, these energy exchanges are unintentional and unbalanced. You might give too much of yourself, literally, to others, leaving little for your own needs, nourishment, and growth. In such situations, energy healers can help restore your personal energy balance.

Life as an Energy Exchange

Every contact you have with other people, with other living things, is an exchange of energy. Sometimes this exchange is palpable. You feel a surge, almost like an electrical charge, when you shake the hand of a person who has an outgoing personality and great vigor or feel the warmth of love surround you when you share a big hug with your BFF from childhood.

The English Romantic poet John Keats (1795-1821), who passed away young from tuberculosis, understood well the vibrancy of life force energy. His poetry and letters demonstrated his belief in the timeless, sacred divinity underwriting all life. However fleeting on Earth, that life is endowed with an everlasting integrity that reaches beyond the grave. The poet's gesture, his imagination, written in the language of his hand, whether "warm and capable" or resting in "icy silence," reaches to greet the reader in an exchange of animating life force energy. It is a greeting that touches us beyond the limits of Earthly life and death.

Read aloud this poem fragment, which Keats wrote in the margins of a longer late work. Here the poet reaches through the immortality of language, to grasp the warm, red-blooded hand of the reader, vital and alive:

> This living hand, now warm and capable
> Of earnest grasping, would, if it were cold
> And in the icy silence of the tomb,
> So haunt thy days and chill thy dreaming nights
> That thou would wish thine own heart dry of blood
> So in my veins red life might stream again,
> And thou be conscience-calmed—see here it is—
> I hold it towards you.

We "read" energy exchanges, gestures of transference, and a shared life force. We use them both to communicate with and make assessments about each other. What do you notice, for example, about a couple that tells you they are deeply in love? They might walk along or sit together, holding hands, touching, and sharing each other's physical space, so they appear to be more as one than as two. As you get near, you can feel the energy of their togetherness like you might feel the charged air beneath a high-tension power line. This is such wonderful energy that you might feel like walking past this couple again, just to connect with it!

Life craves life—the Divine life force energy of Spirit.

Energy You Give to Others

You give energy to others nearly every moment of the day in each interaction you have with someone else. When this process stays a fairly balanced give-and-take situation, you don't notice much about it. You give, and you receive, and your energy stays supportive of you physically, emotionally, and spiritually.

When the balance shifts to giving more than to receiving, you might feel tired, run-down, and edgy. Everyone around you wants, wants, and wants. No one seems to care what *you* might want or need. This constant demand drains your energy, and it's no longer sufficient to support your body, mind, and spirit.

You might start to see indications of this in your health and attitude. Your immune system could become more susceptible to infection, and you could find yourself suffering assorted minor ailments. You might discover you become clumsier (even than usual!) and prone to small injuries as a result. It's not that these problems are your fault. Rather, you're not able to resist them.

You might even feel like your energy is being taken away from you, withdrawn from you, instead of you willingly giving it. Sometimes people have such intense needs that they draw energy from those around them but have little to give back to make the process an exchange.

Have you ever said: "I just can't deal with this relationship anymore. It takes too much energy." You might be thinking in terms of the work you put out to sustain the relationship, the amount of time you spend trying to manage your behaviors and emotions. But you're also sensing a loss of energy, literally. It's like the other person is a magnet, and every time you go near, it feels like little fragments of you go flying toward it. You can protect yourself by visualizing yourself surrounded by light.

Energy You Acquire from Others

Exchange is a process of giving and receiving. Just as you give your energy to others, you receive energy from others. The strongest, most positive, most supportive energy is love. When love thrives in any of its multiple dimensions, energy blossoms. It's almost as though you can feel and watch your life force energy intensify.

Sometimes it sounds trite to talk of "the power of love." From sonnets to rock songs, the phrase is everywhere. So much so that the spell checker in your word processing program might identify it as a cliché and ask you if you want to change it! But love is the foundation of the Universe's Divine energy, and its power is very real.

When you feel happy and good in the presence of someone else, you're drawing from an energy that is based in love. It is this energy base, the energy of love, that heals. When you feel it, you know it. It recharges and replenishes you. It restores your sense of well-being and happiness. It makes you whole and unites all parts of your being.

Can you receive "bad" or negative energy from others? Certainly. This is the hallmark of what psychologists call dysfunctional relationships. No one really understands why if we *can* choose the energy of love that we sometimes don't. There are as many explanations for this as there are people. Often this cycle of dysfunction is baggage carried from past lives. Perhaps the struggle to love is related to your soul's lesson in this life.

What's more important than the *why* of such choices is the recognition that they *are* choices. You don't have to accept negative energy as false love from others! Not from anyone! Change is not always easy, but it is possible. And there's plenty of positive energy—the power of true love—out there in the Universe to support you in choosing to refuse negative energy.

Bioenergy: Your Aura

Your aura is the energy field that surrounds your body. All living beings have auras—plants, animals, and humans. Auras contain the energy of biological life. When energy from Spirit connects with your physical self, it does so through your aura. This is how Spirit heals—it flows into your aura, replenishing and strengthening your personal life force energy. Your aura also acts to protect you. When you pray or meditate to connect with the God of your understanding, your aura enlarges. People who can see auras can see this happen.

Your True Colors

Auras appear as colors. If this seems odd to you, think about electrical storms. They often produce lightning of different colors depending on what other substances are in the air at the time lightning strikes. Energy, when it takes a form the human eye can detect, is quite colorful.

The color of your aura provides clues about your physical, emotional, and spiritual states. The vibrancy of the color—whether it's bold and vivid or subdued and flat—and the thickness of its layer influence the meaning of it. Color interpretations, like the symbolism of dreams, are general. What particular colors mean to you can vary. The energy emission of your aura is very low range, beyond the range of normal vision. But with practice, you can learn to extend the reach of visual detection. (We have an exercise for you in the next section.) Here are common colors and their general meanings:

- **Yellow.** When vibrant, yellow represents success, intelligence, wisdom, and creativity. Dull yellow suggests selfishness and negativity.

- **Red.** When vibrant, red suggests blood, sensuality, and passion. Dull red suggests anger, fear, and anxiety. If you become angry during a conversation, your aura might show a spike of red, reflecting the intensity of emotion you're feeling.

- **Green.** Green is related to healing, suggesting balance and health.

- **Blue.** A blue aura says you're searching for spiritual information and answers. Light blue indicates your quest is just beginning; dark blue suggests you've chosen the path you want to follow, and you are now seeking enlightenment. Dull blue (dark or light) indicates self-righteousness.

- **Purple.** A purple aura suggests you have high spiritual awareness and are broadly accepting of others. Purple indicates balance, patience, and helpfulness.

- **Orange.** You are likely friendly and open toward others when your aura is orange. Vivid, dark orange suggests ambition and drive.

- **Pink.** As you might suspect, pink relates to affection and love. A pink aura also suggests you are calm and have the ability to soothe and calm others.

- **Brown.** When your aura is brown, you are likely confused, discouraged, or frustrated. Brown tends to be a stress color, suggesting things are out of balance in your life.

- **Black.** A black aura says your energy is blocked from view. Some people do this intentionally to protect themselves from dysfunctional energy. A black aura can also suggest an inner search for meaning. Other times, a near-black or a loamy aura suggests the rich organic soil that is the medium for sustaining growth.

- **White.** A white aura indicates intense energy and protection. White light comprises all the hues on the visible light spectrum. Your aura might be white when you are meditating, praying, or intentionally giving energy to others.

An aura camera doesn't really capture your energy, although the images it produces can be stunning. Rather, it uses infrared film to record the heat you are generating. The more heat is present, the more vivid the colors.

Because your life is constantly changing, so is your aura. It changes with the physical and emotional changes that occur during your daily life. An aura that's bright and vivid indicates your health is good, and your energy is strong. An aura that's gray or neutralized shows someone in need. There sometimes seems to be a hole in the aura or darkness in that area during illness, or the aura can become weak in color and density. The aura's color changes and may become muddy, but there is no particular color associated with illness. Auras can display manifestations of both physical and mental health problems.

You can send healing energy to someone you know is in need. However, that person's spirit (sometimes called Higher Being in the context of energy healing) decides whether to accept it. Although this is a process of choice, it's not one that you participate in consciously. Similarly, if someone sends you healing energy, your spirit determines whether to accept it. This is another way that your energy protects you.

Explore Your Aura

Do you want to see your own aura? It's easy to do, and you can do it alone! All you need is a white or black (preferred) nonreflective surface, such as a piece of poster board, a darkened room, and a candle.

1. Put the candle in the center of the room and light it. It should be the only light source in the room.

2. Standing with the candlelight behind you, hold your hand in front of the nonreflective surface, about 10 to 12 inches away. Focus on your hand. You'll soon see energy appear around it, like a halo.

3. Now, prop the nonreflective surface against the wall so you can hold both hands together. Place your hands as if you're holding a ball of energy and sending healing back and forth between them. You can actually see energy move between your two hands.

If another person is present, you can have that person stand in front of the nonreflective surface (which must be large enough to function as a screen). What colors do you see around this person?

The Aura and Healing

Semyon Kirlian, the Russian electrician and inventor now famous for the form of photography that bears his name (we introduced Kirlian and his work in Chapter 16), discovered that the auras of health and illness have distinct illuminations. Diseased leaves projected auras differently when photographed than healthy leaves of the same species. Even though the leaf itself appeared healthy, the leaf's aura showed that it had already been infected.

Although Kirlian was certainly not the first person to explore the correlation between energy and illness, he was the first to provide evidence of it. This was a significant discovery step in understanding as well as validating energy healing.

A predecessor of Kirlian, Walter J. Kilner, invented a special lens through which the aura becomes visible. Called a dicyanin screen, the device filters light rays to make the very low spectrum rays of the aura more easily visible to the human eye.

Energy Healing

Energy healing works through spirit chemists, spirit physicians, and other healers to physically, emotionally, and spiritually heal someone on the Earth plane. A spirit chemist is a guide who works through healing Spirit energy to change the biochemistry within the body. A spirit physician is a guide who works as a physician on the Earth plane might while using Spirit energy for healing. Certain healers have "specialist" Spirit guides. A healer might have a "bone specialist" Spirit guide, and so the healing related to bone problems is especially effective.

Energy healing makes a profound difference in people. The changes are physical, emotional, and spiritual—you need all three for complete healing to happen. It's also essential to release any anger you're holding. Holding onto anger creates a constant cause and effect—you send out dysfunctional energy, and so it returns to you. The result is a physical or emotional breakdown of some sort.

Energy healing is not about making everything better; it is about reaching your highest and best. Sometimes the outcome isn't quite what you might expect. Rita once worked as a psychologist with troubled adolescents. A boy told her something he was going to do to break the law and asked her to pray for him. She told him if she did so, he would be caught and arrested because this would be the highest and best outcome for him. He did go out to do it, and he did get arrested! He ended up going to jail but then managed to turn his life around and is now doing fine.

Energy healing also is not a substitute for conventional medical care! If you are sick or injured, always see the appropriate health care practitioner for diagnosis and treatment. Energy healing works to supplement all other forms of healing, not replace them. Although there are numerous specialized forms of energy healing, all people have the ability to do energy healing with Spirit. As always, it's essential to begin with setting your intent for the highest good for the other person and to conclude with thanks to your healers, your Spirit guides, and the God of your understanding.

Hands-On Focus: Reiki

Reiki is an ancient system of hands-on energy healing. The word means "universal energy." Reiki originated in Buddhist practices in ancient India, then was lost for several centuries. It resurfaced in Japan in the 1800s. In contemporary Reiki practice, the four levels of practitioner are identified as level 1, level 2, level 3, and master.

Reiki treatment involves having a Reiki practitioner place their hands over your body, so the energy passing through them activates the energy in the body part that is hurt or diseased. The premise is similar to that of acupuncture: to restore the proper flow of energy. As you feel the energy that the Reiki practitioner is guiding through your body, you talk about the images that appear in your mind. This releases trapped energy and allows the natural flow to resume.

In the United States, Reiki therapy is often combined with psychotherapy. The Reiki practitioner is also a trained psychologist or talk therapist. As with all forms of energy healing, the outcome can be quite profound. Reiki can be quite effective at relieving chronic pain.

Spiritualist Healing

Energy healing is a fundamental element of Spiritualism, which believes that healing is part of all contact and communication with Spirit. Each service includes healing, as do most circles. During healing, the medium or leader asks healing Spirit guides to come close. Each healer also asks their specific Spirit guide healers to come close.

In the Spiritualist church service, members of the church who are known to have strong healing abilities are invited to stand behind chairs designated as healing chairs to direct energy to people in need. The person who comes up to sit in the chair receives the directed healing.

The healer lightly touches the head and shoulders of the person in the chair to let the healing energy flow into them. The prevailing thought about this is that the energy is "intelligent" and will go to where the person needs it. The person receiving healing should relax and release anything they hold onto that is no longer needed. When the healing session is finished, the healer gently brushes the shoulders to clear the space.

Intent matters! A man in Rita's congregation was told by a medium (not Rita) that he would be taking a healing chair and meet the love of his life by standing behind the chair. So every Sunday, he would stand behind the chair, hoping he would meet the love of his life. Although he was a good energy healer, he did not fulfill the promised message. He came to Rita in frustration, and she explained to him that his intent should be to heal, not to meet a partner. The intent of healing is to help the other person. And who knows, maybe the love of this man's life *is* healing! Rita knows what it's like to be on both sides of the healing chair. As a Spiritualist minister, she regularly conducts healings. Many years ago, Rita neared completion of chemotherapy for breast cancer. The chemotherapy left her feeling very sick and drained. She felt so sick during the church service that she asked someone else to drive her home after the service. Rita came to a healing chair, and her friend and mentor, Bob Miller, stood behind it.

Bob lightly touched Rita's shoulders and then raised his hands above her. She felt like an enormous vacuum was sucking everything out of her. Then another member of the church came forward and added healing energy … and then other healers did the same, one after the other, adding the energies and resources of their Spirit guides to Rita's healing.

"I felt like all of the love in the Universe came into me," Rita says about the experience. At the end of the service, Rita's nausea and tiredness disappeared. She no longer felt weakened from her cancer treatments. The following day she even put in a full day's work. (Today, Rita remains cancer-free.)

What people experience during healing with energy from Spirit ranges from feeling very calm to feeling better either immediately or after some time. Spirit healing can't and isn't meant to heal everything; the purpose is always for the highest and the best. There are spiritual lessons in illness and many things that we don't understand. We are sometimes volunteers for people around us to learn their lessons. We don't always know the Divine purpose of a particular situation: this truth is beyond our human capacity.

People sometimes want to separate medical and spiritual healing, but really, they remain connected. Doctors are spirits, too, and medicine is spiritual. It's important to seek healing as a whole, unified experience. Energy healing is only one part of the process; seeing a medical doctor and getting treatment is also part of the process, and the two must be combined.

For Lorie, the image is of Janice when she was already ill, and the resemblance is striking.

Joey was his mother's favorite, so there was no surprise when Lorie came through wearing the flowered dress she wore to Joey's wedding.

Lorie came to Rita for a sitting and drawing at the First Spiritualist Church of Quincy. Her stepmother, Janice, came through from Spirit. Lorie had been close to her stepmother, and Janice kept reporting herself to Rita as mother vibration. Janice has come through in drawings from Spirit for different family members, appearing for each person at different stages of her life.

Absent Healing

Absent healing is healing energy you send to someone who doesn't necessarily know that you're sending healing to them. You might offer healing prayers for a friend who's sick. You might do a healing meditation for the cashier at the grocery store or the mail carrier after hearing that the person is having surgery. There are dozens of times every day that you learn of or encounter people who need healing.

If you are an experienced energy healer, you may be able to administer healing remotely. We know a Reiki master, for example, who delivers healing regularly to her best and oldest friend from childhood, who suffers from chronic pain following a difficult lung surgery. The remote Reiki healing can be done together at a scheduled time, the receiver of healing relaxing and meditating on acceptance and healing while the Reiki master works. Or, the Reiki master can send healing at any time for the receiver's highest and best for recovery and relief from pain.

Rita has had many powerful experiences in her work as a counselor to troubled adolescent boys. One evening, someone broke into her office and stole, among other things, her leather jacket. It was a cold night, and Rita had to walk to her car without a coat. She was aggravated, and on the drive home, she vented to her Spirit guides.

"What do I do about this?" she asked. "How do I deal with these boys?" In answer, she heard, "Send them healing." She said, "You've got to be kidding!" But she got the message again, so that's what she did. When Rita got to work the next morning, her jacket had been returned! Although thefts were quite common, this was the first time in the facility's history that stolen property had been returned. There's no doubt in Rita's mind that the reason it came back was because she sent the healing. Turn back to Chapter 12 and take another look at Rita's painting, *We Worked So Hard*, which depicts the spirit she believes led her to this challenging but fulfilling work with troubled youth.

Maintaining Energy Balance

When you use your own energy for healing, you're using magnetic energy. This is a powerful source, but it quickly depletes. When you send healing to others, learn to use universal energy rather than your own personal energy. Here's how a Native American healer taught Rita to draw energy *through*, rather than *from* herself:

- Visualize the opening of your Crown chakra (see Chapter 5) and invite in energy from Father God.
- Visualize the energy from Mother Earth coming in through the soles of your feet.
- Allow these energies to meet in your Heart chakra—Father God, Mother Earth— and send the energy out through the palms of your hands.

Remember, healing is always about love, with the highest and best intent. You can recharge depleted energy by raising your left hand, which is the receiving hand, palm upward. Concentrate on allowing the Divine energy of the Universe to flow into you through your palm, letting it recharge and revitalize you.

When Grief Unbalances You

Grief is very real. Since we know that life continues on, the feeling of loss can be overwhelming. Even for mediums who can stay in touch with their loved ones in Spirit quite easily, the loss of a loved one brings tangible pain. This pain needs to be healed. Give yourself the time and the space to feel your emotions. Allow yourself to go through the full process of grieving. If you're having difficulty coping with your grief, seek professional help from a grief counselor or psychotherapist. There is no one way to grieve. And there is no set time period for grieving. Each experience of grief is unique and must be honored.

Remember, Spirit seeks only healing and comfort for the highest good. Your loved ones who have passed to Spirit want you to have a full and wonderful life on the Earth plane. Ask for Divine guidance from Spirit and the Universe will provide its healing love. Be patient, and keep the faith. Balance will be restored. Life continues on.

The Lessons of Healing

Rita prepared to display some of her paintings in a studio show. She rushed around the gallery space, trying to make sure all the paintings hung in place. She still needed to hang some of her art, and time was running short. Hurrying down the stairs, she missed a step and twisted her ankle. Ow! She crumpled in a heap on the stairs. Her ankle hurt, but more than anything, she felt somewhat panicked. This was not a time she could afford to be hobbled by an injury—she had work to do!

Rita lay there for a few minutes, mentally crying, "Why me? Why now?" This, of course, did little to make her ankle feel better. Finally, she said to herself, "What's going on here? Why have I created this in my life?" She put her hands on her ankle and directed energy to it, just as if she were healing someone else. Then she said, "What do I need to learn from this? To stop rushing around so much?!" She forgave herself for creating the situation that allowed her to injure herself and continued directing energy to her ankle. After about 20 minutes, Rita stood up and walked slowly down the rest of the steps. Within two hours, all of the swelling was gone, and she could walk easily.

This isn't to say that injury and illness are consequences of your doing. Or that they can be instantly healed. They are not and cannot. But this is not a process of placing blame. Rather, it's a process of looking at the events that happen and figuring out what lessons they hold and how to make the best of those lessons. No one wishes for cancer or a heart attack. But when these situations of crisis occur, they can become pivotal turning points in your life. You are the creator of your path through this life, and part of your mission is to find your way around the obstacles that seem to block your way.

As actor Michael J. Fox explains on the flap copy of his best-selling memoir, *Lucky Man* (Hyperion, 2002), he would not trade his experience with Parkinson's disease even if given the opportunity to wave a magic wand and erase it all. Living and coping daily with the tough challenges of Parkinson's, for Michael J. Fox and millions of others, can be transformed into a life path of spiritual growth and rich experience. Two decades have passed since the publication of *Lucky Man*. In his latest book *No Time Like the Future: An Optimist Considers Mortality* (Flatiron Books, 2020), Michael acknowledges the role that resilience plays in continuing on even as symptoms worsen and luck may seem to run out. Life is a conscious act of creation, day by day (sometimes hour by hour when you are in chronic pain), and love becomes our optimism.

In essence, healing energy is love. Spirit is love. Our shared humanity is love. The Divine Universe is love. Despite pain, love endures. We find our way to carry on.

Self-Healing

One of the most powerful aspects of energy healing with Spirit is that you can do it for yourself. Try this exercise:

1. Begin by setting your intentions and asking for light and love to surround the healing.

2. If you can touch the part of your body that needs healing, lay your hands on it. If you can't reach it, visualize it. You can also focus on an emotional or relationship problem.

3. Ask the God of your understanding to send love and light to the part of your body or to the situation. Ask what you need to learn from this problem.

4. Consciously release the pain to the Divine Universe.

5. Forgive yourself, forgive others, and bless the process you've just gone through (including the problem for which you've asked for healing).

You don't have to like whatever condition, problem, or pain it is that you have/feel, but blessing it is important because this says you understand its purpose in your life and that you accept it. Release comes with acceptance. Self-healing through Spirit can be very profound. And though the self-healing may not produce a cure, it will surely produce inner peace, nurture comfort, and restore your life force energy.

Drawing Energy from Beyond

The Universe is a generous, abundant, giving source. All that you need is yours for the asking. Most of the time, the trouble is we either don't know what we need or forget that we need to ask for it. The energy of the Universe is always available to help you in many and diverse ways. If you want to make changes in your life, put your intent out to the Divine Spirit of the Universe. What comes back might surprise and delight you.

The regular practice of energy healing and self-healing can only make you a more empathic and compassionate person, both toward your inner self and toward others. *Star Trek's* empath Gem (see Chapter 14), needed to learn that she could channel her healing energy in a way that did not threaten her own life if only she could be brave enough to reach out to those in need. By the time of *Star Trek: The Next Generation* Betazoid empath Deanna Troi had become ship's counselor. In Spirit, we evolve and grow in understanding.

We all contain within us the bravery to embrace empathy and compassion—the courage to heal ourselves and offer energy healing to others, both loved ones and strangers. All we need to do is ask.

As Rita says, "Ask Spirit, and the Universe will provide!"

All Is Spirit, Spirit Is All

Many cultures around the world infuse their physical environments with the life and animation of the Spirit world. Spirit is energy, spirit is everywhere, and energy from Spirit is supportive and healing. These cultures honor the spirits of those who have passed on and the spirit of the Earth.

Many of the practices and rituals of these cultures are finding their way into the everyday lives of many people. Aromatherapy and flower essences use the energy and spirits of plants for healing. Crystals carry the energy of the Earth, a powerful and supportive force alone as well as in combination with other energy forms.

Of the Land: Indigenous Beliefs

In the beginning of human existence, everyone had a close and intimate relationship with the environment. The land supported life. Survival meant connecting with the cycles of nature: the four seasons, day and night, planting seed and harvesting grain, birth and death.

Early cultures moved to follow the natural cycles, trying to keep pace with those that meant life and those that spelled certain doom. Over time and as tribes of the First Nations grew in numbers, moving every few months became impractical. Large groups became easy targets for predators and made it difficult for the group to respond quickly to environmental changes.

To keep up with the changing bounty of the Earth, some tribe members continued in nomadic ways while the rest settled in a location where the land provided fairly steady support—shelter, water, limited food. Those who stayed behind learned to harvest and lay in crops, saving for the lean times when darkness exceeded light and the Earth showed few signs of life.

The hunters—those who left the group to follow their food sources—shadowed migratory herds for hundreds of miles. They learned that the further from home the kill was, the harder they had to work to get the meat, bones, and hides back to the tribe. So they learned to direct the migratory flow, keeping it closer to the home tribe.

For centuries, people lived according to these patterns. They learned to appreciate Spirit, as their forebears had, and to be thankful for the Earth's riches. They identified the energy of the focal points of their celebrations as spirits representing Mother Earth, Father Sky, the birds, the trees, the grasses, the water. Every element had its energy, and every element had its own spirit. And they began to formalize their gratitude through song, dance, and ceremony.

These celebrations became the mythology of humankind that carries forward to modern times in many forms and practices.

Native American Spirit Traditions

As the indigenous culture of North America, Native Americans have always honored the spirit energy of the world around them. Rather than controlling the physical environment, the Native American belief is that we are here to take care of the environment and to take care of the Earth and the bounty it supplies to make life possible.

Within most Native American belief systems, life is seamless, existing across time and space. Those who have passed to Spirit simply exist in a different form than those who have physical bodies. Rituals and ceremonies emphasize the connections between the Earth plane and the Spirit world, and communication between the two is ongoing.

Native American cultures honor the grandfather spirit, and many times, they even refer to God as Grandfather Spirit. Grandfather Spirit is wisdom, strength, and courage. Grandmother Spirit is also wisdom but as the wise nurturer.

The Netflix series *City of Ghosts* features the Ghost Club members in animated documentary-style episodes showcasing six different Los Angeles neighborhoods, their diverse cultures, and their histories. In each episode, the Ghost Club makes contact with a resident spirit who struggles to connect its own lived experience on Earth to the people currently living on the Earth plane, for whom history has moved on. Or, so it would seem that history has moved on.

The episode entitled "Tovaangar" tells the story of the indigenous peoples of Los Angeles, the Tongva. Through a series of puzzles and clues (similar to the "bits and pieces" of information a medium will receive from Spirit during a reading), the Ghost Club members achieve connection with the spirit of the Tongva people, voiced in birdsong. With the help of a Tongva tribe member and a pair of locals historians, the Ghost Club can connect to Los Angeles's Tongva history in a powerful and relevant way. The bird spirit of the Tongva delivers a powerful message from the ancestors to a young boy the Ghost Club has met in the park who recently identifies as Tongva and is also searching for his Tongva identity. The ancestors tell the boy:

> That's your chief gift for the future
>
> That you can never forget who you are.
>
> When times change you will
>
> never be lost,
>
> because you will always know
>
> what holds you
>
> and who holds you.
>
> And that will be
>
> your ancestors and the people around you,
>
> more than you've ever known,
>
> that you are not alone.

The message from Spirit is always the same—Spirit is everywhere, everywhere is Spirit. And you are never alone.

Mayan Spirit Traditions

Many ancient Mayan cultures believed that the dead descended into the Underworld. There was no death, really, just a relocation to this setting. There, they inhabited one of nine Underworld levels. This was similar to the belief systems of other cultures of the same time period, such as the ancient Greeks and Romans.

One Mayan tribe, the Lacandon people, held a belief system that was somewhat different and closer, at least in context, to the Western concept of Heaven. The la Candones people believed that rather than descending to the Underworld, the dead ascended to a place, similar to the land they inhabited on Earth, where they then lived forever without wanting for anything. There was no need to work; everything necessary for a pleasant and worry-free existence was provided. The distinction between this belief and Heaven is that there was no concept of needing to "earn" passage to this ethereal land. Everyone went there after death, not just those deemed deserving.

African Spirit Traditions

The indigenous cultures of Africa are varied and diverse. However, their belief systems share a number of common characteristics. These include the following:

- Belief in a Higher Being or God that exists beyond the realm of humankind's understanding, who is nonetheless able to appear to the people as a visible entity.

- A God who is genderless, although often appears as both male and female.

- Spiritual powers associated with objects and beings (animals, plants, other people) of daily life.

- Many levels of spirits linked to elements of the natural environment, such as spirits of the fire, spirits of the Earth itself, spirits of the air, and spirits of the water.

- Spirit visitors were often those spirit entities, usually ancestors, who acquired Divine energy upon passing and can help their relatives on the Earth plane.

- A cosmology, a culture-specific description of the origin and structure of the Universe, which typically includes explanations of creation, the nature and roles of women and men, and concepts related to death and the dead. It will document a tribe's origins and path to its current existence, presented in the context of myths, legends, and riddles.

Ritual, Ceremony, and Tradition

Rituals are formalized actions we repeat, with certain significance, in conjunction with specific events or situations. Ceremonies incorporate rituals into celebrations. A ceremony often contains multiple rituals. The wedding ceremony, for example, includes the rituals of exchanging vows and rings.

When these celebrations become ingrained in the community culture, they become tradition. We inherit them and participate in them sometimes without fully understanding why but just because the traditional rituals are how we do things. At weddings, we toss rice at the bride and groom as they leave the church. Why? You get 10 points if you know! No? Rice is showered upon newlyweds as a symbol of fertility. But traditions do, after painful effort, expand and evolve with time—sometimes a cause for great joy, such as for the legalization of gay marriage in many countries of the world. As traditions grow, they tend to become more all-inclusive, opening the ritual experience to the greater society.

Such symbolic practices of tradition fill our lives. They connect the small events of our daily lives with the bigger picture of how we fit in the Universe. Tradition dictates how we honor passages from birth through death. Even death rituals are evolving with the times, including a recognition of climate change and the need to use fewer toxic chemicals that can poison our land and water. There is a new movement for green burials that naturally return the body to the soil, nurturing new life in Nature. This natural process is similar to the role of nurse logs—the mighty pines, firs, and spruces of the Pacific Northwest that stand for hundreds of years. After they fall, the evergreen trees become a rich source of growth material for new trees, spending hundreds of more years nurturing new life.

When something happens to disrupt the experience of life's signpost rituals, the rupture can be very painful for those experiencing it. Pandemic grief, such as that experienced during the Ebola crises or during the COVID-19 pandemic that began in 2020, informs an urgent need to adapt society's rituals to rescue much-needed traditions. In Africa, burial rituals involve a large amount of hands-on interaction by the family and community to prepare the deceased's body to be buried. Here in the United States, loved ones are often bedside in the weeks before passing with the person who is ill, and at the moment of passage, the dying one is sharing this profound experience in the loving embrace of family.

When traditional practices cannot be observed because of risk of infection, a process begins of creating new rituals that retain the essence of the lost tradition but continue within the new context. However, for those caught in the crucible of change, the abrupt new realities can be hard to adjust to, causing profound distress and emotional pain. In these times, turning to Spirit can help to ease the pain and provide comfort through the knowledge of continuity of life that connection to Spirit provides.

Birthdays celebrate the joyous day of entry into physical life and the countdown to the day of departure to Spirit, as yet unknown. Each new year reminds us that we are all connected to a greater energy, the energy of the Divine life force from which we come, in which we exist, and to which we return.

Ritual and ceremony can also establish energy connections, such as for contact with Spirit. When you set your intent for communication with spirits to come for the highest and the best, you're "tuning" the energy of your connection to support this. Prayer, meditation, and other focused practices accomplish similar purposes and comfort.

Rites of Passage

The vision quest is integral to many cultures that hold a deep connection to the Earth. In such cultures, like many aboriginal tribes of Australia and Native American tribes, spirit guidance is an essential part of the rite of passage to adulthood.

In Western cultures, external events such as obtaining a driver's license and reaching legal age of consent (or drinking alcohol) are the hallmarks of the transition from child to adult. However, in many indigenous cultures, becoming an adult means demonstrating that you have reached maturity physically, emotionally, and spiritually.

Physical maturation is apparent—you see it when you look at someone. Emotional maturation reflects in attitudes and behaviors; it can't as easily be seen by appearances alone. Spiritual maturation occurs when the young person has the adult experience of connecting with their spirit heritage and the Earth's Spirit energy. Only when young people connect with their origins and ancestors in Spirit can they fully take their places as adults within their communities.

On the typical vision quest, one goal is for you to meet and identify your power animal—an animal spirit with special traits or characteristics that represent attributes or qualities you have or need. Power animals are deeply symbolic. As the quest gets underway, you begin to see signs and indications that, as they accumulate, point toward a particular animal. As you start out, you might see a crow fly across your path, a squirrel run up a pine tree at the edge of the woods, and a rabbit bound off into the underbrush. Which might be your power animal? At this point, any … or none.

Over the span of your vision quest other animals, or representations of them, appear. After a time, one stands out and your attention focuses on this animal. And at some point, there's an encounter—such as through a vision or a dream—in which you know that this is your power animal, and the animal's spirit tells you why. (See the "Power Animal Journey: A Guided Meditation" section later in this chapter for another way to identify and meet your power animal.)

Shaman Soul Release

Shamanism is an Earth-based religion, meaning that it's integrated with its environment. It's quite complex, and we're just going to briefly talk about a small portion of Shamanism, soul release (also called soul retrieval). Shamanistic belief systems hold that as we go through our lives and are traumatized in various ways, we lose little bits of ourselves. This depletes personal energy, causing physical, emotional, and spiritual problems.

Through guided meditation, Shamans help you identify what those missing parts are and bring them back to return them to you. This lets you experience the healing that takes place when that essence of you comes back and is yours again. In some ways, the process is similar to Western psychology's inner child work or therapy to reconnect with and bring back your inner child, the parts of you that you've lost. Most of us have been told throughout our lives that there are things we can't do, which is trauma. So we lose those parts—creativity, musical ability, whatever, or we lose some piece of ourselves to a bad relationship or through working for a cruel taskmaster. Through psychotherapy that sometimes includes hypnosis, you reconnect with these missing parts of yourself to restore your sense of wholeness and balance. Shamans sometimes call this process "journeying." In this process the Spirit world is called to journey, that is, to search the Universe for those parts of you that were lost or stolen by others, and to return them to you so you will be whole again.

Shaman soul release helps you find and bring back the missing spirit, or energy, elements. The shaman leads you in a very light meditative state, from which you can then identify what's bothering you. You make this identification, not the shaman. Say that you suffer debilitating migraine headaches. In this light, altered state, you go inside of yourself, so to speak, to look at this pain. You might touch it or determine who or what it is. Then you ask your Spirit guides to take the source of the pain away and replace it with healing light. This last part is very important for restoring your energy balance; you can't just take away energy without putting something back to fill the void.

Self-Mastery Through Conscious Autosuggestion

The book by the same title, by French psychologist and pharmacist Emile Coue (1857-1926) who developed in 1920 a method he popularized as "autosuggestion," where he worked with clinical staff at the Faculte de Medecine at the University of Nancy. Coue believed energy could be manifested or released through the power of the imagination, not the will. If willpower is not in agreement with imagination, energy cannot be raised to action. Coue believed that imagination wins over willpower, *without any exception.*

And so, if you are suffering a physical or emotional pain, Coue recommends that you: "Shut yourself up alone in a room, seat yourself in an armchair, close your eyes to avoid any distraction, and concentrate your mind for a few moments on thinking: *Such and such a thing is going to disappear,* or, *Such and such a thing is coming to pass."* Repeat this ten times as a kind of mantra, and then move on with your day. Autosuggestion alone cannot cure cancer, but it can engage your spirit and imagination in realigning and restoring your life force energy in a beneficial way. As we believe, so we are directed.

For a general practice of conscious autosuggestion: "Every morning before you get up and every evening as soon as you are in bed, shut your eyes, and repeat twenty times in succession, *moving your lips* (this is indispensable), and counting *mechanically* on a long string with twenty knots, the following phrase: *Day by day, in every way, I am getting better and better.* Do not think of anything in particular, as the words *in every way* apply to everything."

For Coue, the saying is true that *willpower is not enough*. Only when we dispassionately engage our imagination, integrating imagination with Spirit, can we begin to manifest achievable change in our lives. Conscious autosuggestion calls to the highest and best within ourselves, directing our energy toward alignment with the Divine life force for nurturing growth and goodness.

Earth Energy

The Earth itself is a tremendous source of energy. Magnets, gemstones, and crystals carry the Earth's energy, which has many applications in conventional as well as Spirit for healing. And of course, Earth energy supports all other energy on the Earth plane.

Because of their capability to store, amplify, and transfer energy, crystals have many applications in modern science. Crystals made the first radio transmissions possible, for example. Today crystals appear in everything from the liquid crystal display on your watch to sophisticated medical imaging technology. The energy of Earth's crystals helps to power our world.

Animal Energy

Animals contain great Spirit energy. In many indigenous cultures, animal spirits represent the connection between the Earth and the Divine. The spirits of certain animals have special significance. Native American tribes had animal Spirit guides that helped them in nearly all functions of daily life.

These beliefs carry over into modern life in many ways. The United States has the bald eagle as its official symbol, which represents power and grace. Golfing fans know the great American golfer Jack Nicklaus as the golden bear. Classic fast cars are Mustangs, Jaguars, and Cougars.

Power Animals

Like Spirit guides, Power Animals bring special energy connections to your life. And like Spirit guides from the Higher side, your Power Animals change according to your needs (physical, emotional, and spiritual) and what is going on in your life. Power Animals are also called totem animals or just totems. A totem is an emblem or a symbol that has spiritual significance.

A totem pole is a tradition specific to the Native American tribes of the Pacific Northwest. Carved from a cedar tree, a totem pole contains the images or representations of the Power Animals important to a family group or clan. It serves to identify the group's history and heritage, told through the symbolism of the totems carved into the pole.

Any animal can be a Power Animal; each animal has particular traits and characteristics. When this animal is your power animal, it shares these attributes with you to give you the energy they provide. When you are learning something, such as when you are in school, your Power Animal might be an owl for wisdom. If you feel someone is threatening your child or your family, perhaps you draw from the energy of the bear. When you are working creatively, such as writing or painting, the Power Animal supporting you might be a spider or a crow.

You don't choose your Power Animals. They choose you. Familiar power animals such as bears, wolves, and owls have become almost archetypal in their representations of certain attributes:

- *Ant*—teamwork, patience, focused action
- *Armadillo*—safety, protection
- *Bear*—power, strength, healing, protectiveness
- *Beaver*—determination, productivity, persistence
- *Buffalo*—abundance, the natural order of things
- *Butterfly*—change, metamorphosis, transformation, joy, freedom
- *Crow*—spiritual strength, creativity
- *Dove*—peace, calmness, unity
- *Dragonfly*—carefree, good luck
- *Eagle*—vision, strength, flight, divine
- *Elephant*—strength, power, royalty, family
- *Frog*—cleansing, rebirth, transformation
- *Hawk*—guide, vision
- *Hummingbird*—welcome, peace, happy home
- *Lion*—intuition, imagination, family, courage
- *Owl*—wisdom, seeing what others can't
- *Peacock*—immortality, pride
- *Salmon*—pride, intensity
- *Snake*—rebirth, change, healing, shrewdness
- *Spider*—creativity, fate
- *Turtle*—steady, loyal, protected

Power Animal Journey: A Guided Meditation

Rita's good friend Martha Tierney wrote the following guided meditation for meeting your Power Animals, especially for this book. As a certified metaphysical hypnotherapist, spirit-trained shamanic facilitator, and medium, Martha maintains a private practice, Soul Healing, in Boston, Massachusetts. For more information about Martha and her practice, you can connect with her profile on LinkedIn. Thanks, Martha!

We recommend that you read this guided meditation into a recorder, so you can listen and follow its suggestions. If you don't want to listen to your own voice, ask someone whose voice you find soothing and calming to record it for you.

To prepare for listening to your recording and the journey it will take you on, follow these tips:

- Be sure you will not be disturbed during this process (turn your smartphone ringtone down or off, or turn off all other electronic devices, and silence your smart speaker by placing it on "do not disturb").
- Dim the lights.
- Put on some background music: Soothing or patterned drumming music (for journeying) can assist in altering your state of consciousness/awareness.
- Begin to slow your breathing.
- Choose a sitting position; this will likely keep you more focused and awake.
- Make sure your posture is straight and that you're not feeling restricted in any way—get comfortable.

Do not listen to your "Power Animal Journey" recording while driving a car, operating heavy equipment, or doing anything else that requires your full attention. This guided meditation will affect and alter your perceptions.

Here is the guided meditation. Read it through a couple of times, so it's familiar, and you can read it smoothly. Where you see *<pause>*, pause for two or three seconds and then continue. This might seem awkward while you're doing the reading, but when you're listening to the recording, it gives you time to follow the suggestion. Read in a steady, calm voice.

POWER ANIMAL JOURNEY

Continue to focus upon your slow *<pause>*

comfortable *<pause>*

breathing *<pause>*

allowing yourself to drop your shoulders *<pause>*

and warmly relax your back *<pause>*

you may begin to relax your body starting at the top of your head *<pause>*

relaxing your scalp *<pause>*

forehead, eyes, nose, and mouth *<pause>*

letting your cheeks and jaw relax and drop your jaw slightly *<pause>*resting your tongue naturally, at the top of your mouth and behind your front teeth. *<pause>*

☆

Feel how relaxed you are from your throat, up through your head, to the top of your scalp *<pause>*

so relaxed *<pause>*

and continue on down *<pause>*

relaxing the throat *<pause>*

warming and relaxing your shoulders, arms, and hands *<pause>*

noticing how wonderful you feel as you continue to release all inner tension from the top of your head, right down through to your shoulders and arms *<pause>*

bring your attention to your chest *<pause>*

allow yourself to let go of all of today's stress, simply let it melt away *<pause>*

freeing you to relax so much more than before *<pause>*

and with every breath *<pause>*

you are able to release *all* of today's unhealthy tension that you may have held within your body *<pause>*

as you relax your waist, your organs, colon, and genitals *<pause>*

warming and relaxing your pelvis *<pause>*

your hips *<pause>*

and as you move down through your thighs *<pause>*

the front *and* the back of your knees feel so much more relaxed *<pause>*

as you continue to release the day's tension *<pause>*

relaxing your calves, the muscles supporting your chins *<pause>*

your ankles are relaxed, you may rotate them if you wish *<pause>*

and the warmth of relaxation *<pause>*

continues on down through the arches of your feet *<pause>*

the soles of your feet, and on down into each toe. *<pause>*

Check your body and see if there is any tension still left, *<pause>*

and if there is, simply release it by warming it with your intention. That's right, let it go *<long pause>*

Now try to imagine your relaxed energy growing out from of the bottoms of your feet, *<pause>*

like a tree growing roots, into Mother Earth *<pause>*

your roots can be as straight or windy as you wish *<pause>*

and as deep or shallow as you wish *<pause>*

allow yourself a moment to feel the energy of love and balance *<pause>*

touching *<pause>*

nourishing *<pause>*

your lovely roots. *<pause>*

☆

Bringing your attention to the top of your head, allow your relaxed energy to reach toward Father Sky *<pause>*

feeling the warmth of the sun relaxing you *<pause>*

nourishing you *<pause>*

and when you feel you have touched upon the right area of Father Sky, bring that wonderful loving feeling down into the crown of your head down through your body *<pause>*

washing away any worry *<pause>*

any tension or discomfort *<pause>*

if you wish, you may allow Father Sky to meet and blend with Mother Earth within you *<pause>*

and as you do *<pause>*

feel how radiant and beautiful you feel *<pause>*

let this energy of healing love continue to feed and nourish your body, mind, and spirit *<pause>*

as you allow yourself to imagine yourself in a calm sacred space *<pause>*

it can be somewhere you've been before *<pause>*

or somewhere you discover here today *<pause>*

that's right, allow yourself to travel anywhere you wish *<pause>*

as you begin to get comfortable in your nice safe *<pause>*

calm *<pause>*

sacred space. *<pause>*

a space that is all yours right now *<pause>*

a place where no one will interrupt you. *<pause>*

Relax in your nice spot and feel the beauty that surrounds you *<pause>*

take a moment to smell the air *<pause>*

feel the warm gentle winds upon your face *<pause>*

there may be sounds of nature around you *<pause>*

maybe there is a babbling brook nearby that you can hear,

or a bird singing its song to his mate *<pause>*

whatever you wish here is fine *<pause>*

for this is your sacred spot in the Universe. *<pause>*

As you continue to feel the energy of nature all around you, supporting you *<pause>*

this is your time to journey to meet with your Power Animal *<pause>*

they will come to you to guide you *<pause>*

and protect you *<pause>*

they will become a companion to you and you a companion to them *<pause>*

It can be any animal you feel comfortable with at this time *<pause>*

off in the distance, you see an animal moving slowly toward you *<pause>*

if you wish, you may move forward to meet them on their way *<pause>*

If, for any reason *<pause>*

you do not feel right with the first animal you see *<pause>*

there will be another one who comes along *<pause>*

to greet you. *<pause>*

As the two of you meet, just take a moment to sense one another *<long pause>*

you may communicate with one another simply with your thoughts *<long pause>*

you will and do understand one another easily *<pause>*

if you feel ready and you would like to extend yourself in friendship at this time, *<pause>*

you may *<long pause>*

perhaps you would like to walk, or fly, or swim with your new friend, to get to know how they live, go ahead *<long pause>*

you may relax with your friend *<pause>*

or play with your friend *<pause>*

or explore with your friend. *<pause>*

Take the time you wish together, for a few moments *<pause>*

when it is time, I will call you back. *<pause>*

<three-minute pause>

The two of you will have a uniquely personal relationship together *\<pause\>*

a relationship of reciprocity *\<pause\>*

you may visit one another at any time you wish simply by calling to one another *\<one-minute pause\>*

It is time to take your leave now *\<pause\>*

give thanks to your new friend *\<pause\>*

give thanks to Great Spirit for this wonderful experience with your Power Animal. *\<pause\>*

Remember your Power Animal can change into any size, larger or smaller, when you need protection. *\<pause\>*

they can and will work in any way the situation calls for to protect you. *\<pause\>*

You may ask if your Power Animal would like to return with you to your sacred space so they will know where to meet you the next time *\<pause\>*

if you are comfortable with that. *\<pause\>*

☆

Return now to the point where the two of you met *\<long pause\>*

going back to your journeying point *\<pause\>*

and return now to your sacred space. *\<pause\>*

If your Power Animal is with you take a moment to exchange goodbyes for now. *<pause>*

☆

Until you meet again *<pause>*

alone now, return to the room in your home where you started this special journey *<pause>*

feel the room around you *<pause>*

feel the energy of Mother Earth and Father Sky *<pause>*

Join them *<pause>*

thank them for healing you and for holding your place during your journey *<pause>*

Release Father Sky with love and pull down your relaxed energy *<pause>*

that's right, pull it all back, right back to the crown of your head where it started from *<pause>*

feel your relaxed energy strengthening again *<pause>*

tightening *<pause>*

like a loose mesh weave closing up *<pause>*

Release Mother Earth with love and gratitude *<pause>*

and as she releases, call back your roots *<pause>*

all your roots *<pause>*

and bring your relaxed energy right back into your feet again where it started from *<pause>*

feel your relaxed energy strengthening again *<pause>*

tightening *<pause>*

like a loose mesh weave closing up *<pause>*

(Read the remaining lines more quickly.)

Feel your feet now *<pause>*

your shins, calves, and knees *<pause>*

your thighs, hips, and pelvis *<pause>*

your colon, genitals, and organs *<pause>*

your chest and back *<pause>*

your shoulders, arms, and hands *<pause>*

your throat and tongue *<pause>*

your cheeks and jaw *<pause>*

mouth, nose, eyes, and forehead *<pause>*

the top of your head and your scalp. *<pause>*

I am going to count to three, and when I do, *<pause>*

you will open your eyes and feel confident, loved, fresh, and revitalized, *<pause>*

ready to continue on with your day. *<pause>*

☆

You will remember the experience with your Power Animal in full detail. *<pause>*

yes, that's right, you will remember in detail your experience with your Power Animal. *<pause>*

1 *<pause>* feeling alert and aware *<pause>*

2 *<pause>* feeling happy and vital *<pause>*

3 *<pause>* open your eyes now *<pause>*

and you are feeling alert and refreshed *<pause>*

happy to continue on with your day.

You can repeat this guided meditation as often as you like. After a while, you'll see certain patterns begin to emerge. You might have an owl as your power animal for as long as several years and then have the ant. Your power animals change according to your needs so that their energy fulfills where yours is lacking.

When Animals Pass to Spirit

Pets are loyal and loving companions. Like all living things, they have vital energy. Often when Rita does readings, spirits come through with their favorite pets accompanying them, such as the beloved Maltese dog, Buff, in Chapter 13. Pets do follow us to the Higher side.

At an evening Spiritualist church service, Rita came to a woman in the congregation and started to chuckle. She said, "I don't know how to tell you this, but I have a dog here that's coming through for you. It's a wire-haired terrier." Then Rita said, "He behaves as if he has springs attached to the bottoms of his feet! He's jumping straight up; it's as if I can hear the word *boing!*" The woman was overjoyed and burst into tears. Her beloved dog had passed to Spirit a month earlier ... a wire-haired terrier that she always told people behaved as though he had springs on the bottoms of his feet.

Often, a pet is so identifiable that it becomes a key piece of identifying the person who's coming through when that's not clear. Pets show themselves by species (dog, cat), size, and personality. It's wonderful to know that our beloved pets, like human loved ones, are still around us, even when they pass to the Higher side.

So, when you are with your pet at passing, their spirit is released to the Higher side, just as a human spirit is released. You are able to be with your pet and make the profound connection, spirit to spirit, honoring your pet's transition from the Earth plane to the Spirit plane. Even as there is much grief we experience at a beloved pet's passing, there is also the joy of feeling your pet's spirit lose its hold on the physical body and move under your hands to the Spirit world. We feel it happen and know that continuity of life exists for our pets as well. They are safe, in Spirit.

If you cannot be with your pet at passing, do not worry. Your pet is able to be with you in Spirit. If you feel your pet's presence, see flashes of your pet, or dream about your pet, it could be that you are being visited by your pet's spirit. How lovely—be comforted in your grief, knowing your pet is with you still and always through Spirit.

Rita met with Kim via the telephone. She called after the passing of her dear friend John and asked for a spirit drawing of him. Rita always tells clients that she cannot promise that a specific spirit will come through, but John was there and was very willing to communicate. John chose to show himself as a younger man, although he had been much more mature when he passed to spirit. John talked about the month of March and showed the number eight. Kim confirmed that John celebrated a very special eighth anniversary in March. Rita identified lungs filled with smoke, and Kim confirmed that John had been a heavy smoker. John also appeared with his beloved beige cat. Yes, animals go to spirit, too!

Plant Energy

Many times, a spirit will show a particular plant as a symbol, such as roses as love or daisies as new beginnings. As with all symbols, each medium will create their own herbarium, or plant dictionary.

Plants give us all life-sustaining energy every day. The whole wheat bread you drop in the toaster in the morning … plant energy. The avocado that tops it…plant energy. The spinach salad you eat for lunch … plant energy. The sautéed mushrooms and green bean casserole you enjoy for dinner … plant energy. The bowl of fresh mixed berries you scarf down for dessert… plant energy. Plants—grains, fruits, vegetables—are the fuels that give your body the energy it needs to carry out the functions of living.

Many plants have additional energies that often are not apparent unless you are tuned in and know about these special qualities. Some of these qualities can be explained through biochemistry. We can look at the plant's chemical composition and know the effect it will have on the body. But all plants have healing energy properties on the energy level. You can't see, taste, or smell these properties. They act on your aura to influence your personal life force energy.

Medicinal Plants

Medicinal herbs and botanicals, for example, contain chemicals that function as drugs. The plant foxglove contains digitalis, which is the chemical now used in the drug digoxin, which is prescribed to strengthen and regulate the heartbeat. There are thousands of such plants, many of which are the basis for the drugs of modern medicine as well as ancient medical systems such as traditional Chinese medicine (TCM).

Plants with medicinal qualities act on your physical body to influence physical functions. The resulting changes can affect emotional and spiritual aspects of your health as well.

Flower Essences

Flower essences use water to capture the energy imprints of plants. In most plants, the flower is the most potent energy source because it is the plant's structure of regeneration. Flower essences come in liquid form and have no taste or smell. They work by interacting with your personal life force energy field through your aura. Flower essences influence your spiritual and emotional dimensions.

Dr. Edward Bach, a British bacteriologist, discovered flower essences in the 1930s while researching the then-new field of vaccines. He began to find evidence that the plants he was using in his culture mediums actually influenced health by interacting on an energy level.

Each plant has specific qualities that act on certain issues. Essence of pine, for example, influences self-acceptance. Roses, so familiar as symbols of romance, not surprisingly influence compassion and love. Bach's Rescue Remedy, a mixture of five flower essences—rock rose, impatiens, clematis, star of Bethlehem, and cherry plum, works to ease acute stress or anxiety. Bach's ever-popular trademarked flower essences still are sold today and can be found in holistic or natural food stores.

Aromatherapy

Aromatherapy has become popular in Western cultures because it smells good. You can enjoy aromatherapy whether or not you understand its energy foundation. Many people enjoy the fragrances associated with aromatherapy. From a scientific perspective, the smells of various substances elicit responses in the brain that cause biochemical changes. From an energy perspective, aromatherapy acts on the body's energy field in the same ways as flower essences. Rosemary, mint, and eucalyptus wake up the body, mind, and spirit and are widely used in lotions, shampoos, soaps, and body washes.

Honoring Spirit

You *are* Spirit, and you are *of* Spirit. The essence of your being is Spirit energy in its own right. Your energy also connects with the Spirit of the physical world around you and the Universe at large. Spirit and energy are inseparable. They exist contiguously, across the Earth plane and the Spirit world. Spirit energy links us to the natural environment that supports our physical needs, to each other, and to loved ones who no longer walk the Earth plane.

This is the foundation of belief for many indigenous cultures, and it is the foundation that supports contact with Spirit and communication with spirits. Honoring this foundation, in yourself and in others, makes it possible for Spirit to continue supporting you—in your everyday life as well as during times of special need, especially times of grieving.

Near-Death Experiences

A bright, beckoning light. A welcoming circle of family and friends. Peace, tranquility, and joy. Many people recount these common elements when their souls travel to the brink of the Higher side and then return.

We call this experience "near-death" because you return from it to life. What makes it "near" instead of permanent? What happens to keep you from passing over when it's not quite your time to leave your physical life? Why would you be allowed to go, or be summoned to, the very brink and then be sent back? Who, or what, sends you to, or from, that brink? Or, is it *you* who makes the decision to turn back to life … is it *your decision to make?*

When you find yourself in the veil between the living and the dead, between Earth and Spirit, as all that lives must inexorably do, what is actually happening then—in the moments near death?

Stepping to the Edge

Each *near-death experience* (also called an *NDE*) is unique, yet most near-death experiences share common characteristics. These typically include the following:

- Sudden trauma that precipitates the experience
- The sensation of rising out of your body and observing it, as well as the activity going on around you, as an entity separate from your body
- An end to any pain you might have been experiencing in your physical body and an overwhelming sense of lightness and peace
- The experience of floating through a dark tunnel or corridor
- A bright light that draws you to it as if with a magnetic force
- The presence of loved ones gathered to greet and welcome you, just on the Higher side of the bright white light

A near-death experience (NDE) occurs when the physical body experiences clinical death and the spirit leaves, and then life returns to the body and the spirit returns. By definition, at near-death, you will reach the point of clinical death. Your heart stops, your breathing stops, your brain stops. All signs of physical life cease ... and then return. Although the medical view is that brain cells begin to die after three minutes without oxygen, people have existed in a state of clinical death for as long as 90 minutes, depending upon the circumstances and conditions surrounding the situation.

How is this possible? From the Earth plane perspective, doctors have lots of ideas but no conclusive explanations. From the Higher side perspective, when it's not your time, it's not your time.

The Shock That Separates

Most of the time, a physical trauma precipitates a near-death experience. This might be a life-threatening injury, a crisis during surgery, a heart attack, a severe allergic reaction—any number of circumstances that strike suddenly and without warning. Such trauma shocks or jolts your being, separating it into its three component subtle bodies. The physical, of course, remains on the Earth plane. The astral body is your energy body and includes your chakras and meridians that supply the physical body with Divine life force. Your causal body permeates and interpenetrates your physical and astral bodies, connecting the "seed" energy of your essence, your soul, to the Spirit plane. As the three subtle bodies jolt to awareness, your soul, your causal body, prepares to do what it's perhaps "programmed" to do as death approaches, it leaves.

But the Higher side is not prepared for your arrival because, despite the events unfolding on the Earth plane, it's not your time to leave your physical existence. Of course, your spirit always exists with one foot (so to speak!) in the Spirit world and the other on the Earth plane. This is the essence of physical life as we've discussed it throughout this book. Your physical body is the vehicle for your spirit in its travels on the Earth plane, but your spirit is still part of and connected to the bigger Divine life force energy of the Universe.

Although your spirit might freely travel during your dream state (many spirits do; see Chapter 17), it does so with intent. Not that you know your spirit is about to take off to go visiting, but your *spirit* (your Higher being) knows. It disengages carefully from your physical and astral dimensions—and returns in similar fashion.

During a near-death experience, your spirit is lifted from your physical body. There is no intent: it just happens. Little wonder human beings find the experience bewildering at first! Many people report that one of the first sensations they become aware of is that the pain they were feeling in their bodies, usually intense because it was caused by trauma and shock, is suddenly gone.

A near-death experience is a spirit communication of the most direct kind. One of the first spirit drawings Rita did was for a woman who had been critically injured in a car accident. When Rita took Harriet's hand in hers, both of them expected a loved one of Harriet's would come through. Much to their surprise, however, the contact involved Harriet herself. "What I'm seeing is an angel come and lift you out of your body in your accident," Rita said. "This was to protect you from feeling the pain from your many injuries, which would have been overwhelming to you." "Yes," said Harriet. "I remember. I came back to my body in the hospital."

I See ME!

There you are, just looking around, and suddenly what you see is … you! No mirrors, no tricks. It's really you in the flesh, as seen from Spirit. This is a consistent part of near-death experiences. Some people feel themselves lifting from their bodies and floating toward the ceiling, then looking down to see themselves as the focal points of desperate efforts to cut the journey of passing over short by restoring you to life. For many people, this is quite a spiritual jolt to experience. One moment everything is as it should be, and the next moment nothing is as it was. And there you are, looking at yourself from a view you've never had before!

Some people report they can look down on their physical bodies during near-death experiences, watching the flurry of activity taking place in the efforts to revive them. A person who has had a near-death experience often can describe, in considerable detail, events that, if still within the physical body, they would not be able to see or hear. These events might include watching the doctors and nurses prepare and give injections, shock the heart, and place breathing tubes. The disembodied spirit can often hear conversations taking place in hallways and other places distant from the body's location. When they return to physical life, people report these conversations.

Near-death experiences, of course, do not only occur in hospitals and healthcare settings. Awareness expands at the scene, and the near-death spirit can see and hear the scene of the accident, witness those present and their actions, and see loved ones waiting on the Higher side. The near-death spirit who passes at home may view in vivid detail the contents of their bedroom, the reaction of their loved ones to what they are interpreting as their passing, as well as the faces of loved ones waiting beyond the brightness on the Higher side.

The events of near-death experiences that take place in the physical world are easy to verify because other people participate in them and can recall their own lived experiences of the traumatic near-death event with you. Some of the most intriguing insights we have into existence beyond the Earth plane come from people who experience physical death and then come back, or those who witness it happen to someone they love. This is yet further evidence of the continuity of life.

The Goodness and Love of the Higher Side

A body that has experienced severe trauma—injury, heart attack, shock from illness, and the like—is nearly always in great pain. These are assaults on the integrity of the body, and they leave damage in their wake. When their spirits withdraw from these damaged bodies, people who have near-death experiences report that the pain goes away. They can look at their bodies and wonder if they really want to return, especially when so much goodness and love beckons from the Higher side.

This is the "good" we request when we ask that spirit contact and spirit healing come through for the greatest good and the highest intent. It is a welcoming, benevolent sense of absolute love—which makes sense because it is a representation of the Divine.

This goodness is pure; it is the energy of pure love. It exists only for learning and healing. It is this goodness that manifests when spirits come through with messages. And it is the goodness that welcomes spirits as they are passing over.

When it is time for your spirit to join your loved ones on the Higher side, there is also sense of transition. Spirit communicators tell us there is a sense of moving from one place to another and a sense of moving into the light. The spirits waiting to greet you on the Higher side differ with the passing person's desires, needs (on the Higher side), and soul's mission. You could cross over to an old-fashioned, backyard picnic … or find your dearly departed lover offering you a dance.

Tunnel Travel

Many people describe a distinctive tunnel or corridor, usually darkened, where they find themselves in when their spirits leave their bodies. At the end of this tunnel, they can see a bright, white light, and they know this is the portal to the Higher side.

Some people report feeling fearful or frightened while in this tunnel, while others experience it as nothing more than a passageway that links the Earth plane with the Spirit world. No one really knows what this tunnel is or represents, but it is common to many near-death experiences.

Tunnels are a metaphor for time travel in Diana Gabaldon's eighth book in the *Outlander* series, *Written in My Own Heart's Blood*. In this book, Claire and Jamie's time-traveling grandson Jemmy finds himself operating a train deep under a hydroelectric tunnel that seems to demarcate and reveal the line between past and future, the Spirit world:

> He couldn't really see it, not with his eyes, not exactly. He squinted, trying to think how he <u>was </u>seeing it, but there wasn't a word for what he was doing. Kind of like hearing or smelling or touching, but not really any of those.

> But he knew where it was. It was right <u>there</u>, a kind of…shiver…in the air, and when he stared at it, he had a feeling in the back of his mind like really pretty sparkly things, like sun on the sea and the way a candle-flame looked when it shone through a ruby, but he knew he wasn't really <u>seeing</u> anything like that.

> It went all the way across the tunnel, and up to the high roof, too, he could tell. But it wasn't thick at all, it was thin as air.

The tunnel, the veil—*yea, though I walk through the valley…*, the river Chiron, the metaphor is one of passage, a journey from the Earth plane to the Spirit plane. Enigmatic, frightening, beautiful, indescribable, we all must cross over to the light. We all must pass through to the Divine.

Into the Light

In near-death experiences, people often report seeing a bright light with friends and family who have passed to the Higher side already gathered around its edges. This is the light of Divine energy. This is the light that reassures you that the Goddess or God of your understanding is near and all is well. There is love, warmth, peace, and joy, and a strong feeling of desire to move into the light to complete the passage. Most people report feeling an overwhelming sense of pure love.

Of course, because it is not yet your time, you cannot complete the passage no matter how enticing the light and the love. And this is clear to your spirit, however much it might want to make the crossing. Spirits on the Higher side know, too. And as much as they want to communicate joy and goodness, they are there just to let you know they *are* there … and they'll be waiting for you when truly it is your time to complete your passage to Spirit.

For many people who have near-death experiences, the light fosters a resurgence of faith in their Goddess/God of understanding and a renewed commitment to following a spiritual path for the rest of their Earth plane journey. It is an amazing and powerful thing to connect with such goodness and love!

So Many Welcoming Spirits!

Typically in a near-death experience, the spirits gathered on the Higher side of this light are smiling and happy to see their loved one, but they aren't beckoning for you to join them. They know it's not quite your time. But they want you to know all is well with them. This is like a spirit communication of the most wondrous and direct sort!

Seeing the loved ones already passed to Spirit is joyous, but this is often where sadness enters in: You want to stay. It's been a long time since you've seen many of them, perhaps, and you want to visit at least.

After a near-death experience, a reading with a medium like Rita, can help connect you with loved ones who have passed over to the Higher side in a way that allows messages to be exchanged, love shared. The sadness you feel in having come so close to the surrender of direct contact with Divine life force energy—as manifested by the spirits of beloved ones who have passed, can be transformed into a celebration of the joy of living. Spirit drawings give proof you've experienced the continuity of life, and that you will reunite with your loved ones in Spirit when your time comes to complete your passage.

Connie brought her brother to Rita for a drawing from Spirit, and a drawing of their grandmother came through for him. He saw his grandmother's eyes and began to cry. It is sometimes overwhelming when one can see the eyes of a deceased loved one appear on a sheet of drawing paper. A year later, Connie, owner of the New Age gift shop Magick Mirror in Bristol, Rhode Island, came to see Rita, and the matching picture of Connie's grandfather came through for her. The connection to a loved one who has passed to Spirit, even in a drawing made here on the Earth plane, is profound, powerful, and full of love. It's no wonder it's the loved ones who are there to greet us when indeed it is our time to pass to Spirit. How wonderful it is to be together again.

Here and There ... at the Same Time

During a near-death experience, you're not really in this world or the next. You're sort of in-between, existing a little in each but in neither completely. You aren't aware of this to any great extent. It's your spirit that appears to have the recall of events that happen during the near-death experience, which is how you return to your physical body on the Earth plane with a memory of events you couldn't possibly have witnessed or experienced.

Often, a person can relate, in verbatim detail, conversations taking place among others in hallways and physical locations outside the room where their physical body lies. The people engaged in these conversations might be different groups discussing the situation—doctors and nurses in one group in one location, family and friends sequestered in another.

The spirit has a simultaneous experience of all events related to the near-death. It witnesses the frantic activity to bring the physical body back to life and sees events and overhears discussions that aren't possible to experience from the physical body's location. At the same time, the spirit's causal body is moving through the tunnel toward the bright light and the waiting spirit entities at its other end. There is no time; there is no space. There is just energy and existence. There is Divine love.

Not Quite Time to Go

With continuing advances in medical knowledge and technology, near-death experiences are becoming increasingly common. People who just ten years ago would have been declared dead from their conditions are now routinely "brought back" to life. Many then go on to full recovery from their physical injuries and enjoy long, full lives.

Are they truly "brought back" or is it the Divine order of the Universe that their spirits are communing with the Higher side? Of course, this is difficult to answer with certainty. But it seems that if it was your time to go, you would go—no matter what technology was being used to prevent such an outcome. And conversely, if it's *not* your time to go, you won't—not because technology saves your life, even if that's how it looks, but simply because it's *not your time to go*.

When it becomes clear that their spirits are instead returning to their physical bodies rather than completing the passage, people often report a sense of sadness and even resistance. They have "seen the light" and want to become one with it, to move into the warmth, peace, and joy that they feel.

Other people feel a sense of relief. Their lives on the Earth plane are unfinished, and they know this. They are eager to return to complete those lives and are comforted in knowing what lies ahead for them when their time to make the crossing does come.

Divine Order ... or Accident?

If there is a Divine order, how can "accidents" such as near-death experiences happen? This is a valid question, and one many people ask in trying to understand or explain the phenomenon of near-death experience. Remember, however, the critically important role of freewill. Your actions determine your movement along your life's path. Your destiny is a journey and is not an endpoint.

We could engage in debate about whether anything happens by accident. Perhaps your near-death experience is as much a part of the Divine order of the Universe as was your birth. Perhaps there are lessons for you that you can only learn by coming so close to making the crossing.

The Edge of Death

So what, exactly, happens when your body dies but the Higher side says you're not ready to make the crossing? There are biological phenomena, of course. Once your heart stops beating, blood stops circulating through your body. Vital organs feel the oxygen shortage immediately, and your body's shock response leaps into action. This response sends epinephrine coursing to your heart, with the intent of jolting it into action, and simultaneously shuts down all body functions not necessary to support life. Epinephrine is a natural chemical your body makes that stimulates heartbeat and breathing. Its release is part of your body's "fight or flight" survival response.

It seems odd to think that so much of this intricate design, which is your physical body, could have so many dispensable functions. But the core functions necessary to just keep your body alive are few: heart, lungs, circulation, and brain. Everything else can wait—because if these core functions go, nothing else matters.

This is what we think of as the edge of death—one more shutdown function, and it's all over. In a near-death experience, that "one more" happens. The physical body dies, at least briefly. It's at this point, it seems, that the spirit makes its exit.

The Nobel-prizewinning novelist Ernest Hemingway experienced a near-death experience during World War I; it was an experience he would use to inform his writing of the classic novel *A Farewell to Arms.* On July 8, 1918, not long before the Great War's end, Hemingway rode his bicycle up to the frontline at Fossalta to deliver coffee, cigarettes, chocolate, and postcards to Italian soldiers in the trenches. A mortar shell detonated three feet away from him, sending 220 shards of shrapnel into his legs and scalp. As he lay dazed, Hemingway recounts, *"I died then, I felt my soul or something coming right out of my body like you'd pull a silk handkerchief out of a pocket by one corner—it flew around and then came back and went in again, and I wasn't dead anymore."*

For many years, the medical explanation for the experiences people have during the time they're technically "dead" has focused on the various chemical and electrical changes taking place in the brain as it attempts to cope with catastrophic oxygen loss. Nonessential parts of the brain begin to shut down almost immediately when oxygen levels reach a certain point. Among them are the parts of the brain responsible for cognition—thought and memory.

The rapid chemical and electrical changes that occur during this process cause brain cells to flare and die, activating memory and thought fragments. According to this explanation model, these flares account for the images of loved ones people believe they see during near-death experiences.

You don't actually *see* anyone; you just experience the activation of *your memory of that person*. This is the same process that causes you to "see" your entire life flash as snapshots in a cosmic slide show before your eyes when facing what you believe is imminent death.

It's an intriguing concept. Until research in the late 1990s and early part of the twenty-first century, it was widely accepted by medical personnel as the physiological explanation for near-death experiences. But this recent research shows that the brain's shutdown is more rapid and more complete than previously thought. Once oxygen levels fall below critical levels, brain function virtually ceases. It doesn't appear that even these chemical and electrical actions take place; there's no fuel source (oxygen) to make them happen.

Another clinical theory puts forth the idea that the brain's return to function following a near-death experience causes the activations that trigger memories and thoughts. As brain cells fire back up, they initially over-respond, like the flare of throwing straw on a fire, before they settle back into normal function.

In a metaphysical understanding, your three bodies—physical, astral, and causal, settle together in harmony once more. As the elements of your astral body—fire, earth, air, and water, channel life force energy through the meridians of the physical body, their qualities manifest to animate your whole being. That is, the slideshow of your life that passes before your eyes in a flash is created by your life force energy stimulating memory. As you experience this, you draw your causal body back to the Earth plane. All as a young Hemingway expressed on that awful day in July 1918, as he lay wounded—and for a few precious moments…he was gone.

Coming Back

Coming back to physical life is often quite a shock. Suddenly you're reunited with the pain your physical body is experiencing, and that's not pleasant. It's a clear indication you are still alive.

Many people report a sense of joy and exhilaration at being reunited with their physical bodies despite the pain because it means they will continue in their physical lives. At this point, people often think of loved ones on the Earth plane, such as children, and feel grateful they can remain with them.

There is sometimes sadness at leaving, once again, the loved ones who have passed to the Higher side. Seeing them again is joyous, and even though it tells you that they'll still be waiting for you when it is your turn to make the crossing, it's not easy to leave them.

Often, loved ones in Spirit maintain their contact from the Higher side, appearing in visitations. It's not that they weren't willing to do this before the near-death experience; rather, the NDE makes people more receptive to contact with spirits.

A Transforming Experience

Just as a near-death experience gives a person who has one a new lease on life, it also provides a glimpse across what we've always perceived to be an impenetrable barrier. A near-death experience is profoundly moving and often life-changing for someone who has one. Many people who experience them find that they return to existence on the Earth plane with awakened psychic and spiritual sensitivities. They see firsthand that death is a gateway, not an end.

Some people return to physical existence a bit reluctantly, not especially willing to leave the joy and peace they've experienced as they've stood in the portal that links the Earth plane and the Higher side. Others return with a renewed sense of mission and destiny, confident in the continuity of life and certain of their places in the Divine order of existence.

Heightened Spiritual Sensitivity

Spirit communication of any sort often heightens spiritual sensitivity. Evidence of the continuity of life is awe-inspiring. It affirms life continues beyond physical death and also there is a Divine energy that is the animating source of all existence. This represents the Goddess/God of your understanding. As it becomes irrefutable that existence continues, so, too, does it become undeniable that a Higher Power exists (again, this is the Goddess/God of your understanding; there is one Divine being but there are many presentations and perspectives of its existence).

Doris stopped in to see Rita on a lark, thinking it would be fun and funny to get a drawing from Spirit. Doris thought she would get a drawing of some Native American guide that couldn't be proven and would have no meaning. Both Doris and her husband considered themselves to be atheists and purported to practice no religion. When Rita began to draw, the face of an older woman came through. Doris was stunned: It was her mother-in-law! Doris returned to see Rita a few times afterward, saying that she and her husband could no longer deny an afterlife.

Heightened or New Psychic Senses

Your psychic senses are how you link to, experience, and understand communication that takes place on an energy level. The intensified metaphysical energy of a near-death experience often makes permanent changes in the abilities of your psychic senses.

It's as though there's been an electrical current surge through your energy field, rearranging its alignment and strengthening its charge. Your psychic senses, as part of this energy field, pick this up. You may find yourself able to tap into greater sources of compassion and empathy.

Even your physical senses can demonstrate how this kind of emotional, astral body growth might work. Think back to the last time you had an intestinal virus. Not a pleasant recollection, for sure! Do you still remember the last food you ate before you became ill? Can you taste it, see it, smell it? When something becomes associated with a strong experience, we remember it long after the experience ends! In a clinical sense, your nervous system imprints the experience along its neural pathways of your physical body. Correspondingly, the energy pathways of the astral body become more sensitive, also influenced by your near-death experience. Your causal, or spirit body, remembers its encounter with Spirit and preserves a new openness to the Spirit world.

Near-Death Lessons

Why do we have near-death experiences? No doubt, one answer is to prove the continuity of life. Nothing is more compelling than going beyond the boundaries of physical life yourself and returning to remember and talk about it! Because near-death experience is a form of spirit communication, it is also about healing. Lessons are intended to reconnect you with spirit, with God, with love—however it is that you need to re-establish these connections in your life and existence. Only you will know, in the end, the lesson of your near-death experience.

Every near-death experience has a unique lesson for the person who experiences it. It is a personal and intimate communication between you and the Spirit world. The lessons of near-death experience are many and varied; the only lesson that matters to you, however, is the one of *your* near-death experience.

Although most people who survive to tell of their experiences seem to recover completely, nearly everyone is changed. It's an extraordinarily profound experience. Some people do find themselves confronting physical changes as a result of the events that caused the near-death experience. There might be partial paralysis from a stroke, or the injuries suffered in a car accident. There could be loss of limb or function.

But even in these situations, people tend to feel very positive about the experience. The physical reminders are also about learning and healing. No one wishes for such changes, of course. But when they happen, they tend to strengthen the conviction that life continues beyond physical death and that life—everyone's life—has equal value and purpose.

Growth on the Earth Plane

It seems virtually impossible to go through a near-death experience and not grow from it in this life. As difficult as the circumstances might be, your brush with death is a gift to you from the Universe, from the Higher side, from the Goddess/God of your understanding. You could turn away from the opportunities returning from near-death offers you. But why would you? You've already had the experience … let it fulfill its intent!

Millions of people walking the Earth plane today have had near-death experiences. The collective lessons of their experiences can change the world and make the world a better place through depth of new understanding. These are the lessons of love, compassion, and empathy for one another. To say to the world, *"I am here!"* You express the meaning of life by living it: to dance, to sing, to write novels, to discover scientific breakthroughs, to invent, to imagine … to take care of one another, you are living your life to the fullest! You do this so that when returning again to the Spirit world, you can say to your loved ones on the Higher side as you meet them again, *"Truly, I have lived."*

Time, Space, and the Soul's Life

Just how old is your soul, and what has it experienced before this incarnation? The idea that Spirit lives indefinitely is intriguing enough. It may be comforting to know there is more to our existence than the physical life we now live, however much our spirits enjoy life on the Earth plane. But to think of living multiple *physical* lives and to contemplate reincarnation in a new physical body with a new conscious awareness ... that's a concept that has been fascinating humanity for centuries.

What happens when a spirit enters a new life? Is it possible to contact spirits that have passed on in this way, that is, that have reincarnated? For example, if your father has reincarnated, can you still contact him as your father in the spirit world? Do you (can you), in your present life, remember your past lives? Do the experiences of those past lives extend in some way into this life—can you contact one of your own past (or future) selves? Do certain souls travel together? This chapter examines the concepts of past lives and reincarnation and relates them to communicating with the dead and to past-life therapy.

The Cycle of Existence

Cycles are the natural order of existence—day and night, planting and harvest, sleep and waking, birth and death. As early cultures observed these cycles, they noticed that they repeat. Spring follows winter, autumn follows summer, light follows darkness, and waking follows dreams. Over and over again, the pattern repeats. Why, then, would this not be the pattern or cycle of human life?

The concept of reincarnation dates back to the earliest recorded history and extends across various cultures. Reincarnation is the return of the spirit after death to a new incarnation in a physical body and physical existence. The word "incarnate" means "in the flesh." The Greek philosopher Plato believed—and taught—that the soul was separate from the body. While the body clearly was mortal—it lived and died—the soul was not. The soul, according to Plato, was immortal and continually reincarnated.

Reincarnation is a fundamental tenet of many Eastern religions. Hinduism believes that the soul returns to physical existence in various forms, depending on the lessons it still needs to learn. Such forms might be animal, plant, or human. A key element of reincarnation in many Eastern belief systems is karma. The principle of karma is simple: what you give is what you get! Karma is the energy of cause and effect you put out into the Universe that comes back to you in this and other lifetimes, and it's always about learning.

In its religious context, karma shapes reincarnation and defines the lessons of the next incarnation. In a broader context, karma is energy. Your thoughts, as well as your actions, are patterns of energy. Everything you think, everything you do, affects the Universe in infinitesimal ways. Karma, as energy, has a ripple effect that extends far beyond logical comprehension.

Your Soul's Journeys

Your spirit has a Divine mission, a way it fits in the grand scheme of the Universe. To fulfill its mission, your spirit chooses paths and journeys. It chooses its time of entry into this life and the circumstances into which it will make its entrance. Your soul chose your parents to be the physical entities responsible for giving you physical life.

These are choices and decisions that take place well beyond the realm of your conscious mind. They often take place before what you identify as your conscious mind actually exists! In a way, it's like your spirit sits with Goddess/God, co-creates your path with Goddess/God, and plans the next phase of your existence. Continued existence on the Higher side? Life on the Earth plane? It depends on what lessons your spirit needs to learn. These determinations take place not only before you enter your current physical life, but they also take place throughout your existence as a physical being, even though you have no conscious awareness of them.

Past life regression, which we talk about later in this chapter, is one way you can gain a sense of your spirit's travels. Experiences that you chalk up to déjà vu (the sense that you've been to a particular place or met a certain person before) could well be connections you had in previous lives.

You come to this lifetime to learn, and you decide on the lessons of this lifetime before you arrive. This doesn't mean these lessons happen automatically. Every choice you make, every decision you make, determines the next path you take along your journey. This is free will: you choose the direction of your life. Even if it doesn't seem that your life is one of choice at all, your spirit has made decisions about how it will learn the lessons of this lifetime.

The really great thing is that you don't have to go it alone! Each morning when you get up, say out loud, "Goddess/God, show me the pebbles I need to step over, show me the boulders I need to walk around." You don't have to bang your head against the wall to "get" it! When we ask for help and guidance, we can more easily learn the lessons we came here to life on Earth to learn.

What about challenging lives? Of course, no one would choose a life of pain and suffering! Would they?! If the soul has choice and has freewill, why does so much suffering exist in our physical world? For reasons we can't comprehend, this is somehow part of the Divine order and the soul's lessons. We know that through communication with Spirit, the learning that occurs as a result of life's hard lessons becomes part of the spirit's evolution. While drawing Emma Rose's Spirit guides, Rita told her that she would run as fast as possible in the opposite direction if she knew what lay ahead. "How can this be a *good thing?*" Emma Rose asked. But Spirit assured her that it would be so. (See Chapter 24 for more on life's journey, a life of service, and Spirit's lessons.)

Soul Companions

Are there people in your life you feel you're just destined to be with? Friends, lovers, and even your siblings and children might feel like they are intended to be a part of your life. You know each other at a level of intimacy that seems to transcend your relationship. You have intuitive and even psychic connections. You finish each other's sentences, and you call or stop by when one is thinking about the other. You live life in loving service to one another. You are connected to each other in ways that even other people notice. You are likely members of the same soul group—a cosmic family of sorts, spirits that travel together through existence.

Even if you don't consciously know your connections to the physical lives of others in your soul group, you eventually encounter them during your life. This might be a stranger you meet in a coffee shop who seems so familiar you begin talking as though you've known each other forever—which might indeed be the case! It's usually a great delight to connect with the members of your soul group. You're all traveling together on your spirit journeys for a reason—you have lessons to share with each other or a shared mission.

After one of Emma Rose's friends had passed too young and too soon to a difficult disease, she attended a special wake for her friend who had been beloved in the local music scene. There she was introduced to another great friend of the woman who had passed. Though the two had never met before the day of the wake, they spoke to each other as if they had always been acquainted. The solemnity and the joy of the occasion allowed the two to talk freely about all manner of subjects. Their immediate connection shocked and amazed them, as it did others who looked on and listened. A new friendship born in sorrow and forged in honest dialog began that day—guided by Spirit through the spirit of their beloved mutual friend.

Soul relationships are not always the same. The characteristics of physical life that we consider important—such as gender and family lines—are just outer trappings. You are man or woman in this life, and you likely were woman and man in other lives. You and a soul partner might have been husband and wife in one life, and brother and sister in another. As awkward as this might feel when you think about it, remember that existence in Spirit doesn't have the constraints of our physical world. Details like gender identity and relationship have little bearing, in the context of spirit growth and evolution, beyond their roles in bringing together the spirits who need to learn together.

Lessons of the Spirit

What are these lessons your spirit needs to learn? Each of us has different lessons; each soul has a unique mission. The more highly evolved your spirit, the more likely it is that your mission involves helping others with the lessons of their missions. Those who leave their legacies in history as great people—from religious figures like Gandhi, the Virgin Mary, and Buddha to political leaders who direct the lives of millions of people—are highly evolved. Their spirits choose to return to physical lives to help direct the lives of others toward the highest and the best.

Highly evolved spirits are not just the famous and the powerful in their earthly lives, however. Who do you know in your life who seems to have wisdom and insight beyond their years? We sometimes say of such a person, "She has an old soul." Intuitively, we understand that on a Spirit level, this person has traveled many lives. In Buddhism, a *bodhisattva* is someone who had delayed their own enlightenment to stay here on Earth to help other souls. In Western terms, we might call this a life of service.

We believe that the ultimate goal of Spirit evolution—and by extension, the lessons our spirits learn—is to work toward becoming one with the Divine. A lofty ideal, to be sure! But if existence is about the spirit's evolution, it is the only ideal that is possible. All lessons move toward increasing understanding and compassion—for ourselves and for others.

The Continuity of Time

It's hard for us to conceptualize timelessness. Yet this is the paradox of the continuity of time: when time is endless, it isn't time. Time, by definition, is a limitation. We ascribe characteristics to it that make it seem finite, but these are artificial. Minutes, days, months, years—methods of measuring time were made for the linear human mind.

Even as we think of the cycles of life, the seasons, and the generations, we think of time as a linear element. We speak of past lives and future lives, lives that exist along a linear continuum. This implies that time has a beginning and an end.

Our familiar calendar is called the Julian calendar. The Romans developed it during the rule of Julius Caesar (around 46 B.C.E.). It divides the year into 365 days (except every fourth year, when there are 366 days) and organizes those days into 12 months. As the Romans conquered much of what was then the Western world, they imposed this system of structured time on other cultures.

Again, this reflects the limitations of our physical existence; as spirits tell us, there is no time on the Higher side! Only in the physical world does time frame existence.

Connecting with Your Past ... and Your Future

The connections of your past continue in the present. They also link you to your future, even though as yet you have no perception of it. The experiences and lessons of the past shape both the present and the future.

The idea of connecting with future lives is quite intriguing. Wouldn't it be wonderful to know the future? The problem is that because it hasn't happened yet, you can't verify it. With past life experiences, there's often a way to affirm what you sense were your experiences. Through contact with Spirit, you might receive information that validates perceptions you have about a past life. You can connect this information and your perceptions to events and circumstances in your current life.

With future lives, this validation process is not in place. You can't verify what you haven't yet experienced. Further, these are glimpses of *possible* futures. Remember, free will determines the paths of your life. You choose the directions you take ... in this life and in other lives. This makes your future lives moving targets. Each decision you make (consciously or on the level of Spirit) influences the path of this Earthly life and subsequently the paths of future lives.

Sometimes in your current life, you find yourself in a situation with someone that is difficult. When Rita worked with troubled youth, she found one young man particularly difficult. Tony seemed to seek her out, yet he continually challenged whatever she told him. For reasons Rita didn't understand, she was especially tolerant of Tony—which she found frustrating because he took far more of her time and effort than it seemed she should give him.

Asking her Spirit guides, "Why is this kid in my life?" Rita did a meditation to explore a possible past life relationship with Tony. The connection came to her quickly: In a past life, Tony had saved her life.

In this past life that took place in the mid-1800s, Rita's father was a wealthy plantation owner. Rita had married an apparently gracious Southern gentleman, only to discover too late that a wicked temper dispelled any qualities of grace. In this life, Tony was an enslaved person, and in his duties, he happened by the house one day when Rita's husband was beating her. Tony hid until Rita was alone and then helped her to flee from the house.

After this meditation, Rita knew that no matter how difficult Tony was, she would never send him away in her current lifetime. Their trauma from that lifetime had echoed across the generations. Images from the meditation stayed on Rita's mind, and she decided to paint them. When the painting was finished, she hung it in her studio. The next time Tony came to the studio, he walked over to the painting and stood in front of it.

"I've been there," he said. "Where is it? It's not around here, but I know I've been there." The painting he recognized was of the vision of himself in a past life and his act of compassion toward Rita.

Past Life Therapy

Exploring your past lives can have great therapeutic value. Often, we carry around much guilt, anxiousness, and fear that we can't pin to specific causes. Sometimes these feelings link back to past life experiences. Finding the connection can help you understand and resolve the issues responsible for the feelings.

Past life therapy, or past life regression, is a recognized form of therapeutic counseling. Many professionals of diverse backgrounds—physicians, psychologists, psychoanalysts, hypnotherapists, among others—offer past life regression as part of an overall counseling approach.

In past-life therapy, the therapist puts you into a light hypnotic state. The therapist talks to you. Although you are deeply relaxed, you are not beyond consciousness. You are just at the level where your conscious mind is not intruding into the process.

During the session, you might see yourself in a different time and place with people who look similar to (but are not the same as) people in your current life. The therapist might ask you questions about what you see. When the therapist brings you out of the hypnotic state, you usually still remember the past life information that surfaced.

Past life therapy is often very profound. You might be amazed by how quickly you understand the connections between things that happened in past lives and things that are happening in your present life. You gain understanding and intuitive insight into why you behave in certain ways, even when your behavior doesn't seem to make "logical" sense.

If you have an overwhelming romantic attraction to someone you meet, it doesn't necessarily mean you're a match made in Heaven! It might mean there are still lessons for you to work out with this person. Karmic connections aren't necessarily romantic. If you feel a sudden, intense attraction, go into meditation and see if you can connect to a past life relationship to understand what you returned to teach each other.

Connecting with Your Past: A Guided Meditation

Past life therapy is only one way to connect with your past. You can call on your Spirit guide to help you explore this dimension of your soul's existence. This guided meditation can get you started. It is similar to the guided meditations in Chapter 7.

1. Make yourself comfortable in a location where you won't have any distractions or interruptions.

2. Take three slow, deep breaths, in through your nose and out through your mouth. Let the first breath clear your body, let the second breath open your mind, and let the third breath free your spirit.

3. Consciously form the thought: "This is my time to be one with Goddess/God and for Goddess/God to be one with me." Set an intent that your Spirit guide will help you to explore a past life.

4. In your mind's eye, see yourself sitting on a bench in an open, beautiful garden. There are flowers and trees, and the air smells fresh and clean. It is peaceful and calm. Across from your bench is another bench, also inviting and peaceful.

5. Watch as your Spirit guide approaches. Welcome your guide, and thank them for coming. Invite your Spirit guide to sit on the bench across from you.

6. Open your mind and your heart. Open your psychic and spiritual senses to allow communication with your guide.

7. Ask your Spirit guide to introduce you to a past life. Listen to your guide with your inner hearing and watch what your Spirit guide shows you with your inner vision.

8. Observe yourself. Look at what you are wearing. Observe other people who are around you. Observe what events are taking place. Listen. Observe … understand that the meanings and connections will come.

9. Ask what lessons you brought from this past life that you are working on in your present life.

10. When your past life experience seems finished, thank your Spirit guide.

11. Take three slow, deep breaths, in through your nose and out through your mouth. Feel yourself back in your body, become conscious of your breathing. Wiggle your fingers and your toes, open your eyes.

After you are fully aware, pull out your journal and write about your meditation and the past life experiences it showed to you. Some people prefer to think about the experience for a while before writing in their journal about it; do what's comfortable for you. Here are some questions to help you understand your experience.

1. What did you look like? What clothes were you wearing? How were you wearing your hair? Do you have a sense for what period of time it is? Is everything in context for the time? Everything needs to be in the correct context to make sure this is really a past life. Describe what you see.

_____

_____

_____

2. Who else was present in the experience? Did any of these people look familiar? Describe each person in as much detail as you can recall. Include clothing, hairstyles, and other characteristics.

_____

_____

_____

3. Now that you've written detailed descriptions of the other people to whom you were linked in the past life, do any of them seem familiar? Disregard factors such as gender and relationship; instead, focus on the things in their character seem familiar.

_____

_____

_____

4. What were you doing in this past life? Did you get a sense of your occupation? Write down all that comes to your mind about your job or daily activities in the past life.

_____

_____

_____

5. What cultural heritage did you have in this past life? Is this a culture similar to or very different from the one you have in your current life?

_____

_____

_____

6. What was your family like? How many children did you have? Do these people seem familiar? How many generations did you encounter?

_____

_____

_____

7. Did anybody speak? Did they have accents? What language did they speak? If they spoke a language other than a language you speak, could you understand them?

_____

_____

_____

8. How did you interact with the others in this past life connection? What seemed to be your relationship to them?

_____

_____

_____

9. Did you get any sense for your name or any other identifying characteristics about yourself? How old did it seem that you were?

_____

_____

_____

10. What did your surroundings look like? Could you hear any distinctive sounds or noises? Did you smell anything particular?

_____

_____

_____

11. Write down any other significant details you recall about the experience of your past life.

_____

_____

_____

Often it takes time to fully understand the connections between your current life and your past lives. Recalling past life details doesn't always paint a complete picture; you might have to wait for some of the pieces to settle into place for you.

After you've encountered a past life, you can do additional meditations that focus on the connections you've discovered. With each exploration, you'll learn more about your spirit's travels, and you'll understand more about your journey through this life.

Understanding Your Soul's Mission

Each physical life that your spirit inhabits has a purpose and a role in your soul's mission. Exploring past lives gives you additional pieces to add to the picture. Eventually, patterns will emerge that will help you get a better sense of what your spirit's mission is in this life and beyond.

Spirit Artist

In this life, as in at least one previous life, Rita is an artist. Through exploring her past life connections, Rita has come to understand that part of her spirit's mission—and her mission in this life—is to prove, through art, the continuity of life. Her drawings from Spirit have touched countless lives, affirming her sense that this is the reason for this life's journey. Do you know your soul's mission?

Hilda had arranged for a spirit drawing for her husband Arthur as a gift. When Arthur arrived, Rita began to draw, and a beautiful mature woman appeared on the paper. Arthur wasn't sure who this could be, so he brought it home to show to his wife. Hilda looked at it and showed the portrait to her mother, who immediately took a photo from her wallet, which matched exactly, including the woman's dress. Rita had drawn Hilda's grandmother, Maria. Yes, in-laws come, too!

The Joy of Living

In the Oscar-winning Pixar animated feature *Soul*, Joe Gardner, a high-school band teacher who's lives for jazz, finds himself ready to transform his life when he gets a chance to play with a jazz legend, Dorothea Williams. But…one misstep and Joe finds himself moving toward the Great Beyond. Desperate to get back to life, Joe escapes to the Great Before where he meets new soul 22 and begins an adventure to explore what gives a soul its purpose. Together, Joe and 22 discover the jazz of life, the wonder of small moments writ large—a falling leaf, a sucker pop, your mom's kindness, a trombone riff, your first piece of pizza—put together, all these unexpected moments give life the spark that makes soul music.

So no matter your soul's mission in this or that life, your challenges or lessons, the constant throughout is the joy of living, the joy of life itself. Spirit confirms for us the continuity of life, the knowledge that life and time are infinite and Divine, that we are here on the Earth plane to be of service and solace—and joy—to one another, and that all is peace, light, and love.

Soul Lessons and Karmic Cycles

Do you feel like you've been this way before? Quite possibly you have! Your spirit's mission might take you through numerous lifetimes. The lessons you need to learn in this lifetime might very well be matters left unresolved in your previous lifetimes. Let's look at how you can bring together your psychical and mediumistic abilities and newfound understanding to draw healing Spirit energy for yourself and to send healing energy to others—both those on the Earth plane and those who have passed to Spirit.

As an individual, your energy is powerful. When individuals join their collective energy, the effect could literally change the world. At a time of profound loss, we crave the sight of a beloved's cherished face, seek our solace from nature, and seek reassurance from our own family as well as our family of community, country, and world. These times of profound loss open a portal through the veil separating Earth and Spirit, offering peace and understanding and a way forward with grace and confidence. Every moment of life is precious, and Spirit is with us—wishing us the highest and best life we can make here on Earth.

CHAPTER
22

Fine-Tuning Your Spirit Gifts

Everyone has the mediumistic abilities that can bridge the veil between the physical and Spirit worlds. Using these gifts is simply a matter of opening yourself to the possibilities. You'll find you are naturally stronger in some abilities than in others. Focusing to develop these skills leads to improvements in all parts of life. As you've learned, everything is energy, and all is connected.

Your gifts from Spirit open new vistas to you, which are often quite profound. Certainly, it's entertaining to develop some gifts, such as telepathy. But it's also a process of discovery, learning, empathy, and helping yourself and others. These are gifts of love, compassion, and of healing, and using them in these ways leads only to good—to the experiencing of the highest and best for everyone.

When you start to open up through meditation and feel what attracts you, you start to put all the pieces together. We get different pieces to master in this or other lives. As we work on understanding each gift that comes to us through psychic connection or communication with Spirit, we bring them together to create a whole picture. This picture unfolds over many lifetimes and in concert with many other fellow caring journeyers (both on the Earth and Spirit planes). This is not a process to fear; it is a process to welcome and cherish. It is part of the Divine order of the Universe.

Identifying Your Spirit Gifts

Although you likely excel in certain gifts from Spirit and lack interest or refinement in others, spiritual gifts are blessings that exist in unity. Also, there is an integration between what you might view as your tangible gifts and your Spirit gifts. Rita, for example, is blessed (and humbled) with artistic talent. Combining her art with her mediumistic abilities provides an avenue for development in both areas. We all have roles in spreading the message that life is continuous.

Do you know your particular Spirit gifts? In the chapters of Part 4, "Activating Your Spirit Senses," you began to explore the many ways human beings are able to connect directly to Spirit energy. By now in your journey, you probably have some idea of the areas in which you seem to have an inherent ability. These are good areas to start your spiritual unfoldment, and there is an exercise later in this chapter to help you start engaging with your process.

Using Your Spirit Gifts

First and foremost, your Spirit gifts exist for goodness and healing. No matter what those gifts from Spirit are or to what extent you choose to develop them, they are your link to an energy much larger than you are. Your gifts from Spirit connect you to the Divine and to all existence. Self-exploration becomes very important. As you travel a spiritual path of discovering your psychical and mediumistic gifts and fine-tuning your skills (the path of enlightenment), you will discover yourself—your Divine self.

Perhaps you feel you really don't want to expand your own mediumistic senses, but instead you'd rather tap into the ways someone else's abilities—a psychic's or a medium's—can bring new information from Spirit into your life. Connecting to Spirit through a psychic or medium is a wonderful start. Because, of course, you can experience contact with Spirit through readings. But, understand that even this new connection to Spirit through a psychic or medium will still change you *and your mediumistic abilities, too,* because everything is spiritual energy, and everything is connected.

Think of all the many ways you use your physical senses during the course of a day—or even an hour. That's a good exercise: For an afternoon, write down every time you use a particular physical sense in the normal passage of time. Start with taste because we tend to think of this as an isolated, intermittent sense. After all, you don't go through your day tasting everything; you use your sense of taste only when you eat. Or do you? You might be surprised! Perhaps even the air you breathe has a taste. Move onto your sense of smell, your sense of sight, your sense of hearing. Experience your sense of touch: how do you touch your world? When you walk past a bakery, the smell might invite you in. Driving down the highway, you may see a hawk fly, and it gives you a sense of freedom. You taste cinnamon and think of your partner's heirloom apple pie.

What happens to you when you enter a new environment or situation? Do you feel like all of your senses are heightened? People who engage in high-risk adventures such as free diving or free-climbing often report intensified sensory experiences. When such an adventure takes you close to what you perceive is the brink of death (though not a near-death experience), you might indeed feel that you can taste the air! You also might feel like you can hear colors and see sounds. The energy of the experience is so strong that it crosses conventional sensory borders.

Cats offer a good observation of the integration of physical senses. Felines have heightened sensory perception in their mouths through which they smell what they taste. Have you ever watched the breathing of a cat in a new experience or environment? It crouches with its mouth slightly open, giving the appearance of panting. This isn't just to bring more oxygen into its system to accommodate its "fight or flight" response. All of those extra air molecules bring information to the cat's sensory systems, expanding what information it can collect about this new challenge.

The same happens with your psychic senses. As you explore and develop them, they become more integrated with your physical senses, which increases the amount of information you can gather about your environment, your experiences, and, really, your life. If you're paying attention, this is all information that increases your understanding of what it means to be alive.

Naturally Curious

The expression might be "curious as a cat," but in reality, no creature on this Earth is more curious than the one who stares back at you in the mirror. We humans want to know *everything*. *How does that work? Why does it do that? What happens if …?*

In childhood, we ask precisely these sorts of questions about how the world works. By the time we become adults, we have learned *not* to ask these questions because they don't always have ready or apparent answers. But often, it is the question that matters more than the answer because asking the question honors the quest—the journey—for knowledge and understanding.

Reclaim your natural curiosity! This is how you grow and develop as a human being and evolve as a being of Spirit. Life is a dynamic adventure, an exploration best shared on both the Earth and Spirit planes. Your psychical abilities are additional tools available for you to use and appreciate.

Shaping Your Future

You hold your future in your hands, regardless of the extent to which you choose to develop and use your psychical gifts. Each choice you have, every decision you make, influences the next step you take along the path of your soul's mission. You don't consciously think about this the vast majority of the time. (Or, who knows, maybe you *do!*) Your Higher being—your spirit in interaction with the thought energy of your subconscious mind—makes many of the choices and decisions that guide your direction. On a conscious level, you can participate actively by using Emile Coue's prescribed daily practice of autosuggestion to set your intent. *Every day, in every way, from every point of view, I'm getting better and better.*

Setting your conscious intent is powerful! The all-encompassing nature of *in every way* imagines every instance that manifests your spirit's highest and best. It's a good thing to move toward your spirit's mission even when you are unaware on a conscious level of what is occurring on a cellular, subconscious level; progress in life seems easy and smooth when this happens. When you might find challenge and frustration along your path, nothing seems to quite work out for you. You feel a half step off—and maybe you are because you can't see the path. Imagine how different your journey would be if you could see each step and where it takes you! Once you start setting your intent, you can harness autosuggestion's power of the imagination. It is important to remember that setting intent is different from using the brute force of willpower. Willpower will never be a match for the creative potential of the imagination. Set your intent, and let Spirit lead you to your highest and best.

Peter came for a sitting and drawing in 1996 at the First Spiritualist Church of Quincy. He immediately recognized the drawing but laughed and said that his Uncle Walter would never be caught in a suit and tie. When Peter searched for a photo, the only one he could find was a picture where Walter wore a suit and tie! When appearing from Spirit for a portrait, Rita finds certain people consider it to be a formal occasion and dress accordingly.

A New World View

We seek because we sense there is more to our lives and to this Earthly existence than we detect. We know, at some level, that growth and development are important spiritually as well as physically and emotionally. We know that ours is a dynamic, not a static, existence. We see evidence of this all around, from the physical signs we see in the mirror—the changes of growth and aging—to the spiritual changes we feel as we encounter situations such as the passing of loved ones. Your psychical senses help you *make* sense of all of these life experiences.

What concerns you the most about the progress of living? For most people, it is worrying about what lies at the end of the road. All life moves inexorably toward this end; we see this every minute of every day. Once, people were terrified to venture very far from their homes, convinced that the flat Earth disappeared beyond the horizon. There was nothingness, a vast void on the other side of where the sky meets the Earth. Traveling there was … well, beyond comprehension. In those places, the map read: *There be dragons.*

But then Christopher Columbus sailed the ocean blue—and changed the world view for all humanity, as did dozens of other courageous and curious explorers. Christopher Columbus was not the first explorer to expand the view of the world. The Vikings traveled to what is now the northeast United States more than 2,000 years ago. Explorers came from many countries to settle what was referred to as the New World, including the earlier ones who were to become the Native American settlers. Of course, these explorers saw that the Earth continued beyond what the human eye could see. Today, we are incredulous at the perception of a flat Earth; humanity has seen the view of Earth from space, and we know the truth.

You are an explorer, too. And you might fear that your world disappears or ends beyond what you see as its physical boundaries. Spirit contact tells us, as did Columbus's reports back to his royal sponsors, there is no end. Columbus and his fellow explorers found exotic new lands, with new species of plant and animal life and physical surroundings like nothing they'd ever seen and documented. Just as Earth's explorers found a New World, so will you find your spiritual explorations will take you to an infinite Divine Universe.

Your world view is changed by what you learn, whether it is about the geography of the physical world or evidence of the Spirit world. Knowledge changes how you perceive the events in your life. Knowledge changes *you*, the way you live your life, and how you walk with Spirit.

Helping Others

What do you do in life? Think about how you use your tangible Earthly abilities and talents. One way or another, you use them in the service of others. You might do this because it's your job, and someone pays you to do it, but odds are, you do what you do because you enjoy how it helps someone else. Whether you build bridges, perform surgery, choreograph dances, manage pension funds, write books … no matter what you do, it somehow helps others.

Your gifts from Spirit expand your ability to help in different ways. At the very least, your gifts lend you increased insight, empathy, and compassion. You see a bigger picture, which gives you the ability to view the actions of others in a different context. When you know that there is more to life than meets the physical senses, you can be more kind, tolerant, and forgiving. Learning to forgive yourself first, and then to forgive others in your life is a cherished gift; and, yes, forgiveness is *always* possible.

Is there a relationship to someone important in your life—a child, parent, sibling, spouse—who you feel is drifting or is impossible to repair? Nothing is impossible with time, love, and effort. If you already spend several hours a day interacting with social media, you can decide instead to set aside a portion of that time for improving your relationship. Be tenacious and steadfast, even if your efforts are rebuffed at first. After all, you've got endless time across many lives to get it right. And what better time to start than now.

Remember, contact with Spirit is about healing, learning, and love. Love endures all things; love transcends time. There will always be enough time.

Ask the Right Questions—Keep an Open Mind

What do you want to know? Sometimes asking the right questions is the hardest part of seeking answers. The more specific the question, the more directed the answer—and also the more limited. Everyone has unresolved issues. Relationships of any kind are complex and often confusing. Human behavior is even more so! Your questions are personal to you, and their answers are likely to bring about significant change.

Are you ready to know the answers you seek? It seems obvious that you are if you're asking the questions. But sometimes, the questions take us in unexpected directions. The answers often aren't what you anticipate, although they provide the information you ultimately *need*.

Rita talks a lot in this book about proving the continuity of life. This is something that interests most people who want to make contact with Spirit. We miss loved ones who have passed to the Higher side, and at times, we want more than anything to have just one more shared contact—to be held, to be kissed. Love is an all-powerful energy bonding us through space and time, but the sense of loss that accompanies a loved one's passing can be overwhelming and debilitating.

Receiving contact from the Spirit world is a blessing. It is also a life-altering experience for many people. Seeing is believing … and believing isn't always easy. Even when your faith incorporates belief in the continuity of life, you might not be prepared for how evidence of it affects you. Again, remember communication with spirits is for good and healing. And it comes of love, the most powerful energy of all.

Spirit's Ancestral Bond

British actor Mark Rylance, renowned for his portrayals from Shakespeare, wanted to find a deeper connection to his grandfather Osmond Skinner's experience during World War II as a member of the Hong Kong Volunteer Corps. As a small boy, Mark remembered his grandfather ensconced in his country acreage in Kent, including a lovely apple orchard. When Mark was grown and Os was an old man, the two walked together at sunrise and sunset through the orchard leaves. But Mark's beloved grandfather rarely spoke of the war, typical for his generation, especially his part in the Battle of Hong Kong. Captured on Christmas morning 1941, Os spent four years in a Japanese POW camp, Argyle prisoner-of-war camp "H." Discovered in bits and fragments after Os's death, Mark, over time, was able to piece together the details of Os's war experiences, which had been lost to the family memory.

To distract from the tedium, stress, and horrific memories of witnessed camp atrocities, the men of the prison camp put on theatricals, complete with theater programs (The Argyle Hippodrome) and, later, printed reviews. Mark was amazed and delighted to discover Os's talents and participation in the camp's creative endeavors. Not only did Mark see his shared physical resemblance to Os, he believed Os's role in a camp production of *Twelfth Night* "revealed the root of my profession to me." Mark won a Tony award for playing Olivia in *Twelfth Night* on Broadway.

But it wasn't just accumulating the details of Os's wartime history that fascinated Mark and came to mean so much to him. As he learned more, Mark became more vulnerable and exposed to Os's great pain and suffering in the camps and found himself empathically connected to his grandfather's spirit. Just as Os dreamt of an orchard back home he might never live to see, Mark found himself dreaming of Os. "Once, I felt his hand on my shoulder. I turned, and there he was, and he said, *I want you to tell Hazel (your grandmother) that I'm fine,* and I began to weep, and I said, *Os, you're alive!* I missed him terribly when he died. By the way, I'm sitting in my grandfather's chair; that's why there's this creaky noise. When it squeaks, it's him saying, *Nah, that's not true! What is he saying, that idiot?!"* And Mark laughs.

Mark Rylance came to know his grandfather—through setting his intent and traveling to primary sources who/that could tell him more about his grandfather's life—and in so doing, called to his grandfather in Spirit. All the physical and spiritual work to develop Mark's psychical skills, likely honed through his actor's compassion and great empathy. Then, a simple tap on the shoulder, and Os was there.

Where Do You Want Your Psychical Skills to Take You?

What skills do you want to develop? Do you want to become more in tune with your intuition? Explore personal issues? Facilitate contact with spirits for others? Do you want to connect with Earth energy, Spirit energy, or both? The following self-exploration can help you determine where and how to start your psychic development.

1. What psychical or mediumistic abilities do you feel that you have? Circle those that apply.

    Clairaudience

    Clairsentience

    Clairvoyance

    Intuition

    Premonition

    Psychometry

    Spirit contact (loved ones or Spirit guides)

    Telepathy

2. What psychical or mediumistic abilities do others tell you that you have? Circle those that apply.

    Clairaudience

    Clairsentience

    Clairvoyance

    Intuition

    Premonition

    Psychometry

    Spirit contact (loved ones or Spirit guides)

    Telepathy

3. Is this statement true or false for you: *Psychical senses are as much a part of my daily life as are my physical senses.*

    Yes   No

4. If there was just one question you could ask the Goddess/God of your understanding, what would it be?

_____

_____

_____

5. How do you communicate with the Goddess/God of your understanding? Check all that apply.

_____ I pray in times of need

_____ I pray at certain times

_____ I meditate at certain times

_____ I meditate regularly

_____ I feel that I'm in continual communication with the Goddess/God

_____ I don't communicate with the Goddess/God

_____ I don't believe in a Divine being

6. What is your faith or belief system? Has it been consistent throughout your life?

_____

_____

_____

7. Have you had a Near Death Experience (NDE)? If so, what was it like? How did it affect your life?

_____

_____

_____

8. Have you ever experienced a miraculous healing?

_____

_____

_____

9. Have you ever received healing energy and prayers from others? If so, did it seem to have an effect?

_____

_____

_____

10. Have you ever sent healing energy and prayers to someone else? How did you feel about doing it, and did it seem to have an effect?

_____

_____

_____

11. This life is a journey for your soul. What do you want as your soul's experience?

_____

_____

_____

12. Do you feel your life has a sense of mission or purpose beyond the activities of everyday living? Describe it.

_____

_____

_____

13. Are there people in your life right now who you feel you have psychical or intuitive connections? How do you use these connections?

_____

_____

_____

14. What comes to your mind when you think of your own passing to Spirit?

_____

_____

_____

15. Do you have Spirit guides or guardian angels? How do you know, and how do they help you? Have you ever seen them?

_____

_____

_____

16. Do you have dreams that involve visits or communications from loved ones who have passed to the Higher side? Describe the most recent such dream.

_____

_____

_____

17. If you could have any psychical or mediumistic skill, what would it be and why?

_____

_____

_____

Obviously, there are no right or wrong answers here; this is an exercise to help you explore what interests you and how you might develop your abilities to aid that exploration. You can revisit the exercise in Chapter 12 to further identify and develop your psychical skills. See Chapter 24 for more on visits from Spirit guides and loved ones who've passed.

Shaping and Enhancing Your Skills

The best way to develop your psychical and mediumistic skills is to find a good teacher! Start with sources that you trust, and see where they lead you. You might feel there aren't many options in your local area, but keep looking. Eventually, you will find the right opportunities. You might have to drive or travel to find the teachers you need. Don't just wait until something/someone comes to you! If you don't connect, just keep looking. Don't give up, and don't settle for what you know isn't quite the right teacher for you.

If Spirit learning opportunities are abundant in your local area, great! But don't limit yourself to them. Remain receptive to new doors that open. In these times of video conferencing, it is easy to have many different teachers, so you learn more than just the one teacher's way. Each teacher has different abilities and will bring out different abilities *in you*. Be sure that, under all circumstances, *you trust the teacher*. Don't idealize or idolize the teacher, though—teachers are just human, just like you. They're just more consciously aware of their mediumistic skills and have spent time studying and training.

Oh, the Possibilities!

The possibilities of psychical abilities that are open to you are endless! If you find yourself being inspired along a healing path, try different modalities. Experience them, see whether you relate to them or whether they really don't make any sense. It could be that it's not your path or that you're not ready for it yet. Or, perhaps you need the guidance of a teacher to help you make progress.

Whatever else, set your sails and remain an explorer. Self-exploration is especially very important. As you travel this path of enlightenment through Spirit, you will discover your Divine self. You will learn more about your purpose in this life and how you can use your gifts to help others. Make this world a better place. In the end, that's really what life is all about!

Let It Be

Many people know Beatle Paul McCartney's song "Let It Be" is about his mother's dream. McCartney is sure the dream was a visitation from Spirit of his mother during a tough time for him in his life. Paul's dream visitation is a wonderful example of what can happen when a deeply personal encounter with Spirit can be transcended through art to achieve a universal message of love and healing anyone can share. This is Spirit at its highest and best.

We'll close the chapter with Paul McCartney's own words about the experience of his dream and of writing "Let It Be" and its deeper meaning. Such powerful connection to Spirit is there for all of us in our own lives—should we choose to explore and develop the gifts of Spirit we receive.

Here's Paul on "Let It Be" in a video interview for The Iconic Series by GQ: "A lot of people listening to you are going to take seriously what you're saying in a song. I'd been overdoing it; you know it was the '60s. We were just getting crazed and stuff a lot of the time, and so I went to bed, and I wasn't feeling too great in myself. So, my mother came to me in the dream, and she'd died maybe…ten years previously, and so when someone who you've lost comes back to you in a dream, it's a miraculous moment, you know? Because you're with them, and your mind doesn't say, 'Wait a minute, you shouldn't be here.' You're just with them.

"It was really nice because it was my mom—very emotional, and she seemed to realize (this is all going on in my mind, of course, but forget about that…); she seemed to realize that I was going through struggles. And she said, 'It's gonna be okay; it's all really going to be okay.' She …just let it be. I went, 'ahhhhhhhhh.' I felt great and woke up. [I thought to myself,] 'What's that, what? What did she say?' And I remembered the dream, and then I sat down at the piano and wrote the song. It had a lot of emotion because of who'd said it and because of my situation. So, that kind of translated to the record, and I think that's why a lot of people like it. They feel, somehow, that kind of magic comes through."

Rita hopes that your own explorations with Spirit bring you to that kind of magic in your life—a Divine magic of light and love all those you care about may share, on Earth and of Spirit.

CHAPTER
23

Soul Patterns:
Lessons for this Lifetime

Is it hard to make certain changes in your life because the changes are difficult? Or, could it be hard because your soul is putting up a strong resistance to your efforts? Do you feel thwarted or stuck—unable to derail your life from its familiar patterns? Whether you believe you have many lives, or just this one, the awakening of spirituality leads to many questions … and, if you are willing to accept guidance from beyond yourself, Spirit holds many of your answers.

Like learning Tarot or astrology, delving into an exploration of your psychical or mediumistic abilities can be a fun adventure. And whether you're giving a reading or receiving one, gaining insights into questions surrounding the self, life, and relationships, decisions affecting the future can move us beyond set perceptions we (and others) have of who we are and of who *we can be*. Such a prospect is bold and perhaps a bit frightening, and surely, it is exciting to anticipate. It's illuminating to look at someone's aura. It's insightful to read what you find from the life force energy of objects you touch and places you go. Everything that exists connects to Spirit.

The more we search within to find ourselves and to create our paths through life, the more we find All is One—Divine love unites and animates all that is and lights all paths through the Universe. While looking within the far reaches of his human heart, American nineteenth-century poet Walt Whitman wrote in his poem, "Song of Myself," from his book of verse, *Leaves of Grass*.

Do I contradict myself?
Very well then, I contradict myself.
(I am large, I contain multitudes.)
I concentrate toward them that are nigh,
I wait on the door-slab.

Whitman wrote these immortal words in 1855, only four years before Louis Pasteur founded the germ theory in 1859 and published it in 1861—disproving the hypothesis of spontaneous generation, which held that living organisms develop from inert matter. At the near moment Pasteur saw only life under his microscope, Whitman stood on the door-slab of the Universe, multitudes within his soul. Both men saw life in its dissonance and harmonies, life writ large— whether in the movement of tiny microscopic cells, in the expansive thought and feeling of the human heart, or in the very Heavens above.

There is much more beyond the fun adventure of self-discovery in communicating with spirits. We all have serious issues and concerns that drain our life force energy and keep us from finding the joy and happiness our lives can and should contain—the joy of living. Gaining insights into the contradictions that create confusion and discord in life gives you the means to understand and embrace the possibilities for making a truly "joyful noise" in tune with the Universe.

Understanding the continuity of life gives you hope as you look for ways to break through old patterns of living that don't serve you well any longer, as you look to increase the empathy and compassion in your relationships—there is plenty of time to make changes and strike out on new adventures, to find what stimulates and engages your soul, and share it with loved ones. Connecting to Spirit guides and loved ones who have passed allows us to feel the healing energy that sustains us, whether we are on the Earth plane or in the Spirit world. Love is love, and the possibilities we discover are limitless.

Awakening to the Possibilities

Patterns are repeated behaviors we slip into, almost without realizing we've done so. Certain events or situations act as triggers that activate a pattern. You don't consciously think, "Yvonne is home late *again*. I'm going to be upset with her, she'll get upset with and me, and then we'll have a big scene and not speak to each other for the next three days." But that's what happens.

What is behind the reactions for you and for Yvonne? Does it come from Yvonne's or your patterns from earlier in your young adult lives? Are these patterns extending into adulthood from childhood, or might these be newly developing patterns centered on a new place, a new job, or some new dynamic in your relationship? And, yet, could the problem be exacerbated by patterns from previous lives that represent learning still necessary for your spirits to achieve together? No matter the source, gaining an understanding of the bigger picture can help you change your patterns, so they support a more loving, informed, and joyful relationship.

The Energy of Intent

Many good and right things happen to you in your life without your conscious awareness or efforts to structure or plan them. Seemingly through no efforts of your own, you end up in the right place at the right time. You might not even notice when this happens! All you know is that things finally feel *right*. Relationships are easy and fruitful. You're consciously aware that *something* is making things happen; you just don't know what that something is. Once you do become aware of the energetic intent that underlies your progress, however, you can begin to set your intent in conscious ways toward definable goals.

Using Your Psychical Abilities for Insight and Learning

College professors joke (or complain) that students seem to think they can learn by osmosis. Put the textbook under your pillow when you go to sleep at night, and when you wake up you will have absorbed the book's contents. Wouldn't it be wonderful if this could happen? But the reality is that you won't know anything about the contents of that book until you look between the covers: You must *read* the book to understand its message. And you might even need to read additional books and go back to original sources to get enough contextual information to qualify as true learning about your subject.

Learning doesn't happen by osmosis. It requires effort, work, and focus. A hammer doesn't build a house; intuition doesn't fix a struggling relationship. It's up to *you* to use the tools available to you, in ways that allow you to build a life where you develop and grow. You must do the hard work to build a practice of learning. In Chapter 19, you were introduced to Emile Coue's practice of conscious autosuggestion.

Day by day, in every way, I am getting better and better. Starting and ending your day with this mantra sets your intent to create the highest and best for your life. With the words *in every way*, you imagine every circumstance or situation surrounding you, so that the need to declare any specific goal is unnecessary. However, simply repeating the words is not enough to make things happen with success. You must do the hard work of learning to excel at your profession (whatever that may be—student, mother, lawyer, designer…whatever you imagine for yourself). Willpower alone is not enough. You must *imagine* the life you want and then do the hard work to manifest it—all the while supporting your efforts through conscious autosuggestion. *Day by day, in every way, I am getting better and better.*

Call Your Spirit Guides: A Guided Meditation

Your Spirit guides are always available to help you create your future. Often they are at work when you don't realize they are there or even that you need their help. Invite your Spirit guide to give you specific guidance about a particular problem, challenge, or concern. Use this guided meditation to structure your lesson.

1. Make yourself comfortable in a location where you won't have any distractions or interruptions. Prepare yourself for meditation. Take three slow, deep breaths, in through your nose and out through your mouth. Let the first breath clear your body, let the second breath open your mind, and let the third breath free your spirit.

2. Consciously ask your Spirit guide to join you, to help you with your concern or your question.

3. Envision a place of peace and calm. There are two comfortable chairs. You are sitting in one of them. Your Spirit guide enters the room and sits in the other. (You might need a couch if more than one Spirit guide answers your call for assistance.)

4. Focus your thoughts on what it is you want your Spirit guide to help you understand. Be specific. Complete the request, "Spirit, I want you to help me understand ..."

5. Open yourself to receiving your Spirit guide's response, in whatever form it takes. Listen with your inner hearing, observe with your inner vision, understand with your inner knowing.

6. If anything is unclear to you, ask more questions. Ask how you can use this information to resolve your problem. Remain calm and open, even if your Spirit guide's response seems to be missing the point of what you asked.

7. Ask your Spirit guide how to use the information they just provided. Ask for clarification if you are confused by your Spirit guide's message. Trust that the message given is for your highest and best.

8. Thank your Spirit guide for assistance, thank them for their good care, and thank them for walking with you through life to be available for guidance.

9. Feel yourself back in your body, become conscious of your breathing. Wiggle your fingers and your toes, open your eyes. Breathe into the core of your body, lifting your heart. Exhale.

As with any communication with Spirit, it's important to stay open to whatever information comes through for you. You might feel that the information your Spirit guide gave you was interesting but not especially relevant; insight and advice that comes through symbolic interaction is not always clear. Writing in your journal about your Spirit guide lesson can help you to explore the many layers of meaning the message has.

No matter what change you want to make in your life, you can always ask to be guided by a Higher power, your Higher self, your loved ones, and your Spirit guides. They can't make the changes for you, but they can lead you to the lessons you need to learn so that you can acquire the insight and information to make changes.

Are You Doomed to Repeat It Until You Finally Get It?

Throughout history, leaders and philosophers have warned us that unless we learn the lessons of history, we are doomed to repeat them. We turn to this as explanation for the cycles of challenge, strife, and even war, which define human existence. If only we could "get" it, then we could end this seemingly perpetual cycle of doom!

This lifetime we're living right now may be just one piece of our soul's progression. This life is not about being doomed to repeat the lessons we don't get. It's about the journey of "getting" it. It's about having the privilege to keep learning so that we can continue evolving and growing.

Each of us comes to this physical life to learn. Our lessons are not just behavior-oriented lessons like being kind to one another, although certainly these acts of compassion are fundamental to a happy, fulfilled life. Rather, they are lessons of insight and understanding to allow us to make paradigm shifts. Your beliefs and behaviors form your personal paradigm, a model or framework of collective beliefs and behaviors. This is the pattern of your life. What you do represents what you believe, whether you are aware of it. In some ways, paradigms are similar to the symbolism that shows up in dreams and in the symbolic messages that come through communication with Spirit.

The Persistence of Memory

Rita knows the power of art to speak great truths. The Museum of Modern Art in New York City is home to Spanish artist/philosopher Salvador Dali's Surrealist masterpiece, *The Persistence of Memory,* painted in 1931, during the rise of fascism in Europe before World War II. Part of the meaning of this painting has to do with the lessons of time and of history repeating with the persistence of memory. Inspired by Sigmund Freud's work on dreams and the notebooks of Leonardo da Vinci, Dali looked at Surrealism as a method of painting multiple layers of the mind, not of the eye. Freud wrote, "In classic paintings, I look for the unconscious, in a Surrealist painting, for the conscious."

Here, we see the planes of the mind, of consciousness, where the gold watch is swarmed with ants—for Dali, a symbol of decay. The watch faces melt in a "Camembert of time," as Dali called it—"the tender, extravagant and solitary paranoic-critical Camembert of time and space." By this, Dali means the illusion of time, the optical illusions that create a state of paranoia in the consciousness, states of mind that turn time to a soft cheese. At the time the painting was first exhibited, many critics referenced Einstein's Theory of Relativity. Again, in Dali's words, the painting "systemizes confusion and thus helps discredit completely the world of reality."

When we can break free of the unconscious patterns of our lives, to see through the paranoia and confusion that disrupts time and space, then we can make true, systemic changes. It takes deep and persistent work to dislodge the fallacies of mind to reach the true nature of timelessness, of the union between the Earth plane and the Spirit plane. Dali shows us what happens when we do not see or think clearly, when the persistence of memory and the repetition of history blinds and confuses us.

The Energy of Your Thoughts

The most important thing in your life, then, that you can change is the way you think! In reality, this is the *only* thing you can control and change, and yet it's the thing we spend the least amount of our time and effort concentrating on doing.

Your thoughts are energy that create reality. Your thoughts are as tangible as your words and your speech. When you change the way you think (on both a conscious and unconscious level), you change the way you move through your life—just as when you speed or slow your pace when walking, you change the way your body moves through space. When you choose to live your life in the flow of goodness and love, then you change your own energy vibration, you alter the neuropathic, synaptic connections of the brain, which has an amazing ripple effect on you, on your relationship with the Universe, on every person you reach out to touch.

The Negative Energy of Worry

Many of life's challenges come from worrying about the actions and behaviors of other people. You might think that you change your energy, but so what? If the energy of all the people around you stays stuck, how does that help you in the end or help others, for that matter?

You may find you create your life by worrying about what you don't have. All of this worrying sends out negative thoughts. When you change your thoughts, you change your energy. This is the "self-fulfilling prophecy" trap: You worry so much about something that it comes to pass, at which point you can say "See? I told you this would happen!" You become caught in Dali's Surrealist landscape in *The Persistence of Memory*, where time melts in a wasteland of self-repeating paranoia—a landscape where reality is obliterated.

Angie spent a lot of time worrying about having enough money to pay her bills. No matter how hard she and her husband worked, there never seemed to be quite enough. They argued about money; their money concerns seemed to rule their lives. Finally, Angie realized she couldn't continue this way and made the determination that every time such a thought came into her head, she was going to replace it with a positive thought about the good things made possible by the money they did have. Instead of thinking, "I don't have enough money for this," Angie consciously changed her thought to "I have just enough money to meet this need."

This worked fine for Angie. She immediately felt as though a tremendous burden lifted from her. She found that although not worrying about money didn't change how much of it she and her husband had, it did relieve the stress of always feeling like she had to fix things. And oddly enough, it made it seem as though the money they did have was adequate—barely—to meet their minimum needs even if it wasn't as much as they wanted.

As Angie became more attuned to the energy of her thoughts, she realized that even though she had changed her thoughts about money, her husband still had many negative actions and thoughts. She worried for a while about how to change that, and suddenly, it dawned on her: She *couldn't* change his thoughts! She could only change the way she thought and how she related to him. She changed her perceptions.

Accomplishing that shift in perceptions became her next focus. Every time she found herself thinking, "All Richard does is complain about not having enough money," she made the conscious effort to think instead, "Richard is financially comfortable." Eventually, this caused Angie to change the way she reacted toward Richard. Instead of snapping at him, she empathized with his concerns and said things that contained heartfelt support. It wasn't long before Richard also relaxed, and between them they were able to find ways to be economical and efficient. Feeling more confident, Richard found a new job with a better salary. Their financial situation improved considerably.

Changing Negative to Positive

Negative thinking is insidious. Sometimes, even when your actions are positive, the thoughts that drive them come from a challenging or worrisome perspective. This spills out into everyday life in ways you often don't recognize.

We tend to focus on what we don't want to have happen: I don't want to gain more weight; I don't want to be in an accident; I don't want to lose my job; I don't want to get lost when I'm driving; I don't want to fail my test; I really hope there are no delays or restrictions at the airport when I fly next month. Feel how the energy of these concerns shifts when you instead say or think:

- My body is healthy and strong, and I take good care of it to keep it that way. My cells, my tissues, my organs, my systems are all working together.

- I will work with attention and focus and put safety first.

- I like my job, and I want to stay in it as long as it continues to meet my needs and my company's needs. I have good skills and abilities that, combined with the learning of this job, make it possible for me to always have a good job.

- Having GPS for directions is wonderful, but I enjoy getting a good physical description of my destination from whomever I'm driving to visit, so I'll recognize my surroundings and feel welcome when arriving!

- I'm prepared for my test through good study, good sleep, and good intent to do well. I will enjoy the opportunity to discuss my subject by answering the test questions well and cheerfully.

- I've been looking forward to this trip for a long time. The people who work for the airline are eager to make sure my flight is safe and comfortable. The pilot and flight crew are well-trained and efficient.

Athletes, musicians, dancers, actors, and other live performers often use creative visualization to prepare for events. They focus on envisioning themselves moving perfectly through the event, from start to finish, experiencing every move. When they get to the actual event, they've already gone through it so many times the pattern for success is well established. All they have to do is follow its blueprint. There is no need or room to worry about "what if …." Trust and intent have been set for the highest and best to follow through—*no matter what happens in the moment.*

When you find yourself worrying about what you *don't* have, make a conscious choice instead to think about what you *do* have. When you change your perceptions, you change your reality. The key is to change your thinking from focusing on what you want but don't have … to wanting what you have. Hope in the positive and avoid composing your hopes as too difficult or impossible. If you find you conceive your hopes in challenging terms, you may be surprised to find that, in some way, you have set your intent to be challenged, and that you are hoping for something that now is unlikely to happen simply because of the obstacle of your fears! Instead, hope for what *will* happen. Thoughts are life force and Divine energy, and they are *creative.* Positive and hopeful thoughts create the grounding for your *positive and hopeful* reality to manifest.

The Challenges of Change

Real, lasting change is not easy. Although this might seem the epitome of understatement, it's necessary to say this. *Change is not easy.* One of the ironies of insight is that for as wonderful as it is to know why you do something, there isn't a direct link from divining insights to making changes in your life that support your newfound understanding. Insight does lead to decisions about actions, but it doesn't directly result in actions.

The connection between insight and action (between understanding and change) requires conscious attention and continual effort from you. You can decide to make a change, but then you must continue making choices supporting that decision. Tuning in to the energy of the Universe through your psychical senses and through contact with Spirit connects you to endless support. Rita knows when we talk about this vital support it is yours for the asking and that it is there to help you carry out your spirit's mission in this life.

It's important to remember this is true in the context of the bigger picture. There is a grand scheme to existence that none of us can comprehend in this physical, Earthly life. However, it is beyond your power to change everything. We are limited on the Earth plane by our very humanity, our form as human beings. We rely on Divine support to affect change. Many recovery programs and support groups begin their meetings with a simple prayer: *God grant me the serenity to accept the things I cannot change, the courage to change the things I can, and the wisdom to know the difference.*

Breaking Free from Negative Patterns

Negative patterns often develop as a result of *inaction* rather than action. You slide into habits based on *can't, don't, won't.* You *can't* get a better job because you *don't* have an advanced or specialized degree, and you *won't* be able to do all the other things you like doing if you quit your current job to go back to school.

When you read such a statement in a book, it's easy to see the present elements of choice. In real life, "can't" and "don't" situations are those you truly have no control over. If you are paralyzed from the waist down, your legs don't work as they did before, and you can't walk as you did before. No matter how much you want to change this situation, you are not able to do so. These are facts of reality, and there may be little you can change about them.

You can, however, choose the ways you deal with these constraints. You can decide to work out regularly to strengthen and condition your upper body, so you can become fully mobile using a wheelchair. Perhaps prosthetic limbs are an option. If not, surely, you can choose to use weights, stretching, massage, and other physical therapy techniques to tone, as much as possible, the muscles and structures in your legs that no longer work as intended. You can determine you will find ways to transcend your physical limitations, allowing you to keep doing anything you want to do—albeit perhaps in a new way!

A challenging or negative pattern is anything that's causing you difficulty in your life, such as a pattern of disastrous repetition that you realize you fail to understand and interrupt. Why do you keep doing this, you wonder? What is that saying of Einstein's—something about doing the same thing over and over yet expecting to get a new result? Somehow, you miss connection between your past and present actions. You recognize the events or circumstances that puzzle you, but you struggle to perceive the connection these have to your current behaviors and situations. As in Dali's painting, your confusions and contradictions create a paranoia that obscures reality and warps time. You are unable to see clearly. Negative patterns deserve your attention because they are often destructive. When things are going well, it seems we tend to coast along, not really noticing the details. It's only when relationships, jobs, health, and other aspects of life begin to fall apart that you might look for the patterns underlying the problems. Also, "if" is a key concept here; no change is possible "if" the destructive effects go unnoticed. Noticing difficult and destructive soul patterns requires mindful awareness—our conscious intent.

You can choose to recast your thinking in the positive, and you can fully "choose your choices," reinforcing behaviors of strength, confidence, and love. When you want a child to be careful with a drink, you say to the child, "Hold the glass upright" rather than, "Don't spill the milk!" When we voice things in the negative, we open the door for our greatest fears to manifest. Negatives are about fears. Expressing hope in the negative reinforces fear of a negative outcome, however subtly. When you express your hopes in the positive, then you move in a positive direction. And maybe others will be encouraged, both on the Earth plane and the Spirit plane, to move with you!

When you have a painful relationship to resolve that involves someone you love who has passed to the Higher side, it's important to first release despair—let it go. The situation, no matter what it was, was not your fault. This moves both you and your loved one in Spirit toward healing.

If Anything Happens I Love You

The 2021 Oscar-winning animated short film, *If Anything Happens I Love You*, is an elegy on grief written by Will McCormack and Michael Govier. It tells the story of a struggling marriage, a couple suspended in time and unable to function after the loss of their child. In animation, we see the shadows of their spirits rage and cry out while their bodies languish, unable to act or to comfort one another in daily existence. As the film begins to share the details of the family's home life, the personality of the lost daughter begins to enliven, and her spirit gains a lively presence through her parents' memories.

As their grief builds, so does the energy of their daughter, as the circumstances of her death peek through. In time, we watch with the parents as the little girl goes off to school, where what we dread, we hear, and we know a school shooting erupts behind a closed cafeteria door, under an American flag. A text appears on the girl's cell … *If anything happens, I love you.* Grief overwhelms. As the parents seem estranged in anguished despair without hope, the force of the girl's spirit works from the Spirit plane to bring her parents together in love again. The girl's Divine energy unites the little family once more in Spirit with a poignant faith in the joy of living.

Spirit gives us the courage to find and nurture love that seems lost to grief. Destructive patterns of grief can be interrupted and transformed by enduring love. All Spirit is love, and no love is ever lost if it's been held in our arms. Love endures all things, so keep the faith. Know your loved ones passed to Spirit are wrapped in healing comfort and want nothing more than to bring you back to your life, awakening you to new possibilities and new joys.

Establish and Maintain Positive Patterns

One reason challenging patterns are so difficult to change is we focus on putting an end to them but don't know how to go about replacing destructive patterns with healing patterns. We know behaviors and thoughts are energy; when you take energy away, it leaves a void. Without intentional replacement, that void will fill with whatever energy is readily available. More often than not, this will be the same energy you just sent away because it's right at hand. It's the flow of least resistance.

When you dig a hole in the garden and just leave it, what happens? Most of the time, it fills back up with dirt, rocks, debris, and weeds—whatever falls in. The only way to keep this from happening is *intentionally* to put something in the hole to replace the dirt you removed. Energy is the same way. It's great to remove difficult energy, but to keep this energy from returning, you need to replace it with energy of a more positive resonance.

Leonard came to Rita for a reading because he was having extreme relationship difficulties. Now in his 40s, Leonard had never been in a relationship that lasted longer than three or four months. The person who came through to Rita from the Higher side for Leonard was a man Leonard identified as his father. "Was your father a doctor?" Rita asked. "He's showing me a doctor's bag."

Puzzled, Leonard said that his father had been a jeweler. Rita went back to the visitor from Spirit, who again showed her a doctor's bag. This time, there was also a message. "There was something with your mother and a doctor when you were about four years old," Rita said. "Do you remember that?"

Leonard was quiet. He did indeed remember his family talking about the matter. The spirit was not Leonard's father; it was the family doctor. His mother was having an affair with the family doctor, Leonard told Rita, and all the family gossiped about it. Leonard immediately recognized this as the source of his lifetime distrust of women and why none of his relationships lasted. Leonard was able to release the negative energy of mistrust and move forward with his life. He's now been in a loving relationship with the same woman for seven years.

Spiritualists believe in reformation of the human spirit at any time, here on Earth or hereafter in Spirit. What this means is that at any time we have the opportunity to change direction and move toward a positive energy. Our life paths are fluid. Life can always be turned around. If Spirit is telling you the bridge is out, are you going to drive off the cliff? You can take a detour! If any psychic or medium tells you something is carved in stone, run the other way. If Spirit gives you a warning, it means that you have an opportunity to make changes.

Affirming Positive Change

Positive life force energy is powerful. You can use it to shape and focus your future in ways that allow your dreams and hopes to become your reality. What about your life would you like to change? Let this affirmation exercise show you how effective setting positive intent can be!

1. Choose a hope or an aspiration, something you'd like to have as a part of your life that is not a part of your experience right now.

2. Articulate this hope as an affirmation. Be as specific as possible (see Rita's example following the exercise).

3. Write this affirmation in the first person ("I am ..."); then write it in the second person ("he/she is ..."); and then write it in the third person ("Rita is ..."). This is important because it makes the affirmation both internal and external and gives you different perspectives of the same vision. Write each version of your affirmation in longhand five times in a notebook kept specifically for this purpose. Date and sign the affirmation.

4. After writing them down, read your affirmations out loud, one in each person/point of view. How do you feel when you hear the words spoken aloud? Allow yourself to feel where voicing your intent feels awkward to you, and then change the wording of your affirmation until the intent becomes entirely comfortable to you. (It's important to release your affirmation to the Goddess/God of your understanding, for the highest and best intent. Sometimes what you hope for is not for your highest and best; if it were to materialize, it would cause problems for you, such as an affirmation to marry the current love of your life when there are serious issues making it unlikely the relationship would work.)

5. First thing in the morning, write (or say, if you don't have time to write) your affirmations five times in each person/point of view. After you complete the affirmations, consciously release your hope to the highest and the best.

6. Continue this process until your affirmation begins to manifest for the highest and best. Each time, be sure to release your affirmation to the Goddess/God of your understanding.

Rita's Affirmations

The first time Rita did this affirmation exercise, she knew her affirmation would be about her painting. So she went into her studio and wrote:

I show my paintings.

She shows her paintings.

Rita Berkowitz shows her paintings.

Rita wrote this affirmation for a few days and then realized it needed something more. So, she revised it:

I show and sell my paintings.

She shows and sells her paintings.

Rita Berkowitz shows and sells her paintings.

But still this wasn't enough. So, Rita revised the affirmation a third time:

I show and sell excellent paintings.

She shows and sells excellent paintings.

Rita Berkowitz shows and sells excellent paintings.

Rita wrote her affirmation five times a day for several weeks. Then she got the idea for a series called *City Folks*. In the ordinary scheme of the art world, a painter does ten or so paintings, takes slides of them, and then contacts gallery owners to view the slides and try to land shows. It's a challenging and sometimes grueling process Rita had been through a number of times already. Although it's very important for an artist, it was something Rita had trouble looking forward to!

Rita continued to write her affirmations every morning as started working on the paintings in the *City Folk* series. She had just completed the third painting when gallery owners began stopping by her painting studio, seemingly for no apparent reason related to Rita's current cycle of work. They saw the paintings she was working on and started asking when the series would be finished and whether she wanted to show the paintings. This spontaneous offer to show is almost unheard of in the art business, and Rita was astonished. The series turned out to be Rita's most successful, and the paintings sold all over the United States. Rita's affirmation came to pass!

Canvas

Sometimes, finding your way back to a lost love takes more than affirmation; it also takes a leap of faith. In the 2020 animated short film *Canvas,* created by *Toy Story 4* animator Frank E. Abney, III, an elderly widower finds the courage to paint from life once more through the love of his daughter and granddaughter on the Earth plane. His visiting granddaughter (a budding artist herself) finds her grandfather's abandoned art studio, which contains a lovely unfinished portrait of her deceased grandmother. The power of love draws her grandmother's spirit right off the canvas, and her presence from Spirit reminds her beloved husband why he so loved putting paintbrush to canvas.

A loving hand is an artist's hand, is a creative hand, and is a hand that can bring a loved one to life under its touch. That spark of love can be the leap of faith reconnecting us with our lost passions. Continuity of life, the abiding love of generations, touches off the spark engaging our imagination and restores our faith in the future.

Destiny: Your Soul's Changing Path

Your soul negotiates with the Divine (the Goddess/God of your understanding) to establish its mission, and to choose the life paths that will support this mission. This is the element of existence you might think of as capital "D" Destiny—it is the cosmic course of your spirit, something determined as the course of your life events, to unfold over time *no matter what.*

Destiny comes from the Latin word *destare,* which means "to take a stand." This is what Destiny is from your soul's perspective—taking a stand for what it needs to accomplish during this lifetime. Taking a stand requires conviction and action. You'll see it is hard to take a stand by passively allowing life to flow around you. You act with firm conviction to take a stand—to put your Destiny in motion—through the thoughts and actions you choose. In essence, your freewill decisions and actions lay the grounding lifepath work of your Destiny.

Conversely, in Greek mythology, the Fates were three Goddesses whose role was to spin out the threads of life for each person born. The first, Klotho, spun fibers into thread (birth). The second, Lachesis, controlled the length of the thread (life). The third, Atropos, wielded the scissors that cut off the thread (death). Mortals remained powerless to influence the actions of the Fates; the Fates alone determined the metaphysical dimensions of life.

We believe your soul's path is the means by which it takes a stand. Because your freewill actions determine its course, your life path is dynamic and ever-changing. Each decision you make advances your soul toward its mission, or Destiny. Some choices change the direction of your path and the length of time it takes to achieve what is necessary.

When Rita's husband David came home from work way back in December of 1996 and said he had a new perk at his job, tuition reimbursement for spouses, Rita felt great excitement. She had long wanted to go back to school for her master's degree in painting, and this looked like the perfect opportunity, dropped right in her lap.

Rita did a meditation about returning to school for art, and instead got a very different and unmistakably clear message from her Spirit guides: *Go back to school, get your master's degree in psychology.* The message was emphatic and powerful. Rita did two more meditations and got the same message, which affirmed for her this was the right choice. So she went to graduate school and earned her master's degree in psychology. Rita now finds what she learned is a crucial part of her work as a Spirit artist.

It's important to confirm or verify any message that tells you to make big changes in your life. Ask three times, as Rita did. If you get different answers, back off. If this is genuinely an opportunity for change that has your name on it, the change will still be waiting for you whenever you're ready to accept its life-altering message. Always make sure you are 100 percent comfortable with the message before making any changes or taking any actions based on it. You can always make changes; there is always time.

Finding Fulfillment Now—in This Life

Inasmuch as your life on the Earth plane is a piece of the bigger cosmic whole and but one passage in your soul's complete journey, it still is itself a mission. Rita knows it's wonderful to be aware of the ways your life fits into the metaphysics of Divine existence. But Rita also knows your life is the *here and now of your current existence,* and the only way to make this present unfolding of your soul's journey worthwhile is to make it the highest and best experience possible.

You live in the here and now. Life exists in the present moment. Infinite decisions, choices, and actions shape the grounding pathway of Destiny, some of which are within your control and many beyond it. To look toward your future, *look where you want to go.* Keep your mind open! Remain unattached to outcomes, but set your intent for the highest and best. Allow life to happen and to surprise and delight you.

As a Spirit artist, Rita draws the face presenting to you from Spirit, the face that proves for you the continuity of life. And she knows its appearance may not follow some predetermined way, but it shines with the fleeting beauty of a treasured moment plucked from time, challenging memory while embracing time's only constant—*all existence is change.* Your soul's path is dynamic and ever-changing.

Sheree works in Women of Wisdom and has seen many Spirit drawings produced for others. In her drawing, Sheree immediately recognized her grandmother Delia and the description of Delia's home. Delia reported everything to Rita, including her favorite color, insisting as well on being drawn with her hair in a 1970s-style frizz perm. Sheree didn't remember her grandmother with this hairstyle, but when she asked her father, he produced photos of Delia wearing the frizz perm and the same color dress she had insisted upon in the drawing.

The Best Things in Life

Sometimes at our moments of greatest confusion and feelings of loss, we receive the most unexpected, profound blessings from Spirit. Another great example from fiction is the relationship between television's legendary adman, Don Draper (played by Jon Hamm), and his classic boss, Bert Cooper (played by Robert Morse). As the Mad Men series hurtled toward its finale, drawing Don Draper toward California and his greatest inspiration experienced through despair, we saw Don mourning the loss of his mentor and friend, the brilliant eccentric Bert Cooper (who passes while watching the 1969 moon landing on his television). As Don turns to look down the corridor to Bert's office door, Bert himself, in socks, appears with a bevy of singing secretaries.

In a nod to Robert Morse's genius career in musical comedy, Bert and the girls launch into a rousing, endearing rendition of the song, "The Best Things in Life are Free." Spirit has the answers, if only we will see with our inner vision, listen to our inner voice, and understand with our inner knowing. With a heart full of mischievious play, Bert Cooper's spirit sings to Don: The stars in the sky, the moon on high, they're great for you and me…because they're free! The moon belongs to everyone. The best things in life are free.

What a rousing affirmation of the continuity of life, of humanity's place in the Universe, and our continuing exploration of the Heavens! As our spirits learn and evolve, surely do we make our futures. We ourselves are proof of the continuity of life. We continue, moment to moment, lifetime to lifetime, Earth plane to Spirit, and back again. We are Spirit artists, all. We create. Through all change, we live, we love, and are loved.

Spirit Heals the World

Each life, each entity of Spirit, is unique, with its own set of experiences, challenges, and learnings. Yet each life and each entity of Spirit is also a piece of the Earth's collective journey—together, we forge a Darwinian evolution of cooperation (cooperation, almost more important to Darwin than natural selection) marked, given force and direction, by the world's very turning. Our energy shapes the world's future—humanity's future—through the efforts of our collective conscious, whether our spirits are working to the good on this Earthly plane or from the Higher realm of Spirit.

When we evolve to approach enlightenment, we become suffused with life force energy, and we move closer to being at one with the Universe. Souls in their yearning merge into the Divine flow of vital energy found at the Source. As the soul's evolution transcends at last beyond personal identity, individual personalities become less important. We shed the details that have lovingly defined us, our hallmarks of character, moving from "mine" to "ours," from "I" to "we," and from "human" to "Divine." Our physical, Earthly lives give us the opportunities our spirits need to make these all-important transitions. And through them, our collective spiritual conscious influences our beloved Earth, sending healing and love to the soul of the planet that is our entryway to explore the Universe and beyond.

Our Earth in Healing Balance

James Ephraim Lovelock, noted scientist, environmentalist, and natural philosopher, created the Gaia hypothesis, which postulates the Earth is a self-regulating system and will restore homeostasis when needed. Homeostasis is a biological term that denotes harmony and balance, such as in the human body. According to Gaia, the Earth will act with conscious intent to balance its energies. In Greek mythology, Gaia is the Mother Earth, a primordial entity of Nature.

Now, at the start of the twenty-first century, many scientists believe the Earth is entering the Anthropocene Era—a period marked by humankind's influence upon the patterns and life cycles of the Earth. As species die off, it's also believed the Earth is entering its Sixth Great Extinction. The Fifth Mass Extinction occurred about 65 million years ago when the dinosaurs were wiped out. Earth faces unprecedented climate change evidenced by the mass relocation of refugees because of shortages of natural resources, violence, and disease, and by a global pandemic. It also benefits from an explosion of human understanding and innovation (genetics, 3D printing, fertility, rocket technology for commercial space travel, cloning, computing power, agriculture, and so much more).

The great challenge and task of humankind, of Spirit, is to heal our planet, to create and nurture a new planetary balance. We need to be sure our home planet is strong and healthy as we evolve spiritually to contemplate those first steps we must take off the Earth, beyond the Moon to Mars and the other planets of Earth's solar system, out to our galaxy, and beyond. All this, even as we explore our Sun's solar power, divulge the mysteries of black holes, dark matter, and other secrets of the Universe we have yet to uncover.

Our individual role in helping create balance in such an immense—infinite, really—Universe seems daunting … so hard to wrap our senses around. The stress of contemplating it can seem too much to handle, even when the stress of a loved one's transition to Spirit is often experienced as an insurmountable loss. How do we heal the world? Is such an undertaking—for one human spirit—even *possible?*

Micro to Macro

Throughout human history, humankind's relationship to the Divine has changed as our understanding of the Earth and the Heavens has grown and evolved. During prehistory, any unexplainable phenomena must have loomed as a Divine occurrence. Even now, hallmarks of that time, such as the proliferation of standing stones like those at Stonehenge, portend astronomical symbology, though we do not understand who created these structures or understand their function.

Throughout the Middle Ages, humankind revered the Divine, looking to the Goddess/God of their understanding to guide and control humankind's moral and ethical behavior. God's will formed a serious and holy compact that humankind transgressed at their peril. However, with the flowering of the Renaissance and the emergence of scientific theory, Galileo defied the Spanish Inquisition insisting the Earth revolved around the Sun. The workings of the natural world and of the Heavens revealed through scientific discovery served to underscore the beauty and mastery of the Divine. Increasingly, the human beings (mind, body, and soul) became revered for their nobility in the likeness of the Divine.

It was the dawn of Enlightenment, the Age of Reason. Humankind stood, a noble figure, silhouetted against the vastness of Nature and the Heavens. The great cataloging of the world and its species had begun, including Charles Darwin's famous voyage on the HMS Beagle and his book chronicling it. With the world-shaking theory of evolution, Darwin advanced the notion of humankind's place in a progression that challenged the notion of creation. For the first time, God's place in the Universe became that bit more tenuous. The controversy of evolution continues to this day. Many believe it is possible to reconcile evolution with belief in a Divine Goddess/God. Many do not believe so.

Today our notions of humankind are wrapped in both grandeur and insignificance. In an age of artificial intelligence and genetic manipulation, in an age where a computer can accomplish calculations in a matter of moments that would take a human being many years, even decades, to perform, the worth of an individual human life seems diminished. At the same time, it is the human mind that has created all the technological advancements laying the groundwork for a human-induced evolution of the species. For the first time, humans may be able to affect their own evolution through that same process of genetic manipulation and enhanced learning.

From microscopes that see deep into the components of cells to telescopes that see far into the origins of time and the outer reaches of space, humankind now has the ability to explore the nature of Spirit. Are we coming closer to understanding our Divine purpose? Or, will we become alienated from ourselves and from each other? Rita believes our soul's missions have become more important than ever. Now that we can see more deeply, our responsibility to Spirit (and to each other) is ever greater.

The Spring at the Source

Rita is brought to mind of St. Teresa of Avila's work of mystical theology, *Interior Castle*. St. Teresa writes of the two basins of water. One basin is filled through a network of sophisticated conduits designed by humankind that bring the water from a great distance, wending this way and that, through a "Rube Goldberg" contraption, emitting a great noise and vibration. The second basin has been constructed at the very source of the water and fills without a sound. Because the water comes immediately from its source, it flows directly, without impediment, filling and refilling the basin endlessly, without interruption. Of course, the metaphor is clear. Our human intelligence runs the risk of over-complication. Our Divine intelligence springs naturally from the Source.

When we communicate with Spirit we access a direct channel to the Divine Source. We must trust in Spirit, in the flow of our faith, so that we might reach enlightenment. And in so doing, have the strength and focus to heal our planet and to be good and kind stewards of the Earth.

The Bigger Picture

Each of us has an absolutely different soul mission, and each mission has infinitely many paths that can take you to it. The people who enter our lives (on the Earth or Spirit planes) all have reasons for doing so, regardless of how long they stay or what it seems we accomplish as a result of their presence.

It is an amazing choreography. Even though it doesn't always feel that way, the people who come into your life come together for good purposes. Even when you think this is not the case or that the outcome is less than you hoped for, we are all working toward healing. Sometimes the people who have the greatest roles in revealing lessons and leading to progress are the people who are the most challenging. Challenge is a form of questioning of problems that present opportunities.

At one point in her life, Rita worked for a company that was incredibly difficult because the owner liked to play mind games with people. If you were on the employer's good side it wasn't so bad, but when you were on the bad side, this owner made your work life nearly impossible.

After Rita had been at the company for some time, the owner offered her an astonishing promotion. But it immediately became clear there were many strings attached to the offer. Ultimately, Rita felt the only choice she had was to leave the company, so she did. She went to a new job, where her interactions with clients resulted in a series of paintings Rita otherwise would never have thought to do.

The people who push you in these ways are often pushing you toward where you are supposed to be in the bigger picture, even when it seems that all they're doing is pushing your buttons or forcing you toward difficult situations. Imagine you are always one step closer to the Divine Source and that each opportunity leads you to actions that help and heal.

Your Journey's Meaning

Spirit communication provides validation that your life journey has value, purpose, and meaning. Those who have passed to the Higher side can reach back to you to show you there is more to existence than physical life. Your passage through this physical life is an opportunity for your spirit to grow and evolve and for the events of your life to contribute to growth and evolution for others.

For You

Your spirit is here on the Earth plane, living as a physical entity because there are lessons for you to learn. These lessons often come in the form of challenges. You face problems, adversity, even crises. You wouldn't consciously choose these circumstances because they are often hard and painful and involve loss and suffering.

But these are the experiences that are your soul's lessons. They are what you point to as defining moments in your life. From them, you make changes—sometimes forced—in the outward ways of your life. You see and experience these changes. The inward changes that accompany them are not so obvious or visible. They reflect the personal growth that results from confronting the challenge.

This is not the only way your soul can evolve through the lessons of problems and difficulty. Rather, it's that the problems and difficulties are the events that force you to pay attention to your soul's mission. You learn just as much (if not more) from situations of loving kindness and of goodness for the highest and best intent. One goal of healing is to increase the learning that comes from good.

Meditation is a good way to stay in touch with your soul's mission and to explore inwardly the choices and decisions at hand. Astrology is a way to confirm the information you receive through meditation. Because astrology is the blueprint of your life, it shows the path of your spirit's evolution.

For Others

Your life touches the lives of countless others. This is most obvious in your immediate circle of contact—your family, friends, neighbors, co-workers. You form bonds and connections with these people through which you send and receive Divine life force energy.

Sometimes people enter your life, or you enter someone else's life, for a specific purpose, and this is clear from the moment you meet. The purpose might be limited and defined, such as a mechanic who opens a shop on your commute route just when your car needs repair, or a woman ahead of you in line at the grocery store who tells the clerk a position has become available in her company just when you're looking for a job, or a security officer who happens to drive by when you're walking through a nearly deserted parking garage late at night. Circumstances such as these are constant reminders the energy of the Universe is there to help you in times of need, small and large.

Sometimes the contact is amazingly brief. A woman who profoundly changed Rita's life was someone she spent barely five minutes with at a holiday party decades ago. Grace was studying art and wanted to meet Rita because Rita was a professional artist. Grace was 92 years old, a tiny woman who walked a mile and a half from her house to the School of Fine Arts in Boston, where she studied figure drawing.

The Hierophant, August 1991, oil on canvas. Rita worked on a series of paintings based on the Tarot in the early 1990s. In the Tarot deck, the Hierophant card is the symbol of all that is spiritual coming together. Recently a teacher of Rita's sat in a trance and told her of a rabbi in full regalia who was her guide. When Rita showed him the painting, he smiled and said, "That's him."

After talking with Grace, Rita thought to herself, "If she's not too old to learn, I'm not too old to learn!" Rita then made the decision to return to college for her graduate degree, setting aside her worries about possibly being the oldest person in her class (she wasn't).

Other times, your life becomes entwined with the life of someone else for reasons that aren't very clear. This is particularly true for mediums whose role it is to bring people into contact with messages and information that will be profoundly moving and then drop from the picture. From a Spiritualist perspective, this is the key purpose of mediumistic abilities.

Sometimes you think people come into your life for you to help them, and they end up helping you instead, in ways you didn't know you needed help. When Susan met Alan, he had some substance abuse problems. Susan thought she could help him, and before long, she became involved in an extramarital affair with him. Her marriage was difficult, and she found comfort in helping Alan.

But Alan's substance abuse problem was significant, and as he slid into decline, he became less comforting and more challenging. In a flash of insight born of Alan's problems, Susan realized she needed to redirect her energy toward working on the problems in her own marriage. Alan would be better helped by professionals able to assist him in breaking his addiction and returning to a stable, dependable experience of life.

Working Toward a Common Good

As much as we like to focus on the positives of psychical and mediumistic abilities, it's a reality they occasionally reveal challenges and problems. When this happens, surround the situation with as much white light as you can. You probably can't stop the situation from unfolding; clearly, it is necessary for those who will experience learning as a result.

Also, send healing prayers to help those who are caught in the situation to pull from it the information and insight that moves them in the direction of what is for their highest and best intent.

When your psychical or mediumistic abilities show you a negative situation or a disaster, send healing energy immediately. Don't wait to see if your prediction is correct, and don't worry if it doesn't come to pass. You might never know how you made a difference. Always send healing for the highest and the best.

The Anguish of Forebodings

What happens when signs and portents seem to drip with foreboding, as a forewarning of horrible realities and visions rife with futility? There's a heavy question. This kind of thinking and worldview seems to evoke the passionate tragedies in the pages of the great Russian novels. Nowhere better can this be seen than in Mikhail Bulgakov's classic novel, *The Master and Margarita* (tr. Richard Pevear and Larissa Volokhonsky, Penguin Books, 1997, 2001).

Written during the height of Stalin's terror in the twentieth century, the novel contains all manner of dark arts séances, occult happenings, and terrifying goings on. All forms of connection between human beings, whether personal, professional, political, or religious/spiritual are undermined, subverted, and proven untrustworthy. Anguish and fear provoked through terror, especially when experienced through sleight-of-hand tricks and smoke-and-mirrors tricks, keep people from nurturing faith and trusting love.

This, we believe is the key. Whenever faith and love are threatened, truth remains elusive and progress stalls into impossibilities. Keep your core spirit strong, your belief in your Divine light unshakeable. The road to love may be a long one, progress in your life, your community, and your world may be hard and too often out of reach. Keep reaching. Never surrender compassion and humanity. Spirit will not fail you.

Through the humor (irony), lyric poeticism, and magic enchantment of Bulkagov's novel, the author shows us readers that the path to peace in the moonlight is found in seeing life through on our own terms—terms of love and joy, no matter what occurs. U.S. Medal of Honor recipient and Vietnam War POW James Stockdale expressed the concept in these words, what's now known popularly as "Stockdale's Paradox": "You must never confuse faith that you will prevail in the end … with the discipline to confront the most brutal facts of your current reality." Now, that's a little harshly put. But the message is on point. Never give up.

Have faith in the highest and best, for yourself and for the world. Strive always for light, love, peace, and healing—for everyone. If you must, delight in small moves and incremental progress. Ask for Spirit's help, and know you receive it.

The Committee in Spirit

We've talked a lot about Spirit guides and the healing work they do in our lives, especially when we call upon their help. Beyond our Spirit guides are what is known among mediums as our Committee in Spirit. The Committee in Spirit emerges from the Divine Source and exists to support and nurture each one of us. It is a collective of spirits whose role is to facilitate our connection to the Source and direct us toward our higher purpose. Ask in meditation for the name of the guide who speaks to you on behalf of your Committee. Remember, it is a collective of Spirit.

When Rita offered to connect through Spirit to Emma Rose's Committee, she readily agreed. Even though a Committee in Spirit is pretty high up in the Spirit realm, Rita can connect without the rigors of a trance session. This is because an individual's Committee and facilitating guide are here precisely to nurture and shepherd our Divine humanity. As Rita put out the intent to connect with Emma Rose's Committee and facilitating guide, she first saw all the spirits surrounding Emma Rose. But then, she began to ascend as spirits made way for Rita to pass until one Spirit guide emerged, accompanied by five others. The spirit identified as Emma Rose's facilitating guide and agreed to allow her Committee in Spirit to be drawn.

This is an intense-looking group. The facilitating guide expressed a purpose of connecting with Emma Rose's open heart. From left to right in Rita's drawing, the members of the Committee presented as Emma Rose's guides to pathos and compassion, humor, the taskmaster (this guide helps Emma Rose, a publisher, to work with authors and tough out every book schedule to successful completion!), the scientist, and the poet. Emma Rose watched as the faces of her Committee took expression under Rita's drawing hand. Rita smiled as she drew and said, "Emma Rose, if you knew what was coming, you'd run as fast as you could in the opposite direction." Of course, Emma Rose was more than a little skeptical, wondering why or how fleeing could be a good thing. "You won't flee," the Committee's facilitating guide told Rita. "Your heart won't let you." After receiving the blessing of the Committee in Spirit, thank the Committee for their care, and ask their help for your continued unfoldment in Spirit.

Rita's drawing of Emma Rose's Committee in Spirit.

Even if life's path seems difficult or daunting, great spiritual growth and learning is possible. Your Committee in Spirit is there to help you as you consciously walk the walk of spiritual evolution. As you do the hard work of growing in love, empathy, and compassion, you grow in Spirit—and you are better able to help in healing the Earth. Emma Rose checked in with Rita many years later and let her know the Committee's insights proved spot on. Emma Rose has done much heart-and-soul work and credits the strength of her Committee in Spirit to help her stay steady on her path over time.

The World's Energy

Spirit connection is so amazingly powerful. As with all tools, you must first develop expertise in how to use your psychical and mediumistic gifts to bring connection with Spirit into your life. Once you are comfortable in using your mediumistic skills, you can apply their insights for your good and growth, as well as for the common good and growth.

In the space of a few generations, the world's population has grown rapidly as many spirits entered Earth plane existences. According to a study in *The Lancet*, global population could peak at 9.7 billion by 2067 and fall to 8.8 billion by century's end because of overall falling fertility rates. In our lifetimes, we will see the consequences of this population growth on resources, environmental as well as social. Although the energy of the Universe is endless in its capacity to support life, boundaries and limits define the Earth's ability to do the same. As we draw from the Earth to sustain our physical lives, it becomes increasingly important for us to replenish and restore its natural environment.

Practicing personal homeostatic balance leads to good practice of healing homeostatic practices in your home and community. Start small. You might begin by attending Spiritualist church services and participating in open circles. Practice connecting to your Spirit guides and to the facilitating guide of your Committee in Spirit. The more you engage with Spirit, the stronger and more balanced you will be in doing your important work of spiritual evolution.

What Can You Change?

Change, all change, starts with you. You probably could argue that it stays with you, too, because in reality, all you can change is yourself. You can change your thoughts and actions, your beliefs and behaviors. The differences might sometimes seem so small as to be inconsequential, but they have significant ramifications nonetheless. What seems like a small change today may affect large and lasting changes going forward.

The Power of Freewill

We've talked a lot about your freewill and how it shapes your path through this life. Students frequently ask Rita, "What happens when someone else (on the Earth plane) sends you healing, and you don't want to accept it?" Perhaps you sense your time of passing might be near, and you don't want to delay it. Or you just don't want this healing energy that's being sent to you, or don't want energy from this particular person.

Your higher self, in conjunction with your Spirit guide, guard access to your spirit. Your higher self decides whether to let the healing in. This is often related to the journey you've agreed to embark upon in this lifetime. Before entering this life, you agree to what you will do and accept. This agreement frames the choices you make.

If healing comes to you for your highest and best, it's not intended to make everything better. It's simply there for you to use if you choose. It won't interfere with your soul's path. If it's your time to make your transition to the Higher side, then you will, no matter what energy those on the Earth plane try to send to you. And if it's not time for you to pass to Spirit, then you won't.

Healing energy is yours to accept, when and how your freewill decides.

The Power of Love and Goodness

All healing comes in love and goodness. When so much of what we see and hear in our everyday lives seems far removed from either love or goodness, it's sometimes hard to believe this is the core of our existence and the basis of the Universe. This is especially true when war, disease, poverty, and famine are still all too common for much of humanity. Such challenges impoverish us all. Yet where there is great need, we surely will find great love and the imperative for healing.

When we talk about the higher vibration of the Higher side of life, we are talking about a place of light, a place of love and goodness. We come from there! Even in our physical forms, we remain part of this love and light. You come to this Earth plane existence to learn, but you are always connected to the Source of your origin. Before, during, and after incarnation, we are always Spirit.

Teresa, March 1991, oil on canvas. Rita sat with some friends doing readings when above her friend Teresa's head, she saw a vision of a young nun praying. She mentioned it to Teresa and did a quick sketch, which was later to become a painting. Teresa stayed in storage for about nine years when Rita met an astrologer Terese, who was to become a good friend and who was fascinated by Rita's Spirit artwork. Rita told her she painted a painting of a young nun named Teresa and Terese asked Rita if the nun was actually Carmelite nun St. Therese of Lisieux, called "The Little Flower." Being of a different religious origin, Rita had not heard the story, so she showed her friend the painting. Terese became quite excited and brought a book that showed an actual photo of St. Therese; they seemed to match. St. Therese is the patron saint of florists, missionaries, people living with AIDs, and the sick.

Connecting Beyond Yourself for the Greater Good

We are all connected. Some connections are closer than others, but we are all connected as one. If one person hurts, it affects every one of us. Alone, your energy is powerful enough to shape the flow and direction of your personal life. But in combination with the energy of others, you become part of a whole, a collective that is far greater than the sum of its parts. Imagine what could happen if everyone would …

- Send healing to the Earth.
- Send healing to the parts of the world where there are problems.
- Send healing not only to the people they love but the people they don't.
- Send healing to the people they care about as well as those who cause them problems.
- Send healing to those challenged by disaster and tragedy.
- Send healing energy to transmute the problems you see, or read about in the news media. You don't have to change the world … just send healing!

There are no limits to the good that we can accomplish when we pool our individual energies! Make your own list of healing prayers to further focus your energy for the Highest intent. You might send healing when you …

- Drive past an accident on the highway
- Experience or are witness to an abuse of power
- See aid units on their way to a rescue
- See the destruction of the natural world by fire, rising sea levels, and other effects of climate change
- Hear of a family left struggling or homeless
- Hear that a child is missing
- Read that teachers need better classroom resources
- Meditate on the sick or the dying
- Learn that a neighbor lost their job
- Hear that a local business is closing

Add your own reasons to send healing:

_____

_____

_____

_____

_____

Many of us spend a lot of our time worrying about things we believe we cannot change. We don't have to feel helpless in these situations. We can send out healing, do what we can on a spiritual level and on a psychic level and connect with the energy to transmute it to work toward the positive.

There is much strife and discord in our world, and it often seems so overwhelming there is little hope for change. But change takes place one person at a time. And over time, this adds up to an amazing collective energy capable of changing—and that does in truth change—the vibrational pattern of energy throughout the world and the Universe.

As insignificant as it might seem for you, as one person, to change the way you think, it is impossible for such a change to exist in isolation. Every thought, every action, affects the flow of energy in ways both obvious and obscure. More often than not, you don't see the full and multiple outcomes of these changes.

We often use the metaphor of tossing a pebble into a pond and watching the shift in energy ripple outward from the point of impact until ever so faintly those ripples reach the shore and echo back toward their center again. Even when you can no longer see them, the ripples are still moving through the water.

On the Earth Plane

From our lives here on the Earth plane, we cannot always see the outcome as being for the Highest good. We have to trust that when we are working in light and for the Higher good, the energy and the healing will go forth in the direction intended.

Rita's friend and mentor Bob Miller uses every opportunity to send healing energy to people. When walking down the street, if he sees somebody looking very distraught, he goes to them, shakes hands like he knows them, and sends spiritual healing to them! Then he pretends to have confused the person with someone else and gracefully disengages. This gives him the opportunity to make the physical contact to send the healing.

Avoid attachment to outcomes; when we care too much about a certain outcome, that's "I" energy, or ego energy, not healing. Send healing, send love. The body has an intelligence (as does the Earth); the healing will go where it needs to go and manifest for the highest and best (which may result in an outcome not easily imagined beforehand but to be much welcomed).

To the Spirit Plane

The same holds for those on the Spirit plane. They can send healing and love to the Earth plane. You can also send healing and love to the Higher side to help a spirit entity evolve to a higher place.

Many times, those on the Higher side can see the bigger picture. In turning to the Higher side for assistance and guidance, you can go to your Committee in Spirit, to the Spirit guides, and to the Infinite Source (the Goddess/God of your understanding) and ask them to send healing to the Earth plane.

Using Divine Love to Help Others

Rita hopes that as you've read this book, your awareness of Spirit in your life has grown, and your human curiosity is sparked to learn more about communicating with Spirit. Whether you desire to communicate with a loved one who has passed to Spirit, or whether you simply want to know more about Spirit and its workings, Rita hopes you too will come to honor a belief in the continuity of life. As a Spirit artist, Rita knows Spirit is a healing force to help, guide, and nurture all humanity. Rita knows that death is not the end, that the face of love endures.

You may feel still, after all, that one person alone cannot contribute much to what sometimes seems to be a world of troubles. Renowned philosopher, psychologist, and Holocaust survivor, Viktor Frankl, wrote this in his powerful book *Man's Search for Meaning*. "When the impossibility of replacing a person is realized, it allows the responsibility which a (hu)man has for (their) existence and its continuance to appear in all its magnitude." We could not have said it better. Each of us is invaluable. We each and all of us contain multitudes. We love and are loved—in Earthly life and in Spirit. Collectively, we draw upon the awesome power of Spirit that is the essence flowing to us from the Source of all that is. We live by grace with Spirit.

Rita wishes for you the highest and best for your life. May your adventures in communicating with spirits lead you to a personal understanding of the continuity of life that will bring comfort and healing to you and to those you love on the Earth plane or in Spirit.

Let what you've learned through this book help to bring healing, light, and love through Spirit for a better world, right now, in our time on Earth.

When Grief and Sadness Overwhelm

Sometimes, life overwhelms us with experiences that leave us flooded with strong emotions—emotions we have difficulty processing or perhaps even fully understanding. In those times, we look for places to put these difficult thoughts and feelings. These would have to be places strong enough to match the intensity of our emotions and big enough to hold all that charged energy, while keeping us safe so we might begin the work of examining and understanding what and how we feel and what must be done, later to bring our lives back into balance.

Oftentimes, while we rely on the love and compassion of family and friends to see us through, there is a wave of sadness and grief after a loss that is uniquely personal. Some feelings we need to grapple with alone. Managing the potentially overwhelming feelings after a great loss can be confusing and more than a little daunting. Will you *always* feel this way? Many elements of what you are feeling may be resolved during the grieving process, but pieces and fragments of emotion will stay with you, though their intensity may decrease over time.

The Nature of Grief

Grief is an emotion that can follow us throughout our lives. It likely will change focus and perhaps soften as you pass through different stages of life. But your yearning for those you have loved, those who have passed on to Spirit, will stay in your heart. Their presence there at the heart, the core of your compassion, provides a great comfort. You may feel your loved ones are with you, and you would be correct. But the energy of Spirit surrounds us always, whether we feel it there consciously, or not.

In Lee Ann's reading with Rita, Rita made a spirit drawing of Lee Ann's Sicilian great-grandmother Vennera, for whom the family didn't have in hand a photographic image. Lee Ann is no stranger to grief, having been involved in the care of both her parents and of her grandmothers, including being with them all at their times of passing. Vennera had insisted that Rita draw a blue sky behind her spirit portrait to show Lee Ann that blue skies ahead were not only possible for her but were destined. Even as we carry our grief with us for those we have lost on the Earth plane, our bonds to Spirit confirm the continuity of life, opening vistas of opportunity. Spirit affirms the promise of life force energy—so we can experience all that existence on the Earth plane makes possible.

Lee Ann tells Rita that, for all the world, she would not trade those difficult caregiving years, or the pain of grief that followed. It would be easy to feel alone. But as she goes forward in life, Lee Ann believes the memories of care and of the times shared sustain her with a richness of family love and joy that is eternal. She has loved and been loved. That joy of family is not lost; it goes with us, forever after the loss of loved ones on the Earth plane.

But until you can reach for the kind of peace through Spirit that Lee Ann talked about with Rita, what do you do with your intense feelings of grief and sadness? Feelings too big for your body, your heart, and mind to hold?

Sadness at the Start of Grief

At the start of grief, feelings are high. You are searching. As Joan Didion so aptly named it, this is the "year of magical thinking." Our minds, hearts, and bodies stutter in adapting to a world without our loved ones in it. It is a time of questioning and disbelief. All we loved that was particular to our loved one, all the intimacies shared—both large and small—feel lost to us. And if the loss is sudden, the shock of the loss felt is all the more impactful.

It is here at the start of grief, that Rita asks you to call to attention. Now, when the power of the emotions passing through you can seem large enough to devour you—to, as the saying goes, "eat you alive." Whether you find yourself a mass of feelings you can't rein in, or whether you've turned numb in the face of the event's enormity, we react to grief's strong emotions in survival mode. It is at this point, at the start of grief, when a call to attention through Spirit can be helpful.

Rita will explain what is meant by a call to attention, but first: While a period of intense sadness and grief may knock you off-center in the beginning, if you are struggling with feelings that adversely affect your daily experience of life, your work, or your relationships, in an ongoing way, please do see a grief counselor, your personal doctor, or therapist to help you work through your process.

Grief Is Spirit's Call to Attention

One way to begin the process of understanding your grief is to take your overwhelming feelings and point them, with laser focus, directly at Spirit. Now, you might say this is as overwhelming a task as your emotions are overwhelming! The task is too unmanageable. Spirit is vast and eternal. How do you offer the vastness of loss to the vastness of Spirit and attain any kind of manageable focus?

The call to attention is a call to the presence of Spirit in all the things of this world, large and small.

Here's how it works.

The World at Large

A call to attention using the world at large involves finding something on the Earth plane that is large enough to hold your powerful emotions. Anything big or anything truly "awesome," by definition, is what you are looking for. By offering the energy of your strong emotions to the energy of Earthly "awesomeness," you will be reaching for Spirit. The spiritual connection will enliven and comfort you; it will take your strength and match it. With your strength held in Spirit, you, at least temporarily, will be relieved of its burden and reassured by the Eternal Divine.

Following are some awesome worldly calls to attention:

- **Works of Art.** A great symphony, an ethereal ballet, a museum masterpiece—there are many ways to use great works of art as your call to attention. Giving yourself to the passion of the artworks can help you release your emotions to a masterwork worthy of their intensity. These works of art, themselves attempts to reach the Divinity of life, serve as a formidable link to Spirit. In touching the Divine, however briefly, you experience through art the continuity of life, of All that is.

- **Experiencing Nature.** Whether it is a day hike, a camping (or glamping) adventure, a sail, or a walk on the coastline, experiencing Nature is a fast track to Spirit. Let all the things of the Earth comfort and protect you and let the Earth take your pain and transform it, if only for a moment, into peace.

You could make a day hike through the rainforest of Washington State's Hoh River or camp there, experiencing the beauty of old-growth forest and the nurturing power of nurse logs (trees that have fallen and are now organic "wombs" for new growth). The Hoh rainforest is officially the quietest spot in the United States—free of human-made sounds. Standing in a cathedral of old-growth trees, you can feel the life force surrounding you, reaching both to the sky above and down into the ground in a web of nourishing roots. You could take a walk along the coast, and if possible, sit under the stars and watch the course of the moon across the night sky (or bring along your telescope).

- The World's Great Cities. All the cities of the Earth have a unique energy, a hum, and a rhythm that is theirs alone. Consider a walk through Paris's famous parks, up New York City's Fifth Avenue to Central Park and the Metropolitan Museum of Art, through Hanoi's maze of streets in its Old Town with a vibrancy of scooters and pedestrians. Is there a city you love? A day in a beloved city can let you give your emotions to their unique humanity, and the collective human experience of city life can offer you assurance of the continuity of life and a connection to the Spirit that animates all things.

That's just a few ideas of ways to call the world at large to attention through Spirit. You get the idea. What other ways can you imagine?

The World in Miniature

The call to attention using the world in miniature involves finding the infinite in whatever requires our close view. Here, we find the infinite in the smallest things of the world. When you are focused on the finest of details, you become lost in a flow state that connects you to Spirit, to the Divine in the composition of all things. In doing so, it is revealed that the strongest, most unwieldy of emotions can be held in a microcosm. Remember Walt Whitman ... *I contain multitudes*. The smallest detail can be strong enough to hold the largest truth.

Following are some calls to attention in miniature:

- **Reading.** Besides being about the most wonderful thing a person could do, reading is a great way to expand your mind while practicing calm and stillness. There are many medical studies that show both the cognitive and neurological advantages of reading. Whether you are reading the latest book in the *Outlander* series or a philosophical treatise, your mind is learning and making synaptic connections that help you focus, concentrate, and grow. Reading has the power to take your strong emotions and give you calm, escape, and pleasure while repairing and nurturing your body, mind, and soul.

○ **Building.** Okay, you can build anything here. You can join a woodworking group or learn about to do boat-building. You can look under a microscope and see what's there. You can do crafting—beading, needlework, quilting. You can work a puzzle with a thousand pieces. The key here is to lose yourself in making something. Give your strong emotions over to the act of creation, touching Spirit through the most human of all endeavors, the need to build.

○ **Gardening.** Gardening is a beautiful way to connect to the cycle of life. When you walk through a garden, you are actually having a conversation with a community of plants chosen by the gardener. These plants have woven a rich system of interconnected roots that form a shared intelligence. When you create a garden, you put your hands in the soil (a healthy thing to do, studies show), making a direct connection to the Earth itself and to nurturing life upon it. Gardening requires both your body and your mind. You are giving your strong emotions over to a curated expression of natural beauty, the art of nature. You are linked to the life force energy and the Spirit in all that surrounds you and are reminded of the continuity of life and the joy of living.

That's just a few ideas of ways to call the world in miniature to attention through Spirit. You get the idea. What other ways can you imagine?

What calls you to the things of this world? Do you raise your voice with others in a chorus? Do you play in the weekend soccer league? What other things can you imagine that might prove sufficient to hold strong emotion?

Practice the call to attention through Spirit when your grief and sadness overwhelm you. It is a start and a first step toward processing and understanding. While some grief may stay with you, it will be the love that endures.

Index

B

babies, symbolism, 219
balance, energy, 236-237
Barrymore, Lionel, 57
Battle of Alamance, 20
bears (power animal), 249
beavers (power animal), 249
beds, symbolism, 219
Best Things in Life are Free, The, 319
bioenergy, 230-232
birth, spirits before, 72-76
birthing process, 71
black aura, 231
blankets, symbolism, 219
blue aura, 230
bodhisattvas, 280
Breathe of Snow and Ashes, A, 59
bridges, symbolism, 219
Bronte, Charlotte, 194
Brooks, Albert, 58
brown aura, 231
Buddha, 280
buffalos (power animal), 249
Bulgakov, Mikhail, 327
Buried Giant, The, 21, 61
butterflies (power animal), 249

C

Caesar, Julius, 281
Capra, Frank, 57
cars, symbolism, 219
causal subtle body, 64
Cayce, Edgar, 217
Cerberus, 20
ceremonies, spirits, 244-245

chakras, 62
    crown, 64
    heart, 64
    root, 63
    sacral, 63
    solar plexus, 63
    Third Eye, 64
    throat, 64
changes, challenges, 310-312
Charon, 20
Christmas Carol, A, 56, 100
circle of necessity, 22
circles (mediums), safe circles, 150
circles (séances), 136
    closed, 137
    open, 137
    participants, 137-138
    trumpet circles, 142
City Folk series, 315
City of Ghosts, 243
clairaudience, 177-178
clairsentience, 180-181
clairvoyance, 178-180
climbing, symbolism, 219
closed circles, séances, 137
clothing
    energy retention, 201-202
    symbolism, 219
Coleridge, William Taylor, 182
collective unconscious, 212
colors, aura, 230
Columbus, Christopher, 295
Committee in Spirit, 328-330
common good, 327
companions, souls, 279-280
conscious autosuggestion, 247-248

free association, 183
Free Will, 73, 330
Freud, Sigmund, 212, 307
frogs (power animal), 249
furnishings, energy retention, 200-201

G

Gabaldon, Diana, 58
Gandhi, Mahatma, 280
gardens, symbolism, 220
Gardner, Joe, 287
gates, symbolism, 220
Gerwick, Madeline, 73
Ghost Story, A, 105
Ghost, 58
Ghostbusters, 57
global population, 71
Goldberg, Whoopi, 58
goodness, power, 331
Good Soldier, The, 145
Govier, Michael, 312
greater good, connections, 332-333
Greek Mythology, 19
green aura, 230
Gregory IV, Pope, 24
grief, 237
grieving, 237
guided meditation, 89-94
    connecting with your past, 283-286
    power animals, 249-258
    spirit guides, 306-307
gun violence, 102

H

Hades, 20
Halloween, 23-24
Hamlet, 56
Hamm, Jon, 318
hawks (power animal), 249
healing
    aura, 232
    energy, 129, 227-239
    lessons, 237-238
    power of love, 5
    séances, 141
    self-healing, 238
heart chakra, 64
Heaven, 60-61
Hell, 60-61
Hemingway, Ernest, 145, 271
Hemsworth, Chris, 57
Hierophant, The, 325
Higher side, 5
    near-death experiences (NDEs), 266
History of Art, 88
homeostasis, 322
honoring spirits, 261
Houdini, Harry, 31, 134
houses, symbolism, 220
Hudson, Ernie, 57
human energy field, 64-65
human suffering, 145
hummingbirds (power animal), 249
hunters, 242

meditation, 66, 181-182
    connecting with your past, 283-286
    power animals, 249-258
    spirit guides, 306-307
mediumistic abilities, 291
    activating, 11-15
    ancestral bonds, 297
    asking questions, 296
    goals, 298-301
    helping others, 295-296
    honing, 301-302
    identifying, 292
    natural curiosity, 293
    new world view, 295
    shaping future, 293-294
    utilizing, 292-293
mediums, 6, 122, 143
    activating abilities, 145-147
    as facilitators, 132
    automatic writing, 124-125
    becoming, 144-145
    challenges, 154
    choosing, 123
    consciousness, 48
    continuity of life, 128-129
    developing skills, 150-151
    energy healing, 129
    establishing intent, 114-115
    expectations, 153-154
    experience, 122
    experiences during contact, 124
    filtering signals, 148-149
    fraud, 130-132
    healing, 154
    honing skills, 152-153
    human suffering, 145
    intentions, 149-150
    learning focus, 148
    limitations, 149-150
    messages, 129
    psychical vocabulary of symbolism, 48
    psychometry, 126
    reading, 48
    readings, 127-128
    realistic expectations, 153
    safe circles, 150
    spirit drawing, 125-126
    spirit photography, 126-127
    training, 122
    trance, 134
    transfiguration, 126
    versus psychics, 151
mediumship, spiritualism, 32-33
memory
    activation, 9
    persistence, 307, 308
mental phenomena, 33, 116
mental subtle body, 64
Merriam-Webster's Collegiate Dictionary, 68
messages, 157
    clarification, 166
    delivering, 162
    details, 159-162
    emotionally powerful messages, 163-164
    interpreting, 158
    journaling feelings, 164-165
    personal, 166-167
    symbolism, 159
    transforming difficult energy, 162-163
metals, energy retention, 199-200
Mictecacihuatl, 24
Miller, Henry, 79
modern circles, séances, 136-137
Mondrian, Piet, 88
Moore, Demi, 58
Morris Pratt Institute (MPI), 152

Q–R

• •

rapid eye movement (REM) sleep, 210
reading, mediums, 48, 127-128
rebirth, divine purpose, 19
red aura, 230
Reed, Donna, 57
Reiki therapy, 233
reincarnation, 61
Relativity: The Special and the General Theory, 62
Remains of the Day, The, 21
REM (rapid eye movement) sleep, 210
residual energy, 206-207
resurrection, 61
Return of the Soldier, 145
Rhine, J.B., 189-191
Rippentrop, Betsy, 68
rites of passage, spirits, 246
rituals, spirits, 244-245
roaming visitations, 108
Roman Mythology, 19
root chakra, 63
Rose, Emma, 279-280, 328
Rosna, Charles, 29
royal road to the unconscious, 212
Rylance, Mark, 297

S

• • • • • • • • • • • • • • • • • •

sacral chakra, 63
salmon (power animal), 249
séances
    attire, 138-139
    beginning, 134-135
    circle participants, 137-138
    closed circles, 137
    establishing intent, 139
    healing, 141
    identifying yourself, 139-140

    inviting spirit presence, 139
    manifestations, 140-141
    modern circles, 136-137
    phenomena, 136
    positive attitude, 139
    table tipping, 135
    trumpet circles, 142
second chakra, 63
Second Law of Motion, 55
seeing images peripherally, 8
self-healing, 238
self-mastery through conscious autosuggestion, 97, 247, 248
senses
    physical, 172-173
    psychic, 173-183
sensory processing sensitivity (SPS), 185
seventh chakra, 64
Shakespeare, William, 56
shaman soul release, 246-247
Shining, The, 102
Shintō religion, 23
shocks, near-death experiences, 264-265
signals, filtering, 148-149
sixth chakra, 64
Sixth Sense, The, 58
smells, 9
snakes (power animal), 249
Society for Psychical Research, 189
solar plexus chakra, 63
Song of Myself, 303
Soul, 287
souls
    see also *spirits*
    before birth, 72-76
    companions, 279-280
    cycles of existence, 278